The

# Halloween

# Party Host

# HANDBOOK

By

## DR. BONNIE

Create Space Publishing, USA
First Paperback Edition: May 2016
The characters and events portrayed in this novel are fictitious. Any similarity to real
persons, alive or dead, is coincidental and not intended by the author.
Blossman, Bon 1970—
The Official Halloween Party Host Handbook/by Dr. Bonnie
Summary: The ultimate Halloween party handbook for party hosts that includes over
200 party games, menu suggestions and recipes, DIY costume tips, Halloween party
themes, Halloween safety guidelines, and a master checklist for your party.

ISBN: 0-9965248-9-4
ISBN-13: 978-0-9965248-9-6

*[1 Party – Non-Fiction 2. Handbook - Non-Fiction. 3. Halloween - Non-Fiction. 4. Event –
Non-Fiction]*

*Life is one fabulous party at a time.*

# Table of Contents

# I. Introduction

## WHAT IS HALLOWEEN?

Halloween is an annual holiday celebrated on October 31st. It originates from the Christian All Saints Day, the Celtic festival of Samhain, the Roman feast of Pomona (the Goddess of fruits and seeds), or the festival of the dead called Parentalia.

The name Halloween comes from the 16th century referring to the Scottish All Hallows' Eve, which means the night before All Hallows Day - another term for All Saints' Day (November 1st), which is a Western Christian holiday in honor of the Saints. Halloween is also known as Allhalloween, Hallowmas, All Souls' Day and Hallowe'en.

The Celtics believed that on this night, the two realms (this world and the otherworld) allowed spirits to pass between them – both dangerous and harmless alike. Wearing masks became a tradition by the Celtics to ward off these spirits, thereby affording the mask wearer some protection on Halloween night. Also, the Celtic tradition holds that Samhain marks the best time to store food for the upcoming winter. Livestock slaughtering became more common during this time, and bonfires were lit to burn the carcasses.

No matter what the origination of Halloween is, today it is a secular tradition filled with rich tradition such as watching scary movies, pulling pranks, haunted hayrides, murder mystery parties, pumpkin carving contests, Halloween dance parties, haunted houses, and trick-or-treating.

## HOW TO HOST A MEMORABLE PARTY

Sense is a physical phenomenon of the human body. Scientists have noted as many as twenty types of senses in the human body. Focusing on the basic five senses accredited to Aristotle of sight, hearing, taste, smell and touch, you can host a truly memorable event. Leaving one of these out while planning your event can lead to disaster. When your guests walk into your event space, each of the five (primary) senses should be stimulated. If you fail in any one area, you aren't maximizing your guests' sensations, and subconsciously, they won't feel as good about your event as they could have felt.

# The Halloween Party Host Handbook

## Appease the Five Senses:

**Sight:** is essentially the most important sense to embrace during event planning and should account for a good portion of your budget. If you have everything in place for the perfect party, but your guests walk into a drab space of different shades of gray - that will be what they remember. Some people don't realize that everything in the space is contributing to sight. This includes food, furniture, candles, and any other decor you have acquired. Food is part of the decor, so if you are having a themed party of any kind, such as Halloween, it is a must to coordinate the food and make it as pleasing to the eye as possible. Food should make sense along with the theme.

It is easy to purchase decor to fit your theme at party stores, but you may not have the budget to purchase the perfect decor. If you are on a tight budget, make beautiful focal pieces out of metallic or opalescent balloons by fastening a cluster of different hues of the same color balloons, tying them with shimmering ribbon, and attaching them to the ceiling. Using these balloon clusters over tables - either dining or reception - is a smart way to expand your budget. Also, using items collected for free (i.e. tree branches on the ground) - painting them with metallic paint and sprinkling them with glitter would be another suggestion.

Halloween colors are traditionally orange, purple and lime green with black, of course. For younger groups, stick with happy monster faces and some spider webs – but no spiders and refrain from being too scary. Orange and black balloons are great fillers and add festivity to any party. The party space should exude happiness and not be scary unless the minimum age of the group is over ten-years-old.

Tweens can handle a bit of spooky, but don't go for gory just yet. Add some plastic spiders to the webbing, and some LED candelabras. A few scenes such as a science lab with glowing body parts in jars with colored water and maybe a morgue with a stuffed body bag are excellent additions. At this age, a bit of fog is a great touch, but not too much.

Teen to adult, you should create a creepy ambiance to set the mood. Use dim lighting, and as many cobwebs as possible (or that you care to clean up the next day). Line your tables with purple string lights for a fun effect. Fog machines are great - set on a timer to keep the room a bit mysterious. LED candles are a must. View more DIY spooky décor on Pinterest/MyMysteryParty and by visiting our party host site **partyhost411.com/halloweenhandbook** for some more fun tips.

8

# Dr. Bonnie

**Hearing:** sticking with the theme of the event, analyze what style of music fits best with the theme. A Halloween party mix, such as the Party of 2 on iTunes (or any other dance mix) is great to play in the background. Classical music at a low volume is a very traditional choice. Not many people are offended by classical music, and it transcends many generations. Keeping music at a reasonable volume is key. The sound is merely ambiance, not the entertainment. You do not want your guests to expend energy raising their voices to be heard over the music. Before the guests arrive, perform a sound check from all points in the event space before you decide on the appropriate volume. Your guests should be able to talk comfortably without any stress. With a younger crowd, you may go for light pop music, but again, at a minimal volume. Hard rock, rap, hip-hop or electronic dance music is not suggested at an event unless you have a dance floor, and dancing is the primary form of entertainment. In this case, you will need to increase the volume for dancing. Teens will want their style of music.

**Taste:** the party is centered around food whether you want it to or not. Do not host an event without ample provisions for your guests. *Food's gone = party's over.* Whether you are strictly serving appetizers or a full meal, the food must fit the theme of the event. Food is part of the party decor and should not only fit the theme but be part of the visual sensations of your event. With a Halloween party, this is the case!

The host should always sample the choices that are available to the guests. One quick way to ruin the vibe of the party is to serve bad grub. If the fare isn't up to par, make changes. During the planning stages of the event, if you hire a caterer, ask for a tasting. If you are preparing the dishes yourself, practice the recipes in advance. Food is important, so the more memorable your spread, the more impressive your event will be.

Since this is a Halloween party, you should serve a spooky selection of treats. Be as creepy as you want with the food – it's the only day of the year to do that without people finding you weird. There are menu suggestions/recipes later in this handbook. If you don't want to serve the novelty/cliché style treats, at least consider printing out tasteful cards with Halloween-themed names for your food – even if the dish wasn't created to look like a zombie eyeball – label a chafing dish of meatballs *zombie eyeballs*.

**Smell:** when your guests enter the party space, they should inhale subtle yet interesting aromas. Purchase scented candles or even plug-in air fresheners in the scent of your choice, but hit your guests with the aroma upon their arrival and keep the scents away from the food. Scentsy has fragrant candles without a flame. Flames have to be managed as they can be hazardous, especially for large groups.

Do not allow artificial fragrances to compete with food. Never light scented candles on a buffet or dining tables, as the perception of taste is ~ 75% smell, and you will cause your guests' taste to be off with fragrant candles.

**Touch:** this sense will be one of the most difficult to rouse, but is simple at the same time. Think about where your guests will be and what they will have access to touch. Linens for the reception tables or dining tables are a subliminal focus. Choose unique textures for table coverings. Mix up a silk and satin, and add different items to the tabletops, such as large rhinestones, blinged-out skulls, or confetti. For a classier Halloween bash, opt for onyx and orange jewels to scatter about the tables. Look for items at party/Halloween stores that are small and can be scattered on tables to add a cool effect such as tiny plastic skulls. Add rhinestones for the eyes with some E6000 glue, and you've just creating inexpensive filler pieces that the guests can view and handle throughout the night. These go for visual, as well.

Party planning is a delicate process. It is always best to have a partner, or even committee for a large event, to discuss ideas. Follow a party planning checklist, such as the one given in this handbook. Nevertheless, each event is unique so make any additions to your party checklist before you get started.

### Choose the Location:

The most successful parties use two neighboring rooms as well as a restroom/bathroom /loo /privy/water closet – or whatever you call the room with a toilet. The restroom is a necessity, but two separate party spaces are entirely optional. A fun Halloween party can be held in a tiny apartment in a small kitchen if you have the right people there!

If you have access to two adjacent rooms to host your Halloween party, it is preferable to have one area where food is available in a buffet style set up, or this is where you'll put your dinner tables if you are having a seated event. This area should be well-lit and decorated in fun Halloween décor. The more décor that you have at a party, the more your guests will get into the Halloween spirit. This will encourage guests to mingle while eating.

# Dr. Bonnie

A second location should be available (a neighboring room) where it is darker – possibly with a black light and fun neon Halloween décor. The music should be playing in this room and possibly a television playing a scary movie without the sound on. This will encourage fun conversation and dancing (if there is room). In this space, lighten it up to play some games when the time is right.

## Require Costumes:

Even if your guests are approaching 100-years-old, everybody should be encouraged to wear a costume. There are plenty of costumes to make with items in your home and closet, so there's no real need to spend money. However, if the cash is burning a hole in your pocket, it is worth the fun to be someone else for a night! As the party host, schedule a costume contest with various categories.

**Here are some example costume awards:**

| | | | |
|---|---|---|---|
| BEST DIY | CUTEST | SCARIEST | MOST TECHNOLOGICALLY ADVANCED |
| MOST ORIGINAL | BEST OVERALL | BEST GROUP | BEST 5 MINUTE THROW TOGETHER |
| BEST CONCEPT | PRETTIEST | BEST COUPLE/DUO | MOST LIKELY TO HAVE BEEN PURCHASED THIS MORNING |
| MOST INNOVATIVE | WEIRDEST | FUNNIEST | WORST/ UNRECOGNIZABLE |
| REQUIRING THE MOST EXPLANATION | BEST MATERNITY | BEST PROPS/ACCESSORIES | MOST LIKELY TO GET YOU ARRESTED |
| SILLIEST | BEST SMELLING | MOST ENVIRONMENTALLY FRIENDLY | MOST LIKELY TO SCARE THE DOG |
| BEST PUN/PUNNIEST | SEXIEST | CLOSEST TO REAL PERSONALITY | BEST USE OF HALLOWEEN COLORS |
| MOST OFFENSIVE | BEST ANIMAL | BEST TV/MOVIE INSPIRED | MOST TRADITIONAL |
| MOST COLORFUL | GORIEST | MOST REALISTIC | MOST POLITICALLY CORRECT |
| BEST VINTAGE | MOST MANLY | BEST ROCK STAR | MOST FEMININE |
| MOST OUTRAGEOUS | MOST WHIMSICAL | MOST INAPPROPRIATE | BEST MYTHOLOGICAL |

## Make a Statement with your Invitation:

Sure, you can send an eVite or make an event page on whatever social media outlet you choose. However, if you want to be the talk of the town, go an extra mile.

# The Halloween Party Host Handbook

**Consider these following options for your invitations – some picture examples can be found on http://partyhost411.com/halloweenhandbook:**

| |
|---|
| **ZOMBIE HANDS:** purchase zombie hands and place your invitation inside the hand in a scroll. Put your zombie hand on top of red crinkle paper in a box and mail to your guests. |
| **VOODOO DOLLS:** Using burlap, black felt and needle/thread, sew some voodoo dolls and mail to your guests on top of some peat moss in a box with a note pinned to the chest about your party. |
| **TOE TAGS:** purchase some morgue toe tags and tea stain them a few times, allowing drying in between until you get the right 'aged' color. Add your party information onto the tag and then, dip the corner in blood and allow drying. For an added fun effect, purchase fake toes to tie these on and place in a box containing red crinkle paper to mail to your guests. |
| **DON'T FORGET FINGERS:** purchase fake dead finger and tie a black satin ribbon on it with a 'don't forget' titled card with your party information. Place the finger on peat moss in a box to mail to your guests. |
| **WITCH BROOMS:** all you need is a ~6" twig, thin twine and some ~ 2" cuttings from a broom. Gather the broom cuttings and insert your twig into the center, fastening with the twine and gluing the twine down with E6000, superglue or a dab of hot glue. Prepare your invitation per the parchment scroll directions below and secure to your mini broomstick with twine. Deliver to your guests in a box filled with peat moss. |
| **MUMMY CARDS:** using an elongated ivory card, print your invitation on the card. Then, cut strips of cheesecloth or gauze and attach to the back with small dabs of glue and criss-cross the gauze the length of the card to where your guests must move the gauze strips to see the information. Leave space at the top for google eyes for your mummy. |
| **PARCHMENT SCROLLS:** using parchment paper, print your invites with Victorian-style font. Using a tapered candle's flame, burn the edges of the paper (do this outside on concrete in case your paper catches fire). Then, scroll your burned-edge parchment and tie with twine. Top off your look with a candle wax seal and deliver to your guests in a box of peat moss. |
| **SKELETON IN A COFFIN:** using black jewelry boxes (or jewelry boxes painted black or dark brown, line the inside with red satin. They do make paper coffins – try a search online or go to a scrapbooking store. Using stick-on lettering put 'RIP' on the front of your coffin (lid of the box). Print out an invitation on parchment card stock that fits inside of your coffin and place in the bottom, attaching with a couple of dabs of glue. Burn the edges for a cool effect before inserting it. On top of the card stock with your invite, add a mini skeleton. |

# Dr. Bonnie

> **RAVEN SCROLL:** purchase fake ravens and affix a small scroll with your party information onto their claws with glue. Place raven into a box with black crinkle paper. If you have the budget, purchase a sound module for greeting cards, record a message for your guests, and place in the box with a 'push here' message.

## Plan the Entertainment:

Don't forget that in any party – there must be a focal point. You need some form of entertainment for your guests. Hiring a violinist, harpist, or pianist to play during the guests' arrival would be a nice touch and a great first impression, which is important.

Consider what will fill up the bulk of the guests' time at the party. The focal point of the party can be dancing, watching a live band or other performers, or maybe doing a murder mystery game. Download murder mystery games or have a boxed set prepared for you from MyMysteryParty.com. Another entertainment alternative would be to hire a comedian, host an auction for charity, or host a series of fun party games (see the party game section in this handbook).

Halloween games are a must! 'Tis the season for a good murder mystery party followed by fun party games. People never truly grow up – that's where the term 'inner child' comes from! It doesn't matter if your guests are older professionals; they'll still have fun competing in silly challenges. Encourage everyone to show their inner child and have a blast! For a wide selection of party games, see section V. With party games, set house rules before you play, enforcing the rules of safety.

If you are hosting food challenges, ask about allergies up front, so you don't include any dangerous items in not only the party food, but the food used for games. Also, don't use common choked-on items during the food challenges. Some examples of commonly choked-on items include but are not limited to hard candy, seeds, nuts, hot dogs, gumballs, carrots, meat, fish with bones, apples.

Minimize harmful peer pressure by making a rule that if anybody is uncomfortable doing a challenge, they do not have to participate - no questions asked. If anybody says a word about them backing out, they do five push-ups.

Be safe and avoid your players being harmed/injured by assessing your party area for hidden dangers and reading over the party game instructions carefully to see if your party area is suitable for the challenge. Don't host a relay race in a bumpy yard with holes. Don't use extra-hot salsa for game penalties and burn your players'

# The Halloween Party Host Handbook

mouths – that's not fun! Don't have them handle raw eggs or meat, etc. and get sick after your party. Anything that can be dangerous should not be used in a game.

Feel free to bend the game rules to fit the ages of your players – or make special exceptions for the younger ones on the teams. Life isn't fair, but your games can be! Remember your guests are there to have fun, not to be stressed out or injured!

## Cameras:

Digital cameras are relatively cheap nowadays so purchase a few and place them around the party area. Encourage your guests to capture as many memorable moments as possible. After the party, upload these pictures for everyone to share on social media sites, but please get folks' permission before you post anything publicly.

## Themes

Well, it's obvious you're having a Halloween party, but there are many different types and styles of parties. But if you want to spruce it up each year with a new title and themed décor, party food, etc.
**For more detail on party themes, see Section VI.**

**Here are some suggestions for themes:**

| | | |
|---|---|---|
| Mad Science Lab | Haunted Hayride | Witches and Wizards |
| Goblins and Ghouls | Zombie Apocalypse | A Night with Vampires |
| Haunted House | Halloween Glam | Monster Mash |
| Freak Show | Spooky Graveyard | Edgar Allen Poe |
| Space Invaders | All Things Gothic | Mummy's Revenge |
| Black Tie Affair | Pumpkin Patch | Menacing Movie Marathon |
| A Ghostly Gala | Glow Party | Medieval Mayhem |
| Scary Tales | Creepy Carnival | Halloween through the Ages |
| Day of the Dead | Insane Asylum | Skeleton Party |
| Fall Harvest | Villain Bedlam | Maddening Masquerade |
| Blacklight Ball | Goosebumps Gala | The Blood Ball |
| Serial Killer Assembly | Forbidden Forest | The Morgue |
| The Terror Tombs | Victorian Gala | Steampunk Celebration |
| Gypsy Retreat | Haunted Hotel | Creepy Circus |
| Roaring '20s | Limousine Pub Crawl | Only in your Nightmares |
| Zombie Prom | Monster Masquerade | Saints & Sinners |
| Boo Bash | Dusk 'til Dawn | Heroes vs. Villains |
| Let's Boo-Gie | Fire and Ice | Undead Rock Stars |

# Dr. Bonnie

## Party Favors:

Why do party favors just need to be for kids? Many adults are going home to kids later, so give out a fun party favor bag full of silly Halloween party favors, candy, etc. Or maybe even create a takeaway they can use such as a cute Halloween-themed votive holder, holiday tree ornament in a Nightmare Before Christmas theme, etc. Stemless wine glasses may be customized for your event and purchased for less than 2 bucks each.

**Here are some more options for party takeaways (some adult, some kid, some both) – any of these items may be purchased as custom/personalized:**

| | | |
|---|---|---|
| Wine Stoppers | Bottle Openers | Shot Glasses |
| Mini Purse Manicure Sets | Koozies | Votive Candles/Holders |
| Large Swirl Lollipops | Mini Cookie Jars | Mini Gumball Machines |
| Playing Cards | Candy Bags | Syringe Pens |
| Temporary Tattoos | Gourmet Pretzels | Mason Jar with Candies |
| Mini Picture Frames | Hats | Pens |
| Novelty Necklace/Bracelets | Lip Balms | Curio Boxes |
| Soap/Bath Products | Key chains | Glow Sticks/Necklaces |
| Small Arts & Crafts Kits | Measuring Spoons | Novelty Toys |
| Bookmarks | Crystal Figurines | Plastic Cup |
| Luggage Tags | Compasses | Sparklers |
| Helium-Filled Balloons | Hand Sanitizers | Flasks |
| Stickers | Boas | Beads |

# II. Halloween Party Master Checklist

Use the following universal master checklist for any Halloween party. Any item that doesn't apply to your event, check it off as complete or cross it out! Make copies of this list to use this template repeatedly! Using a highlighter to signify a completed item is an effective method.

| TIME BEFORE YOUR EVENT | X | TASK |
|---|---|---|
| 2 MONTHS | | Nail down your budget and realize you will likely go over ~ 15% so set it lower than you can afford. |
| | | Select your party theme. |
| | | Plan party games, make list of items needed (*e.g. props, awards*). |
| | | Determine guests' attire. |
| | | Select music playlist. |
| | | Select location(s), get quotes, and put deposit down *Think about guest seating, parking, restrooms, linens, serving ware, etc. |
| | | Inclement weather accommodations are planned out (*e.g. coat room/rack, umbrella stand*). If you are having an outdoor event, have a contingency plan such as backup location, tent, party cancellation procedure (*boo, but if you have no choice*). |
| | | Plan for guest pedestal and sign in book. |
| | | Plan for gift table if this is a birthday party. |
| | | Hire staff (bartenders, game hosts, chef, valet, security, ticket takers, entertainers, an emcee, photographer, videographer, etc.) |

|  |  |  |
|---|---|---|
|  |  | Make your invitation list and send a save the date *(email/text/social media event page)* to your most important guests. There are typically guests that can *make or break* your party and you cannot do without, so get their buy-in on your proposed date first before you continue with the invitation process. |
|  |  | Based on your guest list, consider special accommodations for your guests: smokers, elderly *(do they have to climb stairs),* wheelchair access, food allergies/preferences, etc. |
|  |  | Once you know food allergies/preferences, contact a caterer/chef and get a quote. Make an estimated head count at this time and be sure your contract states you can give a final count ~ 24 to 48 hours prior. |
|  |  | If you plan to have anything customized for t-shirts, or other giveaways or maybe even a customized costume contest trophy – order it now. |
| **7 WEEKS** |  | Based on your save the date responses make your party date official and finalize your guest list. If you need to extend your guest list to include more, feel free to add them without a save the date. |
|  |  | Sign contract with caterer/chef and select your menu – ask for a tasting – if they refuse, maybe find someone else. Or, if you are DIY - plan your menu, test out recipes. |
| **6 WEEKS** |  | Send party invitations. You've already received commitment from your VIP guests, but now it is time to invite officially. Printed invites are best, but in modern times, a social media event site is acceptable for most casual events. It is proper to include a RSVP card with a SASE for the guests to return it. Or... if you are using an eVite – they will be asked to accept or decline. You will need a guest total to prepare for your party. Also, include a map to the party location. |
|  |  | Sketch your party area and plan your décor. Make it epic, but stay within your budget. |
|  |  | Purchase online décor. If you wait too long, you'll pay higher shipping fees for a speedy delivery. Search for online coupons before you click 'submit order.' Décor may include balloons, a helium tank *(although grabbing one at a party store may be easier),* streamers, candelabras, animatronic monsters, table centerpieces, string lighting, fog machine, LED candles, etc. |

# The Halloween Party Host Handbook

| | | |
|---|---|---|
| | | Purchase/locate your items for DIY Halloween décor and start creating your items. |
| | | Order online party favors, theme-oriented prizes, party game props. |
| | | Purchase the guest sign in book. |
| | | If you are DIY with party food, make a perishable and non-perishable food list. |
| **1 MONTH** | | Download songs legally – the musical artists work hard ;-). Or, order CDs online if you are still using CDs. |
| | | Order rented equipment *(if applicable)*. Rent tables, linens, chafing dishes, plates & utensils, china, and glassware. There may be décor to rent, a photo booth, chocolate fountain, snow cone machine, a resin bar, cotton candy machine, etc. If you are having an outdoor event, it's wise to get pricing on a tent/canopy and availability of it – just in case you get rained out. |
| | | Continue to manage your RSVPs and encourage those guests who haven't responded yet to let you know if they are in. The worst thing is a placeholder! |
| | | Make accommodations for out of town guests: hotel reservations, transportation, etc. |
| **2 WEEKS** | | Give your 'place holding' guests a call and demand an RSVP, as you need a head count. Realize you may have some last minute cancellations, but that cannot be avoided. You may also have a last minute addition. |
| | | Confirm caterer – even though you have a contract, it's best to touch base to avoid last minute drama. |
| | | If you are DIY catering, do an inventory of your kitchen equipment, utensils, chafing dishes, party platters, etc., and remedy any deficiencies. |
| **1 WEEK** | | Confirm rental equipment and make changes as needed. Check the weather forecast and make adjustments based on the weather. |
| | | Confirm staff – rehire if necessary. |
| | | If applicable and you are DIY bartending/catering, purchase your liquor and non-perishable items. |
| | | Purchase Halloween candy for prizes, games, and party favor bags. |
| **48 HOURS** | | Confirm the time you will be able to access the location *(if not a home party)*. |
| | | Give your caterer a final head count – subtracting any last minute cancellations on previously RSVP'd guests &/or additions to your list. |

# Dr. Bonnie

| | | |
|---|---|---|
| | | Purchase perishable items and store properly. |
| | | Check the weather forecast again. |
| **24 HOURS** | | Clean your house and remove any breakables from the area the guests will have access to – accidents happen. |
| | | For home party - decorate and arrange your furniture to be unobtrusive. |
| | | Decorate your entryway. |
| | | Decorate any and all tables in the room – buffet, snack, bar, etc. |
| | | Prepare food which can be stored in the refrigerator for at least 24 h. |
| | | Check your serving trays, dishes, wine glasses, etc. |
| **DAY OF YOUR PARTY** | | Check bathrooms/restrooms for soap, hand towels, toilet tissue to ensure they are stocked. Do this in a public facility, as well – you don't want to be chasing down management for these items. |
| | | Check your coat rack or clear a coat closet for your guests and in the case of inclement weather – have an area for raincoats/umbrellas *(check the forecast one last time)*. |
| | | If you are playing party games, make a master list of the order in which you will play, and arrange props for the games in piles. |
| | | Set up guest pedestal with the sign in book |
| | | Blow up your balloon pieces, bouquets and arrange them in the room. Helium is best less than three hours before the party, so save this for one of the last tasks. |
| | | For DIY catering, get up early and prepare food, and arrange chafing dishes on the buffet/snack table. |
| | | For DIY bartending, prep the bar by getting the fruit garnishes ready, the herb garnishes cleaned, and do an inventory of your liquor and mixers – make sure you have the ingredients for all drinks on your menu. Put some recipes for your cocktails behind the bar on laminated cards in case your bar gets backed up and you need to recruit some bartenders to get you out of the weeds. |
| **< 1 HOUR PRIOR** | | Turn on your LED candles. |
| | | Start your ambiance music. |
| | | Start your DVD or other viewing media with Halloween movies without sound. |
| | | For DIY catering, light chafing dishes on the buffet table. |

19

# The Halloween Party Host Handbook

|  |  | Turn on your animatronic figures and fog machine *(put on a timer and 'less is more' with fog – it can get annoying)*. |
|  |  | For DIY catering, arrange your appetizers on trays for serving or on a table for a serve yourself buffet. If you are making food for dinner, get it in the oven if you haven't already done so – but set a timer on your phone and keep it handy, the worst thing to do is serve charred lasagna. |

# III. Decorating for your Halloween Party

## DIY PROJECTS

Some picture examples can be found on
http://partyhost411.com/halloweenhandbook

### Cardboard | Styrofoam Tombstones

Use cardboard, paint, markers, glue, fishing wire. Cut out tombstone shapes out of the cardboard (or Styrofoam) and paint them a deep gray color. If you are great with shading and painting the weathered cracks, go for it! Then, paint funny sayings on the front with black paint. Allow thorough drying. Tape them to or set against the wall for a fun cemetery effect.

If you have Styrofoam, make double layers of gray-painted Styrofoam with a wooden stake in between them (make a furrow on one of the Styrofoam layers to insert the stake securely, so there is not a gap in between the layers. Glue the layers together and allow drying. Then, paint the front with your funny saying on the front and stick into the front yard as a cemetery!

### Cardboard Flying Bats

Use cardboard, black paint and fishing wire. Cut out bat shapes, paint them black, and hang from the ceiling with fishing wire. You can find templates for bats on Google easily, so print and trace your outline on the cardboard before cutting your shape. Add google eyes to your bats if you wish.

### Spider Trail

Cut out black spiders out of black construction paper or use the cheap plastic ones from the party store. Using a tiny piece of non-stick paint safe tape or paint-safe putty, arrange a trail of spiders from the door knob and make a curvy trail on the door. If you want to creep your guests out – make a trail around the bathroom/restroom/loo.

# The Halloween Party Host Handbook

## Glowing Floats

Using surgical gloves, fill with glow sticks, inflate them, and tie them off. Float in the pool/pond by your party. Also, inflate balloons with various colored glow sticks inserted inside and float on top of the water. Scoop them all up when the party's over!

## Glowing Ice Buckets/Bowls

Before you put any ice in a bucket, bowl, or ice chest, toss in a few glow sticks for a cool effect. Wash and dry the sticks first.

## Skeleton Trophies

If you will host an awards ceremony on Halloween (maybe for a costume contest), purchase 8"–12" plastic skeletons and circular wooden bases (in the unpainted wood section of a hobby store). Affix the skeleton to the base with E6000 and spray with gold, silver &/or bronze paint – the base and skeleton. Or, paint the bases black. Then, create a sash out of the same color metallic card stock for the skeleton to wear and with elegant writing – put the title of your award. Fasten the sash on the skeleton with E6000 glue.

## Seeing Eye Gothic Rose Bouquet

You will need an old wine bottle (or black vase is fine). Paint the wine bottle black and allow drying. Before it is dry, add a dusting of black glitter for a more glitzy piece. Either using bloomed black silk roses or spray painting any silk rose black, press a doll eye into the center of the black rose with E6000 glue. Place something heavy on the eye to ensure it stays pressed down and doesn't pop out while drying. Insert as many roses as can fit into your wine bottle or vase. Add some black painted twigs/sprays along with your rose bouquet to make it fuller.

## Ceiling Spiders

First, using black crepe paper (streamers), tape the center of four 2'-4' sheets (as spider legs) to the wall, ceiling, corner - wherever you want your spider to be. Use an over-inflated (~ 12") black balloon for the body of the spider, and blow up a smaller balloon (~5") for the head and attach it to the large one. Attach the knots together with tape and secure with tape on top of the crepe paper. Then, position the eight leg ends and tape to the ceiling to the corner, ceiling, wall, etc. to where it looks like a spider crawling. The balloons are the body, and the crepe paper sheets makes up the eight legs.

# Dr. Bonnie

### Framed Ghost Faces

These are a cheap yet spooky 3D addition to your haunted décor and you can store them for years to come. These will appear as though a ghost face is pushing through the portrait. You will need large golden antique frames (just the frame, no glass). Purchase Styrofoam heads and cut off the back portion of the head with a serrated knife or hand saw so the face can lay flat. Cover with a thin layer of petroleum jelly to prevent the cheesecloth from sticking to it. On a white poster board (or cardboard spray-painted white) cut to fit the frame, cover with wax paper and place the head in the center. Drape the face with #50 cheesecloth and spread onto the board, spraying with starch and pressing it against the face to ensure the facial features are retained. Allow drying each time, pressing the cheesecloth back onto the poster board, so it appears as though the face is pushing through. Bunch the cheesecloth to give it a slightly wavy appearance against the board. Allow drying at least 24 hours and remove the cheesecloth from the form and secure to the white poster board or painted cardboard with E6000 and allow drying. You may need to trim the edges of the cheesecloth, so it doesn't peek out the back of the frame. Then, place into your frame by using a staple gun on the back.

### Floating Witch Hats

Purchase witch hats from any party store and affix fishing wire to the tip (thread it through without a needle, but if you can't, use a needle and tie it off with a knot. Hang to the ceiling with paint safe clear tape. Make them luminaries by adding a tea light (use E6000 glue) inside of each hat.

### Bat Colony Fly By on the Wall

Using templates downloaded from the internet, either print or cut out bats (~ 8"-10" inch wing spans). Tape the body of the bat to the wall with paint safe tape and then lightly crease the wings where they appear as though the bat is flying. Group these together to make a flock.

### Cheesecloth Ghosts

Grab some cheesecloth, a 2L soda bottle, a wire hanger and anything you can find that is round that you won't mind getting some starch on – maybe a Styrofoam ball if you have one lying around (leave the plastic covering on it if it's there). Glue the ball to the top of the 2L soda bottle.

# The Halloween Party Host Handbook

Unwind the coat hanger (or use wire of any kind that is sturdy enough to hold the fabric) and wrap the center of it around the neck of the bottle. Shape the two extended ends into the arms of the ghost. Drape the cheesecloth over your model and it should appear as a ghost (without the eyes). Do variations without the hanger, as well. Using starch in a spray bottle, spray the cheesecloth until it is covered – the more starch, the stiffer your ghost. Allow drying and repeat until it is stiff enough. Then, using black felt - cut out eyes and affix each eye with a dot of E6000 glue.

## Trash Bag Ghosts

White trash bags (and paper towels, markers, fishing wire) – make great ghosts. Stuff the bottom of a trash bag with a few paper towels and tie at the 'neck' with fishing wire. Draw two hollow eyes on the 'face' region. Attach the fishing wire to the top of the head (or neck) and hang from the ceiling.

## Homemade Spider Webs

Use yarn/crepe paper (gray or white) and create giant spider webs on your wall and ceiling by following the traditional pattern of a spider web (pull it up on Google). It's easy if assembled on the floor (use tape) and then affix to the wall/ceiling with pain-safe tape. However, the store-bought spider webs are relatively cheap and easy to use.

## Floating Ghost Heads

Purchase foam and bald mannequin heads and attach the end of a 6-10 ft. fishing wire into the top of the head with glue, a tack, etc. Using cheesecloth or tulle, drape a yard or two of the fabric over the heads by fishing the fishing wire through the center of the fabric. Make these as long as you'd like. Then, attach the fishing wire to an overhead structure – maybe on your front porch - and you've got one of the creepiest decorations for less than ten bucks. Group a few heads together for an extra spooky scene. Use a fog machine around this scene and you might scare off your trick-or-treaters.

## Scary Porch Greeter

Using old clothes - stuff them with any material (paper towels, other clothes, etc.) and slap a scary mask on a stuffed trash bag for the head. If you have a wig, use it for the hair and if not, use a hat if your mask isn't a full head mask. Prop this effigy on your porch in an old rocking chair to greet trick-or-treaters!

# Dr. Bonnie

## Black Clusters

Grab some random items such as old wine bottles, books, jars, cans, vases, etc. Spray paint them matte black and allow drying. For a glam effect, sprinkle with black glitter while drying.

To set up your display, add a few LED candles in black votive holders to the cluster and assemble the black items around the candles. Go on a hunt for small branches/twigs and paint them black and insert into any open pieces such as the wine bottles, jars. Finish it off with a few cobwebs. Using our instructions to create some Seeing Eye gothic roses, add some of these to the cluster, as well.

## Mummified Candle Holders

Using strips of gauze or cheesecloth, wrap a mason jar or hurricane candle holder with the material, adhering it with Mod Podge. Top with googly eyes and place LED candle inside for a cool effect.

## Alien Eggs

With a safety pin, make a small hole in the top and in the bottom of an egg. Gently blow out the contents by blowing into the top hole and allowing the contents to escape the bottom. Then, paint the shells green and call them 'alien eggs.' Put them in a nest (gather a bunch of grass, twigs and form a nest) on your porch with a sign that says: alien eggs: careful, hatching will occur at any moment!

## Glowing Monster Faces

This one is quick and easy. Save your mayo jars all year (or other mason style jars). Paint them orange and allow drying. Then, using a stencil, paint a face worthy of a Jack O' Lantern on the front. Paint the jar lid either green or black. Throw in an LED tea light and you've got a cute and inexpensive, glowing pumpkin. An alternative is to make monster faces and paint them bright green or purple, as well. Or, maybe even white and make them into ghosts.

## Shrunken Apple Heads

Set out dried apple shrunken heads around the party area or porch if this is for Halloween trick-or-treaters. Here's how you make them: you need apples, whole cloves, a few grains of rice, ½ cup of lemon juice and 2 tsp. of salt. Peel the apple and coat with lemon juice and salt to prevent oxidation and browning. Carefully, with a paring knife or the end of a potato peeler, carve the eye sockets, a nose, a mouth, and ears. Do not worry about wrinkles, dimples, etc. As when the apples dry out – you won't see it. Whole cloves are the eyes and rice grains are the teeth (do them without these items and they'll still look fabulously wicked). Once done, place the apples on a wire rack in a warm, dry location for about two weeks. Speed this up by drying in an oven on the warm setting – but it still takes several days for them to dry out.

### Old Dusty House
Using old white sheets, drape the furniture for an old, haunted mansion ambiance. If you are hosting a party, this décor doubles as furniture protection.

### Shadow Silhouettes
Use large, black butcher paper and cut out silhouettes of people, bats, cats, or other shapes. You can pull up templates online and scale them for larger sizes. Tape the silhouettes to the wall or windows.

### Acorn Pumpkins
Have extra acorns? Grab some orange and black acrylic paint and paint fun pumpkin creations on them. Allow drying and assemble them in a small, decorative glass dish for a fun pumpkin-inspired piece. To glam them up, use black rhinestones for the eyes.

### Floating Candles
There's a few ways to accomplish this effect, and the realism will depend on your budget. Purchase an assortment of LED candles, affix fishing wire to the tip with E6000 adhesive, and then attach to the ceiling securely. With LED candles, purchase the smaller, thin ones to avoid them being too heavy. Also, this will only work when you have something sturdy to tie the fishing wire to – a simple tape job won't cut it, and your guests will get bonked on the head with falling candles all night.

Or, collect cardboard rolls and spray paint them white and affix a lighter tea light LED candle to the top. This will help to reduce the weight and will be less expensive. You might be able to tape these to the ceiling with paint-safe clear tape – but test first to be sure.

### Pickled Dead Heads in a Jar
On Google (or another search engine), search for *flattened face PDF for Halloween jar*. Use what you find and print it, or make your own

using a template – they are out there. Print this out and laminate the photo. Do this at any local printing store if you don't have a laminator. Then, add some water to the jar with a few drops of green or yellow food coloring. Slip the laminated picture into the jar, flattening it against the walls of the jar. You will creep your guests out!

### Mummify the Front Door

Grab some white crepe paper streamers and tape them on your front door in a horizontal criss-cross pattern. Using white and black construction paper, create a pair of eyes and tape them in the upper/center portion of the door on the crepe paper gauze.

### Elegant Balloon Ghosts

Blow up extra-large white balloons. Using white tulle, drape the fabric over the balloon and tie at the 'neck' below the balloon with white ribbon, allowing the tulle and ribbon to drape down. Tie an extra ribbon and allow more to drape down if you wish. Insert fishing wire into the top of the tulle and hang from the ceiling. Make ghostly eyes with black rhinestones by adhering them to the tulle with glue. Or, if you can find large enough rhinestones, use one for each eye. Spray your ghosts with glitter spray for a gorgeous sparkle.

### Candy Corn Bottle Vases

Using old wine bottles - paint them white and allow drying. Using spray paint, spray the middle portion orange and allow drying, being careful not to get too much orange on the white (it's alright if it is a mist because that will add to a cool ombre effect). Allow the orange to dry. Now, using yellow spray paint, spray the bottom portion, again, being careful not to get too much yellow mist on the orange section. Then, grab some thin, autumn tree branches with colorful leaves (or something similar at any craft store) and place them inside the top. Group these together and add some colorful leaves around the bases.

### Chicken Wire Ghost

Nothing says creepy like a random ghost in your yard. This one may take a bit of time and patience, but all you need is chicken wire and some gloves for protection for your hands while you shape it either into a traditional sheet ghost shape or, if you have the time, go for a human shape for an ultra-spooky piece. Shine an LED light toward it &/or inside of it for a crazy effect at night.

# The Halloween Party Host Handbook

### Rats, Everywhere!

Using a template, cut out rats of all positions out of black felt or construction paper. They should be of various sizes. Tape them along your baseboards, on the staircase, climbing your banister, etc. Even make some mouse holes along the baseboards, as well.

### Bleeding Candles

With this project, you'll need a white column-shaped or tapered candle and a red taper candle. Simple burn the red candle and allow the red wax to drip onto the white candle for an awesome bloody effect. Do this over wax paper or other washable surface, as this can get messy.

### Glitzy Ghostly Standees

Have you seen those white tissue paper bells from the wedding aisle? Grab some of those and black construction paper or felt and cut out eyes and mouth from the black material and glue on to the wedding bell. Then, grab some white tulle and make an outer layer on top, draping down to the floor. Spray a bit of an iridescent glitter on top for a bit of glitz.

### Table with Witch or Monster Legs

If you are using a tablecloth, this will complete the look. Search for colorful, striped Halloween-themed tights – you'll need two pairs. Cut off the leg portions of the tights and slip onto your table legs and secure around the top of the leg or underside of the table with furniture safe tape. Either make witch's shoes/boots with paper mache for each table leg (leave a hole for the legs to go through the boot so your table won't be wobbly) or purchase some old black boots and find a way to create a hole through the sole (with a power drill) for the table leg to pop through and reach the floor.

For monster legs, grab some furry lime green or bright blue fuzzy material and fasten it with Velcro around each table leg, stuffing the leg with batting to make it fuller. Then, make a foot (paw) shape out of the same fabric and some large toenails with some black felt – using E6000 or hot glue to attach them. Put the foot around the bottom of each table leg. You'll probably need ~ 1 yard of fabric per table leg.

### Bloody Window Handprints

Elmer's glue, red and blue food coloring and saran wrap are what you need. Place these cling-ons to windows, mirrors, etc. to creep out your guests. Take a firm piece of cardboard and wrap Saran wrap around it,

# Dr. Bonnie

making sure it is taut and there is a smooth surface on one side. Tape the back in place so it won't move once you start. Use a latex glove if you wish, or your bare hand – it won't matter. Mix in drops of red food coloring until you have a deep red color with the glue. Then, drop by drop add the blue coloring until you have a deep reddish burgundy that looks like blood. Coat your palm-side of your hand with the glue and press onto the plastic wrap and allow drying. Repeat this until the cling gets about 1/8 inches thick. Allow drying thoroughly before using. Make some additional blood drips to use next to the handprints, as well.

### Glowing Creepy Eyes
This quick DIY invention is super easy but has a max effect. Collect toilet rolls starting in August or so. When you are ready, cut out various shapes of eyes in the rolls –use diamond shape, semi-circles, rounded circles, vertical ovals, etc. Paint the rolls in camouflage for where you are going to use them. If you are going to hide these in the bushes for a backyard party, spray paint them green, etc. Then, insert a glow stick inside of each, hide them and you've got creepy eyes peeping at you from the shadows.

### Spider Web Balloons
Using a product which extends the life of helium-filled balloons (search Google for helium balloon life extender); you will create the web effect by using a clear balloon, blowing up the balloon and using the product according to the instructions. Then, deflate and re-inflate to a larger balloon size and this coating should peel away from the edges and create what appears to be a web. Then, glue on black plastic spiders to the outside of the balloon to make them even creepier.

### Glowing Jars
For party ambiance, lighting is everything. Save some mayo/pickle jars and clean them out - or purchase mason jars of all sizes. Purchase glow in the dark paint and using a paintbrush, paint small dots all over the inside of the jars. That's it! This will add an amazing effect. Use different colored glow paints and the more dots, the more glow! The day of your party, charge these in the light, so they glow for the duration of your event.

### A Hanging Baby Spider Hatch Piece
Blow up a white 10" balloon about 2/3 of the way. Wrap with white cheesecloth (cut into strips to simulate large silk fibers) soaked in glue/

water mix (1:1) and allow drying completely. This might take a while as you let each side dry before turning and doing the next. Use a bowl to hold the balloon as you cover it in the cheesecloth. Leave a few gaps and then leave an opening at the top (where the balloon is tied) to attach the spider chains.

Using fishing wire, string together various lengths of small plastic spiders (get these at any local party store) by tying the wire to a leg, etc. And then skip down 1-2 inches before putting the next spider in the line.

When the cheesecloth egg sack is completely dry, pop the balloon and remove it. Where you have left a gap, insert fishing line and tie it to secure, leaving a long line to hang from the ceiling. Attach the spider chains to the top by tying to the fishing line at the base (top) of the egg sack. They will cascade down and over the egg sack as if they are newly hatched - dangle beyond the egg sack as if they are falling to the ground. Your guests will certainly avoid this scary sight!

## Mini Pumpkin Black Cats

Purchase mini pumpkins (any color), black paint, white paint, green paint, felt, small boa and toothpicks. Paint the pumpkins black and allow thorough drying. Paint cat eyes on the front of the pumpkin. Cut out small triangles for the ears and glue a black-painted toothpick onto the pack with the pointed side of the toothpick down. Insert the ears with the toothpick in the appropriate locations. Cut the mini boa for the tail (as long as you want it to be). Glue another painted toothpick to the string in the middle of the boa (or tie this onto the toothpick if the string is small enough.) Then, insert the toothpick for the tail in the back.

## Googly-Eyed Votives

Purchase clear votive holders, black construction paper, Mod Podge, black paint, green paint, a hole puncher and a small paintbrush. Cut out strips of black construction paper and place random holes as eyes. Glue these strips onto the votive holder in a random fashion but do not overlap on your 'eyes.' Use the Mod Podge to secure the construction paper to the glass. Once dry, add another layer of Mod Podge on the assembly and allow drying thoroughly. Where your eyes (blank holes with the glass exposed) are located, draw tiny green irises and a black pupil with the paint and the small brush. Do not take up the entire exposed glass as you want the light to shine through and cast eerie eyeball shapes onto the wall! Allow drying, place a votive candle inside and enjoy your creepy ambiance.

# Dr. Bonnie

### Ghostly Chair Covers

If you have white pillowcases or additional white sheets and high back chairs around a table, create a ghostly seat! Slip the pillowcase (or sheet) around the high back chair and glue felt eyes (long, oval shapes) and a misshapen mouth. With cheesecloth, fasten either the sheet or the pillowcase at the base of the chair and tie loose knots to secure it at the bottom. Allow the cheesecloth to drape to the floor. Add multiple strands of cheesecloth to make a jagged, flowing effect.

## STORE-BOUGHT DÉCOR SUGGESTIONS

Many stores will start having sales a week before Halloween. In the case of a party, this might be the economical way to go. However, you won't get to enjoy the full month of October with your eerie delights! Good news is – you'll have them for next year! Remember to hit the after-Halloween sales!

### Lighting

Change out your porch light with a black light for a fun effect on Halloween night. Inside, for a party, lighting should be low. Change out the bulbs for low watt bulbs or darker/colored bulbs. Or for adult parties, switch out for candles but follow safety guidelines with candles!

### Ghoul Head Buffet Centerpieces

On your buffet table at your Halloween party, create a few ghoulish heads looking at the food. Not very appetizing, but Halloween shouldn't be! Make a ghoulish head centerpiece by putting a Halloween mask on a Styrofoam wig head. Or, to make your own, use modeling clay over the Styrofoam wig head with acrylic paints, a wig, and marbles for eyes. Add stitches, fake blood and scabs at will (see the DIY FX section for more details). Oooh, yummy!

### Crime Scene

If you can get a hold of some 'crime scene tape', rope off an area close to your porch and warn trick-or-treaters and party guests not to contaminate the crime scene. (MyMysteryParty.com sells crime scene tape in the mystery prop emporium – as well as some other crime scene decor). Why not grab some chalk and make a body outline?

## Porch Décor

Decorating the porch/front walkway is a must. This sets the stage for both your trick-or-treaters and your guests to your Halloween party. Line the walkway with illuminated carved pumpkins using LED lights, so you don't worry about a fire hazard. As outlined above, stage a stuffed dummy with a mask and/or an alien egg exhibit right by the front door. A smoking carved pumpkin (by using dry ice) is an awesome eerie effect. The smoking witch's cauldron is always a great choice, as well. Place a flashlight with a colored piece of saran wrap on the end (preferably green or red) and dry ice inside of the cauldron. Tape the flashlight away from the dry ice, so it doesn't freeze and direct the flashlight beam towards the back of the cauldron so the indirect light will shine through the top. You can also elect to use glow sticks.

## PUMPKIN CARVING:

Either at the pumpkin patch or the local grocery store, choose your pumpkin carefully! Select the freshest, most colorful pumpkin in a nice, rounded shape. If you prefer tall and oval, go for it! Make this a family tradition each year to find the perfect pumpkin.

With a thin marker, draw a circle around the stem. Make sure it is large enough to fit your hand. Carefully cut through your guide with a pumpkin carving tool with extra caution not to cut your hand.

Remove the stem and scoop out the gooey contents (pulp and seeds) from inside with a large spoon. Also, trim your stem cap's extra seeds/pulp hanging on there. The less you have to rot, the better.

Either using a template (you can Google these) or by free-hand, draw a pattern for the face (or other Halloween shape). If you make a face, make the eyes and nose large enough to cut all of the way through safely and remove the pieces. With great care and caution, follow your pattern all the way through. From the inside, gently pop out the pieces to the front and discard them.

On Halloween night, place some dry ice (adult supervision – dry ice stings and damages tissue if you leave it on your skin). Place a waterproof flashlight or glow sticks inside, but away from the dry ice. Or a simple waterproof votive candle will do for an eerie glow!

Now, if you're proud of your carved masterpiece and want to prevent it from rotting before the big night, soak in bleach after you've carved it in a 5-gallon bucket (or larger if your pumpkin's bigger). Mix 3 gallons of water and 3 tsp. of bleach. Place your pumpkin masterpiece into the bucket for at least two minutes. Then, allow drying on paper towels. This will extend the life of your pumpkin.

Another pumpkin hack (not to be used in conjunction with the bleach) is to use a retail spray for pumpkin freshness (just do a Google search for pumpkin preservative). These solutions usually contain fungicide.

Vaseline (petroleum jelly) will keep your pumpkin fresh and prevent it from drying out and wrinkling. Just apply on the surfaces and that's it – you may need to reapply during the season.

You always have the alternative of not carving the pumpkin to make it last longer. Glam your pumpkin by using rhinestones and glitter spray. Paint a cute or scary face with acrylic paints for a fun, festive Halloween effect.

# IV. Costumes 101

Some picture examples can be found on
http://partyhost411.com/halloweenhandbook

### Rock Star

Wear a brightly-colored, tight shirt, jeans (or shiny spandex leggings if you have them), and tons of bandanas. Tie the bandanas in your hair, around your wrists, and legs. Wear boots – the higher on the leg, the better. Tease your hair as high as it will go, or wear an 'out of control' long-haired wig.

### iPad

This one can be as elaborate or as simple as you wish. Go full cardboard with this and paint the cardboard in a bright color (or stick with black or white) and spend some time making icons to tape to the front. As an alternative, use a white or black shirt and affix various icons made with felt (or printed on paper) to the front.

### Rosie the Riveter

Why not be the cultural icon of the U.S. who represented women who worked in factories during WWII? Easy-breezy. Snag a denim shirt and a red bandana, and you are ready to go!

### Tourist

Hawaiian shirt, zinc oxide on the nose, sunglasses, large-rim hat, Bermuda shorts and flip flops! Hold a map and a camera as optional props!

### Morton Salt Girl

You need a yellow dress, white tights, yellow shoes and a yellow umbrella. Grab a carton of salt from the store to show who you are during the party.

# Dr. Bonnie

### Stadium or Movie Theater Floor

Purchase a black or charcoal gray sweatshirt. Glue random peanut shells, soda lids, popcorn, empty candy boxes, straw wrappers, etc. on to the shirt. Grab a matching beanie and glue some more trash to it. Be prepared to explain yourself.

### Self Portrait

Wear anything glamorous or at least picture-worthy. Carry an empty frame in front of your upper half. Every time you see somebody new, hold up your frame as if you are in the picture.

### Gumball Machine

Purchase a brightly colored tank top (e.g. red) and wear matching pants. At any craft store, buy an assortment of poms and glue them on the shirt to look like gumballs by spacing them evenly and mixing up the colors. Add a sign to a belt that says '25¢.' Wear a red beret for a hat.

### Runaway Bride

If you have a wedding gown in the closet, slip it on with some tennis shoes and sweatbands, and call yourself a runaway bride. Add a hitchhiking sign and a hobo stick for an added effect.

### Former Nudist

Purchase a t-shirt at any craft store and stick-on lettering. Affix the words 'Former Nudist' to the front of your shirt and you are ready to go.

### Tom Cruise in Risky Business

If you wear this costume at a millennial party, nobody will know what's up. However, if you're older – throw on an oversized white oxford button-up, socks, and black glasses. Wear something underneath the shirt (e.g. bike shorts) or you may win the costume contest award: 'most likely to be arrested.'

### Bunch of Grapes

Blow up a ton of purple (or green) balloons and attach them to a matching t-shirt by sewing the ends to the fabric with a few stitches. For the lower grapes, allow the string to hang a bit from the shirt. Make a headpiece out of twig with some leaves (real or make out of felt). Wear matching tights.

### Scarecrow

If you have a straw hat and a flannel shirt or denim overalls – you're good to go. For an added flair, and to be sure people know what you are, Google scarecrow makeup and fix yourself up just like a real straw person. If you access to hay/straw, stick some in your pockets and coming out of your shirt sleeve (if you can stand it).

### Fantasy Football

Get a football helmet of any kind. Now, create the fantasy around it by wearing wizard robes (e.g. a Snuggie if you have one), carrying a scepter and wearing a long, white beard. Be ready to explain this one.

### Get Along Shirt

If you have a partner for the night, purchase a sweatshirt/t-shirt big enough for the two of you and write 'Our Get Along Shirt' on the front. Both of you wear it for the night and pose as siblings in time out.

### The Ultimate Present

Using a large cardboard box, wrap it in the gift wrap of your choice. Cut out a head hole and arm holes. Using construction paper, cut out a gift tag in this shape: 

On the tag, write in whatever cheeky message you wish such as *To: Women From: God*, etc. Don't forget to top this off with a big bow. Please note: this costume may be considered offensive, but maybe there's a costume contest section for that?

### Terrifying Tarantula

Wear any long-sleeved black top and pants. If you can stand wearing black gloves, that will be great. You'll need three pairs of little girl's opaque tights (black). Cut off the legs at the panties of the tights and fill with paper towels to the ends of the feet. With black thread, sew the tops to the back of your shirt – one on the right, one on the left and space them evenly, putting three additional 'legs' on each side. Now, for the cool effect – attach a long strand of fishing wire to the wrist of your shirt and also to each of your spider arms around where the ankle would be if they were tights, leaving enough slack in between them to look like legs when the arm is extended. Do this for the right side and do the same for the left side. That way, when you raise your arms, you bring up the other three arms below on either side.

# Dr. Bonnie

## Pirate

Tie a bandana around your head with the long pieces to the side. If you have boots, great, and if not, grab a piece of black fabric and wrap it around tight-fitting pants on top of black shoes. Wear a loose fitting shirt with a vest (make a vest by cutting an old shirt) and wrap a piece of fabric (or two) around your waist as a belt. Make a pirate eye patch out of felt and a piece of elastic. Wear one hoop earring on the side opposite the long bandana tails.

## Cowboy

Jeans, western (or flannel plaid) shirt and cowboy boots. Western belt and large belt buckle. Cowboy hat, lasso and a bandana tied around the neck make great touches. Chaps and a vest (leather preferably) are perfect!

## Gingerbread Man

If you have red hair or a red wig – strap on some loaves of bread (leave them in the plastic wrap and tape them on with clear shipping tape). Now, you are a Ginger-bread man.

## *Zombify* a Former Costume

Using old costumes in storage – reuse them by ripping them up a bit, getting them dirty in all the right places and wearing zombie makeup.

## Jelly Fish

Dress in all white/light blue. Purchase a matching color umbrella and attach long strands of sheer material/decorative trim/ribbon from your local craft store to the rim of the umbrella so it hangs down to your lower legs. If you have bubble wrap, cut it into thin strips for the tentacles. For a cool lighting effect, attach glow sticks/LED lights inside of the umbrella. If you want to win a costume contest, go all out and purchase battery operated fairy lights and attach to the rim of the umbrella and stream down along with your other streamers.

## Carmen Sandiego

If you have a brimmed hat, red trench coat, and a globe for a prop – you're all set. Wear black clothing underneath and black gloves. Black knee high boots are a great addition. The hat should be red with gold or black brim, but any brimmed hat will get your point across.

# The Halloween Party Host Handbook

## Men in Black

Black suit, white shirt, black tie, and sunglasses. You're set. Maybe make the neuralizer as a prop out of paper mache, or use a silver electronic cigarette?

## Beer on Tap

If you have a pair of tap shoes and a shirt from a beer company – you're all set to be 'beer on tap.' Get ready to perform all night, but make sure there's video of this – we all want to see it.

## Spice Girls

Have a few friends and don't have a ton of cash for costumes? Have fun with a play on words and purchase cheap t-shirts from a craft store and with stick-on lettering (or a Sharpie), write your favorite spice on the front – thyme, oregano, cumin, sage, etc. You're done!

## The Cloud

Dig in the closet for an old hoodie and get some packages of spider webs or quilt batting and glue it to your hoodie until it resembles a cloud – include the hood, as you'll wear it up all night. Then, glue on random pictures of your friends – especially selfies. Now, give yourself some makeup worthy of a cloud with whites, grays, and a light blue eye shadow. Wear white/light gray pants.

## Brawny Paper Towel Man

All you will need for this is a red plaid flannel shirt and a package of Brawny paper towels for reference to show who you are trying to be.

## Social Butterfly

Paste on the icons for various social media outlets onto a black top. Make these icons out of felt. Then, purchase a cheap butterfly wing/headband costume or make it yourself by using a headband and electrical tape and for the wings, make them out of galvanized wire (14 gauge), transparent gift wrap (iridescent is great), ribbon and glitter. Cut the four pieces of wire – two of the same length for the top wings and two for the lower wings (smaller pieces). Shape the top wings into an oval shape (make a point if you wish) and twist the ends together. Tape the twisted ends together with electrical tape. Do the same for the bottom wings. Now, tape the taped portions together and you've made the frame for your wings. Cover them in gift wrap. Cut a near exact piece and hot glue it to the wire on both sides. Do this for each wing. Cover the electrical tape connection with ribbon and glue with E6000. Glue elastic arm bands to the connected piece and reinforce with another wrapping of ribbon. Spray this with as much glitter spray as possible.

### Iron Chef

On any apron, make a periodic table box for iron (Fe 26) – Google the image for reference. Now, you are an 'iron' chef. And, a nerd. But, own it. Why not wear some black-rimmed glasses with a taped bridge as a fun accessory.

### Static Cling

Wear any clothing you wish and pin some random socks and a couple of dryer sheets to you randomly – but not too many! You'll be asked what you are, but be ready for chuckles.

### Patient from the Game Operation

Purchase a flesh-colored sweat suit. Pull up an image of the actual board from the game and cut out the shapes in your sweat suit in the approximate places. Using red felt, cover the holes you just made from the underneath by gluing swatches with E-6000 (or sew it on, glue it, etc.). With white felt, cut out the Adam's apple, broken heart, wishbone, spare ribs, etc. and glue those to the front side inside of the corresponding pockets you've made. If you want to go more authentic, wear a short black wig and make your nose red. Also, buy a light up clown's nose.

### Strawberry

Get an oversized red t-shirt or a plain red dress. Cut out teardrop 'seeds' from white felt and glue in an evenly spaced pattern over the red shirt/dress. Grab a green headband (or paint it green) and cut out some green leafy pieces and glue them to your headband.

### Glowing Stick Figure

Wear all black. Purchase glow stick necklaces. Using the connectors, make a long piece the length of your torso from your neck to your pelvic girdle. Then, connect pieces long enough for your legs and arms. Now, make a large necklace circle and glue it to the neck part of your torso glue stick. Support with clear packing tape if you need to. You've made your stick figure pieces; now you need to sew it with black thread to your black attire. Note: the circle piece for the stick figure's head should be large enough to go around your head. Your costume will be the best when the lights are out.

# The Halloween Party Host Handbook

## Piñata

Grab some colorful crepe paper and tear into strips. Within those strips, make ¼ inch slits ¾ way into the strip all along the length of the strip and affix to a camisole, alternating colors with the 'fringe' side downward and showing. For the skirt, wear bicycle shorts and attach ½ inch wide strips and fashion into a short skirt. Don't forget to cover your camisole straps with the fringed strips, as well. For the hat, use a party hat with the chin strap already attached. In layers, like you did your top, add the fringed crepe paper in alternating colors. Glue some streamers coming out of the top of the hat for an over-the-top effect.

## Wednesday Addams

All you need is a bit of gothic makeup, dark-haired braids, black clothing with a white collar and cuffs.

## Identity Thief

Buy a package of 'Hello, I am' nametag stickers. Write in different names with a Sharpie marker and stick them on your shirt.

## Cactus

Purchase a green sweat suit or latex suit – whatever you wish. Grab some white straws and glue them on, covering the suit, as your prickles (spines).

## Chicken Cordon Bleu

Here is what you need for this punny costume: any cord, a rubber chicken, and a blue shirt. Tie the cord around the chicken's neck and make a large necklace out of the cord to wear – don't make it even close to your neck size and dangle it down your front. Sew in the cord on your shoulders so it stays in place. Now, you are chicken cord – on – blue.

## Minion

Wear a yellow shirt and blue jean overalls. Make the minion symbol out of felt and glue it to the front of the costume. Grab some swim goggles and paint the rim silver and you're ready to go. Black gloves and black rubber boots are great accessories. If you want to go all out, paint your face yellow with sponge-on makeup and make a headband with black felt pieces as sprigs of hair. An alternative to the goggles is to punch out the lenses of an old pair of oversized glasses and paint the frame or wrap with aluminum foil.

# Dr. Bonnie

## 404 Error Page – Costume Not Found

Purchase a cheap white t-shirt from a craft store. With stick-on lettering (or a permanent marker if you don't feel like going through the effort), write ERROR 404 COSTUME NOT FOUND on the front and be done with it. At least you did something.

## Napoleon Dynamite's Girlfriend Deb

Swish your hair into a side pony, wear some puffed-sleeve attire and carry around a fishing lure box full of bead bracelet making supplies.

## Troll Doll

This is all about the hair. Wear anything you wish – such as a red pair of overalls (stuff the tummy a bit). Either grab a colorful wig or use your hair and color it with spray. However, you've got to tease your colorful hair to stand straight up. Use tons of hairspray!

## Medusa

Purchase cheap rubber snakes from any toy store/party store. This costume focuses on the hair. If you have long hair, you should put it in a circle braid around your head and intertwine the rubber snakes through the braids. Or, grab a wig and glue them to it. For your attire, wear something that won't compete with your over-the-top headpiece such as a black witch's gown. Makeup is also a good touch – the sky's the limit so do an adaptation of what you think Medusa's face should look like –go gothic, do a green face, or just wear normal makeup.
An alternative for the snake hair is to spray paint a bunch of rubber/plastic snakes gold and glue them to a painted headband of the same color – that way; you leave your hair out of it and just wear it as a headpiece.

## Serial Killer

If you dislike wearing costumes, and you're being forced to attend a costume party. Go as a serial killer – they look like everybody else. Wear normal attire and get ready to be asked questions.

## Serial Killer (with Effort)

Grab a plain white t-shirt and glue mini cereal boxes on it. Now, take white plastic knives (or any other toy knives) and pierce the cereal boxes, securing with a dab of E6000 glue (allow drying). Take fake blood (make your own using the recipe given to you in this book or buy some from any costume/party store) and spatter it all over the shirt, dripping some down from each knife-cereal box interface. Allow drying before you wear this masterpiece.

## Mother Nature

Mother Nature can be highly variable as nobody knows what she truly looks like - because she doesn't exist. With that said, the more items of nature glued to an Earth-tone costume, the better. A floral headband is a nice touch, as well. Mother Nature would probably never cut her hair – so a long, flowing wig is great.

## Blessing in Disguise

If your name is really Blessing – you've got to do this at least once for Halloween. If your name isn't Blessing, it can be for Halloween this year. Purchase one of those cheap-o black rimmed glasses with the attached nose 'disguises.' Get a plain white t-shirt. Using cut out felt, stick-on letters, or a permanent marker, place/write the word 'Blessing' across your chest.

## Formal Apology

Wear a tuxedo and a sign around your neck that says 'sorry.' You are a formal apology.

## Maroon 5

Maroon 5 is a cool band and can be represented on Halloween easily with a maroon/burgundy shirt or hoodie with a #5 pinned to it. Make the 5 out of felt or simply write it on a sheet of paper, cut it out of construction paper, use a stick-on letter, etc.

## Bag of Eminems

Everybody loves Eminem, right? Jump on the web and print out a bunch of pictures of the awesome rapper's face and cut them out. Then, grab a white trash bag and cut out neck and arm holes. Glue the pictures of Eminem's face all over the trash bag and now you're a 'bag of Eminems.'

## Sims Video Game Character

Wear absolutely anything you want. This costume is all about the headband. Create a bright lime green diamond out of paper that will appear to hover over your head just like it does in the video game. Google *Sims Character DIY* for some helpful tutorials on how to make this headband. Essentially, you just need two sheets of green paper, wire, glue and a cheap plastic headband.

# Dr. Bonnie

### Pippi Longstocking
Wear young, fun, and colorful clothing with colorful tights and socks. Make side braids in your hair and insert a wire into the braids to mold them to stick straight out. Add tons of fun ribbon around the braids, put on some freckles on your cheeks with lip-liner or brow-liner for a finishing touch.

### Cheeky Ceiling Fan
Wearing any fan gear you want such as a face mask, colored wig, foam finger and/or pom pom – make a sign that says 'go ceiling.' Now, you're a ceiling fan.

### Cat Burglar
Wearing all black, purchase a cheap cat-eared headband (and tail, if it comes with it). Then, with burlap fabric, make a money bag. Cut out a dollar sign (or whatever money symbol your country's money uses) and affix to the money bag. Have some toy dollars sticking out of it.

### Bath Pouf
Purchase a ton of colorful tulle and bunch it up in large pleats, sewing it onto a sleeveless shirt until it resembles a pouf (a large ball shape). Do the same with some bike shorts so it melds together when worn. Purchase about a ¾ yard of a white piece of rope and sew the ends to your shirt, allowing it to hang over the tulle. If you wish, grab some small clear balloons and blow them up to look like bubbles and glue them in clusters to the outer tulle. Glue a rubber duck to a matching headband and you're ready to go!

### Cotton Candy
Purchase a ton of light pink or blue tulle and bunch it up in large pleats, sewing it onto a sleeveless shirt. Do the same with some bike shorts so it melds together when worn. Purchase some white felt and make a hat with a thin elastic chin strap sewn on. Add some bunched tulle to the chin strap and the base of the hat. Make the white cone thin and taper to a point to mimic the paper holder of the cotton candy. Spray the hat with as much iridescent glitter as you want to make it more glitzy.

### Ghost
Grab a white sheet (that you don't want anymore) and add eye holes. Measure this! Cut out the eye holes after you mark their location (don't

cut them out while the model is still wearing it). Add black mesh breathable/ see through fabric backing to the eyes.

## Lego

You'll need a cardboard box big enough to get into – cut out a hole for your head and arms and trim off the box flaps on the bottom. Acquire six disposable plastic Tupperware bowls (about 4-5 inches in diameter). Glue the rim side of the Tupperware bowls to the front of the cardboard box with E6000 – measure to ensure they are of equal distance. If you need to refer to a Lego's pattern, pull one up online. Allow the glue to dry. Now, spray the entire thing with white spray paint and allow drying. Pick your Lego's color (e.g. yellow, red, blue, green) and spray paint the costume. Wear matching tights/shoes.

## Chia Pet

Grab a bunch of green, low profile foliage such as clover (or purchase at a craft store), and glue it to a beanie. You should do this the same day you're wearing it so it doesn't yellow/brown. Using orange-based face makeup, sponge on enough to make your face look like orange pottery – Google *Chia Pet* for reference. If you have clothing to match the burnt orange color – wear it. If not, just wear black.

## Deviled Egg

Purchase a ready-made devil horn headband or make one yourself out of any plastic headband, red sequin fabric, and E6000 glue. Make the horns out of paper mache and glue them onto the headband with E6000 and roll in red glitter. For the egg, take a cardboard box and cut out an egg shape the length of your torso. Paint it white and then paint a yolk in the center. Everything is better with glitter, so spray some iridescent glitter spray on your egg. Or, be more specific and add white glitter to the white of the egg and yellow glitter to the yolk. Do the yellow and white areas separately, allowing drying in between. With whatever rope, twine, etc. you can find, punch holes in the egg and insert your ties and tie the egg around your neck, hanging on your chest. Now, you're a deviled egg.

## Crazy Cat Lady

Hair rollers, a pink fluffy robe and tons of beanie cats (or other small stuffed cats). Tease your hair a bit before you add the rollers and add

# Dr. Bonnie

them sporadically. Glue some of the cats to the robe as if they are climbing or going down. Also, as props, hold on to some.

## Nerd

Wear an oxford shirt, preferably short-sleeved, too small, and buttoned to the top. Fasten suspenders to your high-water pants and wear white tube socks and black dress shoes. Pull pants up high and fasten with the most uncool belt you own. If you don't own an uncool belt, get some rope. Add a pocket protector with some pens and maybe a handy protractor. Wear black-rimmed glasses with a taped bridge and apply a bunch of fake pimples on your face. Grease your hair back to look extra nerdilicious. Apply Vaseline on your face for a nice, greasy complexion.

## Comic Book Character

Wear any colorful outfit and this costume is all about the makeup. Google *comic book makeup* for tutorials. If you have a colored wig, particularly a shoulder length, this is spectacular. Comics are all about color!

## Spooky Doll

Wear any colorful dress – best if it is uber-conservative and little girl-like. This is another costume that's all about the makeup. Google *creepy doll makeup* for tutorials. If you have a long, braided wig that looks particularly synthetic - that's great.

## Mummy

Use gauze for this or just toilet paper if you want a more economical option. Cheesecloth will also work. Starting with your legs, wrap and wrap and wrap and wrap until you are mummified. Just remember – you'll need to use the restroom at some point, so wear clothing the same color as your wrap and don't wrap the important parts. Hang some gauze/toilet paper over your lower body so your costume just doesn't stop.

## Black Eyed Pea

Black one of your eyes using black, purple and yellow eye shadow. Put a 'P' on your shirt by cutting it out of felt and pinning it or gluing it if you don't care about the shirt.

# The Halloween Party Host Handbook

### Hobo

Wear ragged, tattered clothing. Create dirt smudges on the face with brown shades of eye shadow. Carry a stick (find a branch outside) with a bandana tied on the end and stuffed with a fake can of food.

### Nickelback

Albeit the band isn't phenomenal – this costume is cute. Wearing any t-shirt, glue a bunch of nickels on your back. There ya go!

### Zombie

Ragged, tattered clothing. Using white makeup as a base, cover your exposed skin with white. Add green and blue eye shadow on top with fake scabs/scars and blood streaks wherever you feel like it.

## ADDITIONAL COSTUME IDEAS:

| | | |
|---|---|---|
| '20s Flapper | Fruit | Paperboy/Girl |
| '20s Mobster | Fruit Hat Lady | Photographer |
| '50s Greaser | G.I. Joe/Jane | Pilgrim |
| '50s Sock Hopper | Gambler | Pilot |
| '60s Mod | Geisha Girl | Pin-Up Girl |
| '70s Disco | Ghost Lady (Victorian) | Pirate |
| '80s Break Dancer | Ghostbuster | Pizza Man |
| '80s Valley Girl | Ghostly Gent (Victorian) | Plastic Surgeon (Carry Plastic Wrap) |
| Absent Minded Professor | Girl Scout | Poison Ivy |
| Addams Family | Glamorous Prom Queen (Dead) | Potato Head |
| Aerobics Girl | Gnome | Power Ranger |
| Alien | Goblin | Predator |
| Angel | Goddess | Priest |
| Animal (Various) | Golfer | Princess/Prince |
| Archer | Gondolier | Proctologist (Dr. Ben Dover) |
| Army Soldier | Gravedigger | Prom Queen |
| Artist | Greek Goddess | Protester |
| Baby | Grim Reaper | Psychic |
| Ballerina | Guinevere | Queen |
| Bandito | | Queen Of Hearts |

# Dr. Bonnie

| | | |
|---|---|---|
| Bank Robber | Guitar Hero | Raggedy Ann |
| Baseball Player | Gunslinger | Rap Artist |
| Bat | Gymnast | Ravenna (Snow White Villain) |
| Beast | Gypsy/Fortune Teller | Referee (Blind) |
| Beauty Queen | Hairdresser | Repairman |
| Belly Dancer | Harem Girl | Roman Toga |
| Biker | Hiker | Sailor |
| Black Widow | Hillbilly | Salesman |
| Bowler | Hippie | Saloon Girl |
| Boxer | Hula Dancer | Scarecrow |
| Boxer Ring Girl | Hunter | Scarlet O'Hara |
| Boy Scout | Ice Queen | School Girl |
| Break-Dancer | Ice Skater | Secret Service |
| Bride/Groom | Insect (Various) | Sesame Street |
| British Red Coat | Jailbird | Sheik |
| Bullfighter | Jersey Shore | Sheriff/Cop |
| Butler | Jester | Shopper |
| Caesar | Juan Valdez | Showgirl |
| Can-Can Dancer | Judge | Skateboarder |
| Candy | King | Skeleton |
| Car Hop | Lady In Waiting (Medieval) | Snowboarder |
| Carpenter | Leprechaun | Soccer Player |
| Cat Woman | Lifeguard | Social Media Star |
| Celebrity | Lilly Munster | Soda Can |
| Chef | Lion Tamer | Space Villain |
| Chimney Sweep | Little Girl's Doll | Spartan |
| Cigarette Girl (20's) | Lizzie Borden | Sports Star |
| Cleopatra | Lobster | Spy |
| Clown | Lumberjack | Stadium Vendor |
| Coal Miner | Mad Butcher | Sumo Wrestler |
| Colonial Man | Mad Scientist | Superhero/Heroine |
| Condiment | Magician | Supermodel |
| Construction Worker | Maid | Swat Team |
| Corpse | Marathon Runner | Swimmer |
| Cowboy/Girl | | |

# The Halloween Party Host Handbook

| | | |
|---|---|---|
| Crash Test Dummy | Mario/Luigi | Tarantula |
| Custodian | Martha Washington | Teacher |
| Dalmatian Villain | Martial Artist (Ninja) | Tooth Fairy |
| Dark Angel | Masquerade | Train Conductor |
| Darth Vadar | Matador | T-Rex |
| Dead Man Walking | Mechanic | Turkey |
| Dead Prom Queen | Medic | Undercover Cop |
| Detective | Medieval Knight | Unabomber |
| Devil | Medusa | Unicorn |
| Disco Diva/Dude | Mermaid | Vampire |
| DJ | Mime | Veterinarian |
| Dr. Evil | Mob Boss | Victorian Lady |
| Drag Racer | Monk | Video Game Princess |
| Emo Teen | Morton Salt Girl | Vintage Hollywood Glam |
| Eskimo | Movie Characters (Various) | Waiter |
| Executioner | Movie/Tv/Cartoon Villain | Warlock |
| Fairy Godmother | | |
| Farm Girl | Mummy | Weatherman |
| Fashion Police | Muppets Character | Welder |
| Fast-Food Mascot | Musketeer | Wild West |
| Firefighter | Native American | Witch |
| Fisherman | Ninja | Witch Doctor |
| Flight Attendant | Nun | Wizard |
| Football Player | Old Lady | Wizard Of Oz |
| French Artist | Olympian | Wolfman |
| French Fries | Painter | Zombie |
| French Maid | Park Ranger | Zookeeper |

## DIY SPECIAL FX

**Some picture examples can be found on
http://partyhost411.com/halloweenhandbook**

### Adhesive - Homemade
**Ingredients:**
Corn syrup
Flour (as needed to thicken it)
**Directions:**
Don't have spirit gum? This quick fix for facial glue should help.

### Beard Stubble
**Ingredients:**
Coffee or tea grounds
Facial glue
**Directions:**
Apply a thin layer of facial glue onto your beard's location and press on the grounds.

### Blood - Homemade (Non-Toxic)
**Ingredients:**
1 cup of water
3 cups of corn syrup
About 10 to 15 drops of red food coloring
About 2-3 drops of blue food coloring
Chocolate syrup to thicken and add a deep color (or cocoa powder)
**Directions:**
Mix the ingredients and allow thickening at room temperature. This fake blood is non-toxic but very sticky! Wash out of hair carefully! Vampires and zombies – take a swig of this in your mouth and allow to gently 'drool' out of your mouth for a cool effect. Wait at least 10 minutes before touching the 'blood tracks.' Because of the food coloring; this can stain!

### Blood Capsules - Homemade (Non-Toxic)
**Ingredients:**
Homemade blood (above)
Marinade injector (you can pick these up online for under 5$ - or you can use a syringe)
Empty gel capsules from any vitamin store

# The Halloween Party Host Handbook

**Directions:**
Need to make blood ooze from your mouth on command? Well, grab some empty gel capsules from any vitamin store and a marinade injector. Make your homemade blood (above) and inject it into the empty capsule.

## Bruises

**Ingredients:**
Red, burgundy, smoky gray and purple crème makeup
A hint of yellow at the edges is a good effect.
Makeup sponge
Powder (either compressed or baby powder)
**Directions:**
Using the makeup sponge, start with the red crème and make the outline of the bruise. Don't apply too much at once, keep it light and smooth. In the case of a bruise – less is more – you want very bare coverage! You want the skin to show through the makeup. Next, use the burgundy and lightly go over most of the red section. Again, you want the red and the skin to show through. Then, do the darkest purple color in an area of the bruise – again, doing it light enough to where the red, burgundy and the skin shows through. Then, set with powder! You always have to powder crème based makeup or it will wipe off, sweat off and look disgusting in mere moments!

## Bullet Holes

**Ingredients:**
Dental floss
Liquid latex
Saran wrap
Black makeup
Fake blood
**Directions:**
Make 1/3 inch circles with dental floss and set aside. Make ½ inch circles on your Saran wrap with latex, and place the circle of dental floss in the center of each one. Add a few more layers of liquid latex and allow drying. Apply to the skin using liquid latex and blend with the skin to ensure it looks realistic. With a makeup sponge, color the inside of the bullet hole with the black makeup and then use the fake blood to surround the bullet hole. Allow some to drip down onto the face, chest – where your bullet hole is located.

# Dr. Bonnie

## Facial Putty

**Ingredients:**
Equal amount of microcrystalline wax (found in art stores) and
Vaseline (petroleum jelly)
Colored facial powder in whatever tint you need

**Directions:**
On low heat and not over an open flame, melt the wax and petroleum
jelly and stir in the powder when melted. When cooled, use to extend
ears, chins, etc. *Wax is flammable, so no flames.

## Guts (Intestines)

**Ingredients:**
Packing peanuts
Thread
Needle
Liquid latex
Old paint brush

**Directions:**
Just like you are making a popcorn garland for a Christmas tree,
thread a threaded needle through the packing peanuts, shaping them
into an intestine as you go. Make it a strand about 3-4 feet in length.
Brush three-four coats of liquid latex over the packing peanut strand
and allow drying, repeat the process at least 3 times. In a mixing bowl,
coat the intestine with fake blood, mixing it around to coat it thoroughly.
Again, allow drying. This will still be sticky, however, and will stain what
it comes into contact with, so be careful.

## Guts (Intestines)
## Volume II

**Ingredients:**
Spaghetti noodles
Red food coloring
Hog casing (sausage casing)
Fake blood
Funnel

**Directions:**
Boil the spaghetti noodles with the food coloring – use a ton. This will
turn the noodles a red-flesh color, which is great for the color of the
intestines. When the noodles are softened, take them out and strain
them. Using a funnel, push the noodles through and fill the casing,
pushing it down the length of the casing to your desired length (a few

feet). Don't forget to tie off the end so your noodles don't escape the other end. After you have your intestines prepared, put them in a mixing bowl with fake blood and coat them thoroughly.

## Latex DIY
**Ingredients:**
¼ cup tapioca flour
Gelatin packet (or up to 2 packets for more firmness)
1 tbsp. solid coconut oil
1 cup water
Colored facial powder in whatever tint you need
**Directions:**
In a saucepan over medium heat, stir the tapioca, facial powder (or foundation), gelatin, and oil into the water and dissolve. Stir until the mixture thickens and then allow cooling. Apply once the latex dries to room temperature. This isn't really 'latex' but it's a good homemade alternative. Use this as an adhesive or make prosthetics for your costume. Apply facial makeup on top of this, as well.

## Mermaid Makeup
**Ingredients:**
Metallic/iridescent cream eye shadow – aqua, blues, silver, and light greens
Fishnet stocking
Makeup sponge
**Directions:**
Put the fishnet stocking over your face. Apply the crème eye shadow with a sponge or your fingertips, being careful to keep the fishnet stocking in place. Create an ombre effect on your forehead and along your cheekbones by changing colors as you move down the face. Highlight with the silver. Carefully remove the fishnet and enjoy your special effects makeup. Don't end there; do some fabulous eye makeup in the same color scheme. Ombre your lips with the darkest blue color as a lip liner, with silver in the center. Top off the look with some Australian crystal pieces glued on with facial glue.

## Oozing Wounds (How to get the Blood to the Wound)
**Ingredients:**
Aquarium tubing
Ear irrigation bulb
Fake blood

# Dr. Bonnie

**Directions:**
Fill the ear irrigation bulb with fake blood and insert the tubing. Put a dab of E6000 around the interface of the bulb/tubing to ensure it doesn't pop out and ooze blood underneath your costume. Navigate the tubing through your costume to the open wound – making sure the tubing isn't visible to the outside (paint the tip of the tubing to match the wound, if needed). When you're ready to bleed, squeeze the bulb!

## Skin – Blistered

**Ingredients:**
Tissue paper
Elmer's glue
Makeup foundation (skin tone)
Alcohol to clean the skin
Vaseline

**Directions:**
Clean the skin where you want your blistered skin. It is best to match your skin color with the foundation. Coat the tissue paper with the foundation and allow drying. Tear the tissue paper into the blister size you would like to make on your skin. Place the 'blister' on your skin and apply Elmer's glue on top and allow drying. Be still, and if you cannot wait it out, use a hair dryer on cool/low to speed up the process. Apply a thin layer of Vaseline over your blistered skin and you're done.

## Skin - Burned

**Ingredients:**
Cotton balls
Liquid latex
Fake blood (from above or other fake blood)
Black face/body makeup
Alcohol to clean the skin

**Directions:**
Clean the skin where you want your fake burn. Adhere strands of cotton to the skin with liquid latex. Keep applying cotton in an irregular fashion until a large enough 'burn' is achieved. Allow the latex to dry completely. Pour fake blood over the burn and allow drying. With a paint brush or makeup applicator, apply the black makeup in splotches to simulate 'charred skin.'

### Skin – Scabby

**Ingredients:**
1 cup water
1 cup gelatin
Fake blood

**Directions:**
Prepare the gelatin and allow cooling partially until lukewarm (it should not too be too hot for the skin! Be careful!) Test the temperature first and then apply the gelatin on the cleaned area of skin (it will harden quickly and won't stick if it is too cool). Color the scabs with the fake blood.

### Skin – Scabby
### Volume II

**Ingredients:**
Water
1 tbsp. corn syrup
Fake blood
Crème blush (burgundy/deep red)
Envelope of unflavored Knox gelatin (prepare according to directions)
Paintbrushes/makeup sponge

**Directions:**
Prepare the gelatin and allow to partially cool until warm (it should not too be too hot for skin! Be careful!) Paint your scab shape on with the paintbrush with corn syrup. Then, coat your 'scab' with cornmeal, lightly blowing off any excess cornmeal after a few minutes. Using a sponge, color the cornmeal very carefully with the crème blush/fake blood. Then, with a cooled gelatin mix, use caution to paint gelatin over the cornmeal. The gelatin will create a seal and hopefully, keep your scab intact. Add a touch of fake blood wherever you think will add to the scab.

### Skin – Wrinkly/Bumpy

**Ingredients:**
Paper towel
Coffee or tea (brewed)
Corn syrup

**Directions:**
Crumple up the paper towel that has been stained with coffee/tea and allowed to dry. To get the best color, you may need to stain 2-3 times.

# Dr. Bonnie

Then, apply to the face with corn syrup. Color with skin-matching foundation by dabbing on with a sponge.

## Skin – Zombie

**Ingredients:**
Elmer's Glue
2-ply toilet tissue
Face makeup/paint (green, black, gray)

**Directions:**
Test for skin sensitivity with the Elmer's glue first by apply a strip to the face and allowing it to dry. When ready, place a small amount of glue on the face and spread very thin. Take a 1.5" by 1.5" square of toilet tissue and place over the glue. Add additional glue at the edges and a thin layer on top, securing it to the face. Repeat and cover as much of the face as you wish. Once you have the toilet tissue/glue layer applied, add the facial makeup on top. Add some oozing blood spots for a cool zombie effect.

## Snot

**Ingredients:**
1 cup cornstarch
½ cup water
Green food coloring

**Directions:**
Mix the ingredients and then have fun with it.

## Tattooed Legs/Arms

**Ingredients:**
Pair of skin-colored pantyhose
PVC pipe – diameter large enough to fill up the pantyhose, but not too big to tear it.
Fabric marker/paint

**Directions:**
Slip the PVC pipe into the pantyhose where you want your tattoo. Apply the tattoo freehand or by using a template with fabric marker/paint and allow drying. Slip the pantyhose on and you are tattooed. Do this for the arms, but get a small enough pair so it isn't baggy. Also, cut the pantyhose on either end, and fasten with spirit gum. For the wrist, wear a large, leather cuff on the interface and put the other end where it ends underneath a short sleeved shirt.

## Various FX - Upholstery Foam
**Ingredients:**
Upholstery Foam
Liquid latex
Spray adhesive
Paint
**Directions:**
At any fabric store, purchase upholstery foam. Use this in many ways for special effects. Cut shapes to make larger muscles, make facial appliances, a mask, etc. Spray on liquid latex &/or paint it. Use fabric adhesive to glue pieces together if you wish to make a large form. The sky is the limit if you are creative.

## White Makeup (Clowns, Ghosts, etc.)
**Ingredients:**
2 tsp. white shortening
5 tsp. cornstarch
1 tsp. all-purpose flour
Glycerin
**Directions:**
Mix the ingredients thoroughly. For a thicker consistency, add more flour. For a creamier base, add more glycerin.

# V. Halloween Party Games

## TIE-BREAKING

### Mouse-Cat-Witch Tiebreaker

When playing party games, you may find yourself in a tie. What do you do? You can do the obvious rock, paper scissor challenge. Or, spice it up a bit with a full body Halloween version: Mouse-Cat-Witch. The opponents must stand back-to-back about 2 feet apart. When the host counts down three, two one – on 'one' they must immediately turn around (clockwise) and show their choice of the following:

**Mouse** – they must put fisted hands under their chin and pretend to gnaw on something as a mouse would do with their front teeth extended.

**Cat** – they must extend one paw in a scratching pose and shout 'meow.'

**Witch** – both hands must be flat on their belly, and they must cackle like a witch.

If anybody changes their original choice of mouse, cat or witch, once they turn around and see/hear what their opponent has chosen, they immediately lose that turn of the round – no questions asked. The host is the final judge.

They do this three times and whoever wins twice is declared the winner. If you play two rounds and the same player wins – no need to do the third round.

## GAMES INCLUDING COSTUMES

### Crazy Costume Challenge:

**Objective**: not to only have the most fabulous costume but strut your stuff on the Halloween fashion runway the best!

**Rules:** all players wearing a costume can participate. Create a fun Halloween fashion runway – either designate an area or line your runway with tied down orange and black balloons, crepe paper, etc. Play a fun Halloween song while each player struts their stuff down the runway – showing off their costume. The host of the party should be the judge. After all of the players have gone, there might be a tie, and the tied players must engage in a tie-breaking dance contest. The tie-

# The Halloween Party Host Handbook

breaker is the player who can dance in the theme of their costume the best to a song of the host's choice. For example, a vampire needs to insert vampire moves in their dance and a werewolf must dance like a werewolf. The remaining players can vote via a ballot for the winner.
**Props needed:** a runway and a fun Halloween song.
**Playing time:** ~20 minutes.

## Competitive Costume Contest:

**Objective**: to wear the most awesome costume to the party and be acknowledged for your efforts.
**Rules:** all players wearing a costume can participate. Create a fun Halloween fashion runway – either simply designate an area or line your runway with tied down orange and black balloons, crepe paper, etc. Play a fun Halloween song while each player models their costume – hopefully in character - down the runway.
This contest is more structured than the 'just for fun' one above. Recruit three judges for this contest, and give them judging sheets. After all of the contestants have modeled their costumes, stand them in line before the judges with the audience behind the judges. Put your hand over each contestant and ask for the audience to clap for their favorites. The judges will use this 'clap-o-meter' to assess points for the audience vote by clap. The judges shall judge on the following criteria:

- **Overall appearance of the costume: (1-10 points)**
- **Makeup/hair**: did they incorporate makeup and a hairstyle into the costume? Special FX makeup should earn the most points. **(1-5 points)**
- **Use of props**: props add flair and vitality to a costume, completing the look. **(1-5 points)**
- **Creativity**: store bought versus DIY. (Good) DIY should receive more points. **(1-5 points)**
- **Acting:** is the participant playing the role of the character? A costume is about the character as a whole not just the fabric and makeup. **(1-10 points)**
- **Audience vote:** by clap. Point value is lower because audiences, especially smaller ones, tend to be biased. **(1-3 points)**

**Props needed:** a runway and a fun Halloween song.
**Playing time:** ~20 minutes.

# Dr. Bonnie

## Costume Monolog Challenge

**Objective**: not to only have the most fabulous costume but to act out a 1-minute scene in character.

**Rules:** all players wearing a costume can participate. Gather the players into an audience with an area designated as the stage. One by one, the players can come up to the stage and perform a 1-minute monolog in the character of their costume. They can do comedy, drama, horror – anything they wish, but it has to be original, make sense with their costume, and they have to act alone. Either allow the host to judge or have the players vote by ballot.

**Props needed:** people in costumes and ballots/pens if you vote by ballot.

**Playing time:** ~20 minutes (depending on how many players you have).

## Costume Dance Off

**Objective**: to be the last one left on the dance floor.

**Rules:** this is an individual challenge. Clear out an area large enough for a dance floor, and play fun Halloween music (search for Party of 2 on iTunes for a good choice). The players are to dance within the theme of their costume. The judge(s) will walk around judging the dancers and tap the dancers on the shoulder who have been eliminated – either because they aren't dancing in the theme of their costume, or they are just not dancing well. For example: if the player is dressed as a witch, they must incorporate witch'y mannerisms into their dance such as stirring a cauldron, riding a broom, etc. If they are dressed up like a cat – they must get on all fours and incorporate cat characteristics into their style of dance such as licking their arms/paws, rubbing against others' legs, arching their backs, hissing, etc. The last one left on the dance floor is the dance champion. The dancers are not allowed just to mimic their character. Each dancer must incorporate the mannerisms of their character into their performed **dance** – this is a *dance* competition. Tell them to be creative.

**Props needed:** people in costumes, dance music.

**Playing time:** ~10 minutes.

## A Night at the Theater

**Objective**: to create the best, original skit by creating characters with your costumes.

**Rules:** all players wearing a costume can participate and are grouped into sets of three to four. For larger groups, extend this to five to six.

Give time for the groups of thespians to meet and come up with the best 1-2 minute skit made up of characters that correspond with their costumes. They are to write it, direct it and act it – they cannot steal anything from the internet – it must be an original masterpiece. When time is called (~10 minutes), the players draw a number to see who will perform first. Once the first group starts to perform, it is forbidden to speak to teammates in any manner whatsoever. The rehearsal time is over. Any team that is caught speaking to each other will be deducted two points for each violation.

**Judging is based on the following:**
5 points for creativity/originality.
5 points for the utilization of the costumes – did they use their costumes to the fullest?
5 points for acting ability.
**Props needed:** an area for the performances and a sheet of paper/pen for judging. Slips of paper – one for each group and numbered – placed into any container for them to draw their order to perform.
**Playing time:** ~30 minutes.

## GETTING TO KNOW YOU GAMES

### Halloween Human Bingo
**Objective:** is to be the first one to 'bingo' by finding players who can answer 'yes' to the squares on your bingo sheet!
**Rules:** Create your bingo sheets, print one for each player, and cut them out (if needed) and hand each player a writing utensil. When you say go, the players will mingle and individually ask each other questions on their bingo cards. If anyone says 'yes' to a question, the player that said 'yes' is to sign the square on the bingo card. If they say 'no' to the question, the one asking the question must move on to ask someone else. The first player to get five across, down or diagonal – wins the first bingo.

The game can continue with the first to get two lines across, down or diagonal and then the first player to black-out. If at any time it is discovered that nobody at the party can answer 'yes' to a question – everyone gets credit for it immediately. In the event of a tie bingo, the tie-breaker will be the first one to get another square signed.

**Examples of gameplay:** Lauren asks Aubrey if she has ever dressed as an animal for Halloween. If Aubrey replies 'no,' then Lauren cannot ask Aubrey another question until she has found someone to answer 'yes' to that question. However, Lauren must first allow Aubrey to ask her a question on her card before she moves on to asking a question to someone else.

Madison asks Ella if her birthday is in October. If Ella replies 'yes,' then she must sign the square on Madison's bingo card. Then, Madison has to allow Ella to ask her a question from her card before Madison can move on to asking someone else another question.

**Props needed:** bingo sheets and a pen/pencil for each player.

**Playing time:** ~ 10 minutes.

**Example bingo card is as follows:**

| Have you ever dressed as a ghost for Halloween? ___ | Are you afraid of ghosts?___ | Have you ever told spooky stories by a campfire? ___ | Have you ever trick-or-treated with a pillowcase? ___ | Is your birthday in October? ___ |
|---|---|---|---|---|
| Have you ever dissected anything in school?___ | Have you ever seen a zombie movie?___ | Do you know all the words to the Monster Mash?___ | Do you know someone named 'Frank?'___ | Have you ever dressed as a Disney character for Halloween? ___ |
| Have you ever worn black nail polish? ___ | Have you ever had a black cat as a pet? ___ | Have you ever read a Goosebumps book? ___ | Have you ever had a snake as a pet? ___ | Have you seen the movie Krampus (2015)?___ |
| Have you seen the movie Cabin in the Woods (2012)? ___ | Do you have a parent (or child) with a birthday in October? ___ | Have you ever dressed as a monster for Halloween? ___ | Have you ever carved a pumpkin by yourself? ___ | Have you ever dressed as a devil for Halloween? ___ |
| Have you ever eaten a pumpkin seed?___ | Have you ever dressed as a sports star for Halloween? ___ | Is Skittles your favorite Halloween candy? ___ | Have you ever had a black bird as a pet?___ | Is Snickers your favorite Halloween candy?___ |

## Love it, Hate it

**Objective:** to rack up the most points by guessing *who said what* correctly.

**Rules:** Give each player two strips of paper and a writing utensil. Ask them to write their name on both slips and then write one thing they love about Halloween and one thing they hate about Halloween on a slip. They put the slips into the designated containers for each (label a love container and hate container – be creative with decorating these). When everybody has submitted their slips into the right place, the host will alternate pulling a slip randomly from the love container, then the hate container, etc.

The host will read the slip to the group and the first player to guess (correctly) who said it – gets the point. A player is not allowed to guess their own and if they do, everybody else gets a point. Any player guessing incorrectly is penalized and may not guess the next slip. This prevents everybody from shouting out answers and causing confusion &/or players from guessing their own to cause chaos.

**Props needed:** a pen/pencil for each player. Two slips for each player and two containers marked *love* and *hate.*

**Playing time:** ~ 10-15 minutes.

## The Name Game

**Objective:** to get as many balls going in the group without dropping them to the ground.

**Rules:** put about ten players in a circle and have them introduce themselves one-by-one. If the group already knows each other, that's fine. Hand one player a ball and ask that they shout a player's name as they throw the ball to them. The player must catch the ball and throw it to someone else in the circle, shouting that person's name. The game host will add a second ball – adding to the chaos, and the same gameplay continues but with two balls being thrown in the circle. A third ball enters the circle, a fourth ball, etc. until a ball hits the ground. Then, record the number of balls in play in the circle. Have the group compete with another circle to see how many balls they can get going and then, for a second round, switch up the circles so everybody can learn each other's names. If, at any time, a player gets stumped and cannot think of anybody's name and ruins the flow – the game is called and the number of balls is counted.

**Props needed:** hand-sized soft bean bag balls to toss in the circle.

**Playing time:** ~ 10-15 minutes.

# Dr. Bonnie

## Descriptive Intros

**Objective:** to introduce your guests to each other.

**Rules:** ask that each player stand up and introduce themselves to the other guests by adding an adjective that matches the first letter of their name. Then, they are to be referred to by this name for the rest of the night (unless you are doing a murder mystery party. If you are, jump right back into the mystery party character after this activity).

For example, if the player's name is Sarah – she can say *hello, my name is Spunky Sarah.* Dan can say *hello; I'm Decisive Dan*, and so on.

**Props needed:** a group of people willing to be a bit silly.

**Playing time:** ~ 10-15 minutes – depending on your amount of guests.

## True or False

**Objective:** to rack up the most points by fooling others with your 'false' statement about yourself.

**Rules:** Give each player a strip of paper and a writing utensil. Ask them to write one truth and one false statement about themselves. Once everybody is finished, have them stand up one at a time and announce their statements in any order they wish. Then, the host will ask for a show of hands for which statement the group believes to be true. The player gets a point for everybody who chooses their false statement. The player with the most points at the end is the winner.

**Props needed:** a pen/pencil for each player. Slip of paper or each player.

**Playing time:** ~ 10-15 minutes.

## Hammering Out Differences

**Objective:** to weed through questions until everybody in the group stands alone.

**Rules:** this exercise is to allow the group to get to know one another while showing how differently people think. Start with the entire group standing in a cluster in the center of the room – you will need a large space for this. Pose the first opposing thoughts and ask the group to choose one and make their choice by stepping 20 or so steps to the right or 20 steps to the left. Those with the same choice remain clustered together until they have a different opinion. Then, ask a second question and instruct the players to step 15 steps to the right or 15 steps to the left depending on their choice. Adjust the # of steps so

the group can spread out accordingly. Play continues until all/most of your players are standing alone.
**Props needed:** a large enough area for the group to spread out when they make choices.
**Playing time:** ~ 10-15 minutes.

**Here are some examples of what to ask the players to choose from:**

| MOVE TO THE RIGHT | MOVE TO THE LEFT |
|---|---|
| Orange | Purple |
| Jeans | Suit |
| Rock 'N Roll | Classical Music |
| Witch | Vampire |
| Past | Present |
| Action | Romance |
| Sedan | SUV |
| Trick | Treat |
| Witch's Broom | Flying Carpet |
| Vampire Bat | Black Cat |
| Sushi | Shepherd's Pie |
| Tornado | Tsunami |

## Who Dat?

**Objective:** to guess the person on the opposing team with the fewest clues.
**Rules:** Give each player an index card and a writing utensil. Divide your players into two even teams. Ask them to write five clues about themselves on the card. Collect the group of cards from each team, shuffle them, and place in a pile for each team (Team A, B). The host will draw a card from Team B and ask Team A to guess who the player is on Team B by reading the clues one by one. For every clue the host reads, they lose a point (starting with five). If the host reads all five clues and they still cannot guess who it is – the team gets no points. They may only guess one time per turn. Then, the host alternates by pulling a Team A card and reading to Team B until all cards have been read. The team with the highest amount of points at the end is the winning team.
**Props needed:** a pen/pencil for each player. Index card for each player.
**Playing time:** ~ 10-15 minutes.

# Dr. Bonnie

### Around the World in 15 Minutes

**Objective:** to be the first one to make it 'around the world' and back to your original chair.

**Rules:** Your players should be seated in a circle of chairs. Then, one person stands in the middle and is the caller. The caller will state random characteristics, and those players who match them may move chairs to the right. For example, if the caller says *all players with brown hair, move to the right* – then anybody with a shade of brown can move. If someone is seated in the chair to the right, they sit on their lap. When the next characteristic is called - only those by themselves in a chair or on someone's lap may move. For example, if the next thing called is people who drive white cars and a white car driver has someone sitting in their lap, they are unable to move. The first person to make it around the circle and back to their original chair will be the winner. In the case of a tie – go to a Mouse-Cat-Witch tiebreaker (see tiebreaking section for details).

**Props needed:** a circle of chairs – one for each player.

**Playing time:** ~ 10-15 minutes.

### I Would Never

**Objective:** to be the one with the most candy at the end.

**Rules:** give each player up to ten pieces of candy and have them sit in a circle. Place a cauldron in the middle of the circle with a large enough opening so the players can toss the candy inside of it. Each player will take turns telling what they would never do. For any player that has done what that player would never do, they have to throw a piece of candy into the cauldron. For example, player A is told to go first, and she says 'I would never get a traffic ticket.' Every player who has gotten a traffic ticket before loses a piece of candy and must throw a piece of candy into the cauldron. As soon as a player is out of candy, they are eliminated from the game. The last player with candy will win and get all the candy in the cauldron.

**Props needed:** five to ten pieces of candy for each player and a large plastic cauldron.

**Playing time:** ~ 10-15 minutes.

### Pennies in History

**Objective:** to draw a penny from the pile and remember something that happened to you that year.

# The Halloween Party Host Handbook

**Rules:** ask your players to sit in a circle. Start with the player's birthday closest to Halloween and ask them to draw a penny from the pile in the center. They view the year and then tell the group something interesting that happened to them that year. If the penny (or another dated coin you choose) is dated before the player's birth, have them draw another one.

**Props needed:** container full of pennies.

**Playing time:** ~ 10-15 minutes – depending on how many players you have.

## Mapping Birth Spots

**Objective:** to make a human-based map of where everybody is from.

**Rules:** first, ask the group to make four clusters based on where they were born – a northern, southern, eastern and western cluster and move accordingly in the room. If they are on the border of two groups, tell them just to choose one. Now, with your country in mind, ask them to spread out according to their birth city. Anyone born in a different country that you are in – ask them to stand as far as possible in the direction in which their country is located. Make adjustments as needed to create a birth map. When your players have finished arranging themselves, take a picture by standing on a chair (or via another vantage point) to capture the human birth map!

**Props needed:** a large enough space to arrange a human map.

**Playing time:** ~ 10-15 minutes – depending on how many players you have.

## The Devil's Chair

**Objective:** to interrogate your players in the Devil's Chair.

**Rules:** this is not a competitive challenge, but more of an ice-breaker. Each player will take turns in the Devil's Chair. When they are seated in the designated chair, a 20-second timer is started. The other players are allowed to ask as many thoughtful & positive questions of the player as they can think of and the player must answer each question quickly. For any question they do not want to answer, they say the phrase 'Not today, Beelzebub.' However, for as many times as they pass on a question by saying the phrase 'Not today, Beelzebub' they must do five pushups for each pass after their turn.

**Props needed:** a chair to call the Devil's Chair.

**Playing time:** ~ 10-15 minutes – depending on your amount of players.

# Dr. Bonnie

## Great Minds Think Alike

**Objective:** to find out what your guests have in common and to win, it is the player with the most prizes at the end of the round.

**Rules:** this is not a competitive challenge, but more of an ice-breaker. Hand each player five wrapped pieces of candy or other small prizes. Set the overall timer for ten minutes (or however long you wish to play this game). The host will call out a certain topic, and the players have 30 seconds to scramble and find people who think alike & have the same favorite. For example, if the host says 'favorite musical artist' – the players have 30 seconds to mingle about and ask each other who their favorite artist is, and once they find someone who has the same favorite, they lock elbows, make a chain, and search for others who have the same favorite. The chain can grow as long as needed to incorporate everybody who has the same favorite of that topic. It is alright if someone stands alone. When the 30 seconds is up, the host has each chain of elbow-locked people announce what their favorite thing is on the topic. If any two groups have the same favorite – meaning they didn't do their due diligence to find all the like-minded people in the room – everybody with that favorite topic loses a piece of candy and must put it in a designated place. The host will continue to call out topics, and this will repeat until the 10-minute timer goes off. Then, the player(s) with the most candy are declared the winners, and they can split the pile of lost candy between them.

**Some example topics are as follows. Favorite...**

| Sport | Pizza Topping | Comedy Movie | Color | Halloween Monster |
|---|---|---|---|---|
| Car | Genre of Food | Local Restaurant | Beverage | Vacation City |
| Occupation | Horror Movie | Ice Cream | Meat | Halloween Candy |

**Props needed:** five pieces of wrapped candy for each player (or another prize).

**Playing time:** ~ 10-15 minutes.

## Lose a Shoe, Make a Friend

**Objective:** to learn something new about each other.

**Rules:** each player is to remove a shoe and put it in a pile. On the count of three, the host says go and each player selects a different shoe from the pile and searches for the owner. When they locate the owner, they must ask their full name (your group may already be familiar). After they hear their name, they ask for three things they didn't know about that person. When they've been told, they can give the shoe back. Play continues until everybody has their shoe back. For the competitive aspect of this game, once everybody has both shoes on, have them stand up and recite their new friend's full name and recite the three things they learned about them. Without telling them you are going to do this, ask each person to stand up and recite each person in the room's full name. The person who can remember the most names correctly is declared the winner.

**Props needed:** players with shoes on.

**Playing time:** ~ 10-15 minutes.

## Skittles Truth Reveal

**Objective:** to learn something new about each other.

**Rules:** Put a container of regular flavored Skittles in the middle of the group. Ask them to grab as many pieces of candy as they wish, but not to eat any – they are to hold them in their hand until the game starts. Then, give the following rules: you must reveal truths about yourself to the group based on the color and number of candy pieces you are holding. You cannot eat the candy until after your turn. If your Skittles' colors vary, just make adjustments.

**For every red**, you must reveal one of your favorite things to do.

**For every yellow**, you must reveal a time when you were afraid of something/current fear.

**For every purple,** you must reveal a favorite childhood memory.

**For every green,** you must reveal your dream occupations – starting from childhood and to present.

**For every orange,** you must reveal a favorite food.

**Props needed:** Skittles candy (~ a handful for each player).

**Playing time:** ~ 10-15 minutes – depending on your amount of players.

## The Friends & Family Game Show

**Objective:** to get the most points by correctly guessing what answer your partner gave to a question.

**Rules:** divide your group into pairs and send their partners into the adjacent room where they will not hear. Give the players a marker and five sheets of paper or mini poster boards (~ 8" by 11"). Have the players write #1-5 on the back of the boards/sheets. Ask them five questions about Halloween and have them write their answers on their boards/sheets in order with one answer per sheet. Ask that they keep their answers in order of occurrence.

# Dr. Bonnie

Ask their partners to return to the room. Pose each question to their partners and ask that they attempt to duplicate their partner's answers. The host will pose the same question and ask each player to say what they believed their partner said, and then their partner may reveal their answer on the board/sheet for that question. Correct answers get one point. As the host, you are the judge whether an answer is a match or not – be as flexible as you wish.

Then, host round two where the partner who just answered is now asked to go to the next room. This round, the points are doubled, and each correct match is given two points, with the final question worth five points. The pair who has the highest points, wins.

**Props needed:** a marker and five mini poster boards (or sheets of paper) for each player.

**Playing time:** ~ 20 minutes.

## WORD BASED GAMES

### From Three to Twenty

**Objective:** to be the team that comes up with increasingly larger words within the given theme the fastest!

**Rules:** divide the group into pairs. Write down a theme for all to see. Set the timer for five minutes.

When the host says go, the teams are to write down words in increasing size (starting with a three-letter word) that fit the given theme. For example, if the host says zoo is the theme, the team will write down bat (3 letters), bear (4 letters), zebra (5 letters), etc., until they reach 20 letters. They can break up the words into a phrase as long as they fit the number of letters. For example, brown bear would be appropriate for nine letters. However, green bear wouldn't make sense and would not be counted. The teams do not have to go in order of increasing size as they fill in the blanks on their answer sheets but the team with the most correctly applied words or phrases wins! The host calls the time, takes up the answer sheets, scores them and declares a winner!

**Props needed:** a pen/pencil and a sheet of paper for each team labeled 3 to 20.

**Playing time:** ~ 20 minutes.

# The Halloween Party Host Handbook

### The Interrogation

**Objective:** to rack up the most points by the other players not guessing your Halloween items.

**Rules:** this is an individual challenge and largely based on the luck of the draw. Write down Halloween-themed items on slips of paper, fold them, and put them into a container for your players to draw. One at a time, a player is to draw a slip and stand in front of the group. Each of the players in the audience has a chance to ask a question that has a yes/no answer to figure out what the player's strip says. The first person in the audience to guess the word/phrase correctly, gets a point. Any player may guess at any time. However, once a player has guessed incorrectly during a round, they are out and may not guess again. If they have been removed from the round but guess correctly anyway by blurting out the answer (you know the type who will do this) – everybody in the game gets a point besides them. The player with the highest point total at the end of the game is the winner.

**Props needed:** slips of paper with Halloween-themed words and phrases on them. Have one to two slips per people in your game. Each player should have the same chances of being the one interrogated.

**Playing time:** ~ 10 minutes – depending on how many players in your game.

### The Great Halloween Scrambler

**Objective:** to be the team that can find and unscramble the most Halloween phrases in the given time.

**Rules:** divide the group into two teams. Before the party, hide scrambled Halloween phrases on sheets of paper. Find some bloody eyeball Easter-style plastic eggs and hide slips of paper containing these scrambled phrases inside. Give your players the boundaries before the hunt. Set a timer for three minutes, and say 'go.' The teams hunt for the eggs and unscramble the words inside of them for a point. The teams can strategize on how they wish to accomplish this – they can try to hog all the eggs and *then* unscramble them, or they can hunt, unscramble, etc. as they go. As they unscramble a phrase, they write the unscrambled word on the back of the slip and place it in the jar. When the timer goes off, the slips are verified as either correct or incorrect and points are awarded for each correctly unscrambled phrase.

**Props needed:** a pen/pencil for each team. Scrambled word slips containing Halloween phrases hidden in a designated boundary. A container for each team to drop their slips.

# Dr. Bonnie

**Playing time:** ~ 10 minutes.

**Examples of some Halloween phrases are below:**

| Bats in the Belfry | Btas Ni Eth Berfly |
|---|---|
| This is Halloween | Hsti Si Haewoelln |
| Fright Night | Fhigrt Ngiht |
| All Hallows Eve | Lal Lhalwos Vee |
| Witch's Cauldron | Iwtsch Alurcond |
| Trick-or-treat | Ktcri Ro Tatre |
| Happy Halloween | Ahypp Oahlelnwe |
| Count Dracula's Castle | Ocnut Carduasl Actlse |
| Bride of Frankenstein | Brdie Of Ennfriekstna |
| The Swamp Thing | Eth Awmsp Gthni |
| A Haunting We Will Go | A Ahuntgni We Iwll Og |
| Jack O'Lantern | Cajk O Arnteln |
| Forbidden Forest | Dorfdiben Roefst |

## Bungling Secretaries

**Objective:** to be the team with the closest resemblance of the original five-word sentence at the end of the line.

**Rules:** the group is divided into two equal teams sitting in a parallel line facing each other. Player #1 is the 'boss,' and the rest are the secretaries passing the message along. When the host says go, the boss (closest to the host) will write down a five-word sentence that is original and created by the player. There is no planning in advance with the team, as that would be cheating. When they have written down their sentence, they will show it only to the next player in line. The next player, on a new piece of paper, will draw an image best depicting the sentence they were shown. No letters, numbers, logos, or symbols in any form are allowed in this image. When complete, this player will show the image only to the next person in line who will try to come up with the original five-word sentence player #1 wrote down.

    **Cheaters:** if a player further down the line attempts to view a sentence image that was not meant to be shown to him or her – they will automatically lose the challenge for their team. If they...uh mmm...'accidentally' see an image or sentence from a player down the line – the round will reset and both teams must start over. The host will determine an accident from a blatant disregard for integrity.

    If you are playing two teams of 3: the host will judge which team has the closest five-word sentences from players #1 and #3. If both teams have an identical sentence to the original or if they are

71

equally terrible and not even close – the host calls it a 'draw' and they will go again, but this time, in reverse order (player #3 becomes the boss and will come up with the sentence, and #2 will draw the image, etc.). If it continues to be a draw after 4 turns (reversing order each turn), they will each select a player from each team to go head-to-head with a Mouse-Cat-Witch tiebreaker (see tiebreaking section).

*If you are playing with two teams of 3 (or with an uneven number of players on each team – i.e. two teams of 5, 7, 9, 11), the instructions above are what you follow and you will match player #1's sentence with the final player's sentence. For example, with 9 players on each team, match player #1 and player #9 to determine how close they are. *If you are playing with two teams of 4 (or more with an even number of players such as 6, 8, 10), player #1 will start with an image and the second player must formulate a five-word sentence from the image. The team who has the closest five-word sentence from player #2 and the final player will win.

**Props needed:** a piece of paper (or more – have backup in case you need to have multiple rounds) for each player and a writing utensil.

**Playing time:** ~ 15 – 20 minutes.

## Halloween Drawathon

**Objective:** to be the first to guess your teammate's drawing.

**Rules:** pair the players into groups of two to three. The team with the oldest member at the party will go first. They are to select a team member to draw a card and show their competitive drawer on the other team(s). They are not to show the members of their team nor tell the member on their team what the item is that they are drawing. The host says go and using a marker and white paper, the drawer on each team will draw the item on their card and have their team guess it before the other teams guess from their respective drawers. They cannot write symbols, letters, or speak while they are drawing. The only people allowed to speak are the host and the team members guessing. Once a team member guesses it correctly, the round is over, and a point is given to the team that guessed it correctly. Repeat the rounds by alternating teams that draw the card and drawers in the groups. Once the cards are all played, the points are added, and a winner is declared.

**Props needed:** white paper/pads for each team with the same number of sheets of blank paper for each card you play in the game. You can elect not to play all of these cards; you can make your own, and/or

# Dr. Bonnie

only play a set number of rounds depending on the time you allow for the game.

**Playing time:** ~ 15 – 30 minutes.

**Examples of drawathon words are:**

| Pumpkin | Black Cat | Skeleton | Haunted House |
|---|---|---|---|
| Bat | Witch's Hat | Frankenstein | Dracula |
| Ghost | Cauldron | Zombie | Goblin |
| Witch's Broom | Coffin | Tombstone | Cemetery |
| Serial Killer | Demon | Candy | Full Moon |
| Scream | Slime | Scary Movie | Monster |
| Werewolf | Mummy | The Munsters | Ghostbuster |
| Blood | Trick-or-treat | Gravedigger | Shadow |
| Frankenstein | Mad Scientist | Bob for Apples | Tarantula |
| Witch's Brew | Skull | Headless Horseman | Mask |
| Hayride | Owl | Eyeball | Tombstone |

## Halloween Charades

**Objective:** to be the first to guess your teammate's word without a word.

**Rules:** divide your group into two teams. One by one, a player will draw from the container of words/phrases and they will get one minute to act out their word to their team. If the team guesses the word correctly, they will get the point. Play alternates with each team allowing a player to be the actor. However, they must stay in the same order during the game – a player may not act a word/phrase twice until everybody on the team has been the actor. The team with the highest point total is the winning team. For the characters – use the words from Halloween Drawathon game.

**Props needed:** charades slips folded and placed into any container

**Playing time:** ~ 15 – 30 minutes.

## Fool Your Friends

**Objective:** to be the one who guesses the correct definition of an obscure word.

**Rules:** this is an individual challenge. Either by handing the host a dictionary, or allowing them to use their smartphone to pull up an online dictionary, the host is to find an obscure word – preferably Halloween-themed. They announce the word and each player is to write down a false definition of the word. However, if they happen to know the correct definition – tell them to write that down, as they will

73

# The Halloween Party Host Handbook

earn an extra point by getting it correct. When everybody is finished, they write their initials on their slip and hand it to the host.

The host will then put the slips in any order along with the correct definition. If anybody writes the correct definition, the host removes it, and gives the player three points but does not announce the correct answer. Then, the host reads the definitions to the group one by one and asks each player (in a pre-determined order) to choose the correct definition from the choices. If they choose the correct definition, they're awarded two points – but do not announce until every player has guessed. The author of a false definition gets a point for each person they fooled into picking their answer each round.

Continue by changing the host player and play until every player has had the opportunity to be the host. Then, total the points and see who is the winner.

**Props needed:** slips of paper for each player (minus one for the host), each round. A dictionary &/or access to a phone to pull up an online dictionary – or pre-make slips of paper with words and definitions and ask the host players to draw from a hat to get their word. Pen/paper to keep score. However, doing it this way, you will be unable to play as you'll know the answers.

**Playing time:** ~ 15 – 30 minutes.

**Examples of obscure words are:**

| WORD | DEFINITION |
|---|---|
| Malneirophrenia | Depression Following a Nightmare |
| Saprogenic | Causing Decay, Produced in Decaying Matter |
| A La Mort | To the Death |
| Acariasis | Infestation with Mites/Ticks |
| Barbastelle | Long-Eared Species of Bat |
| Bathylimnetic | Living At The Bottom of a Body of Water |
| Malnoia | Feeling of Mental Discomfort |
| Talionic | Pertaining to Revenge |
| Tristiloquy | Mournful Manner of Speech |
| Endiablee | To Put the Devil into |
| Daddock | Center of a Rotted Tree |

# Dr. Bonnie

## How Many Words Can You Make?

**Objective**: to make the most words out of a larger word.

**Rules:** write a large word on a wipe-off board or piece of paper and set the timer for two minutes. Pair up your players into teams of two or three and when you say go, they are to make as many smaller words out of the large word. The team that comes up with the most words – wins! In the event of a tie – set the timer for 30 seconds and have them come up with more words. If they keep ending in a tie, a Mouse-Cat-Witch tournament best two out of three will claim a winner (see tiebreaker section of this handbook).

**Props needed:** a wipe-off (dry erase) board or piece of paper, dry erase marker, writing utensils for each team and sheets of paper for each team to write their words on. Also, a timer or a watch with a second hand will do fine.

**Playing time:** ~10 minutes.

## Scary Sentence Scavenger Hunt

**Objective:** to make the most sentences out of the eggs you find during the Halloween scavenger hunt!

**Rules: Phase 1**: using sentence makers (example shown), place the slips containing the words inside of Halloween-themed plastic eggs, and then hide the eggs in a designated area. Tell your hunters the boundaries of the hunt before you say go. Each hunter is to place his or her Halloween treat bag/basket in a designated area before the hunt.

When the host says go, the hunters are to collect as many eggs as possible that they can make full sentences out of but once they find an egg – if they choose to keep it – they must take it to their treat bag/basket and deposit it before finding the next egg. They will not want to take any eggs that contain words inside that they can't use, as they'll be penalized for having them during the next phase of the game. They do have the option to view inside the egg to see what the word is and if they don't want it – they are to place it back in the exact location in which they found it. They are not allowed to re-hide a rejected egg in another location. After the eggs have all been found (you'll know by counting the hunter's eggs) or if the hunters are finished hunting (i.e. there are eggs left, but they have words in them that the hunters can't use) – move to Phase 2.

**Phase 2**: when you say go, the hunters can remove the slips of paper containing the words and arrange them into as many sentences as possible. Players are allowed to add an 's,' 'ing,' or 'ed' to any word.

# The Halloween Party Host Handbook

There is one point given for every word used in a sentence. For any words that are leftover that the hunter does not use – there is a one-point deduction per word. The sentences must be grammatically correct. For example, if Scott collects 20 eggs and makes three sentences with six words each, he will earn 18 points. However, he will be penalized for the remaining two eggs he did not use. His final score will be 16 points.

**Props needed:** sentence maker word squares, Halloween-themed plastic eggs.

**Playing time:** ~ 35 minutes.

**Example sentence maker word squares:**

| The | Orange | Black | Witch |
|---|---|---|---|
| The | Tiny | Cat | Is |
| Halloween | Night | Monster | There |
| I | Want | To | Win |
| You | Can | Not | Make |
| Me | And | I | Am |
| I | Enjoy | Trick | Or |
| Treat | To | Get | And |
| The | Zombies | Scampered | Across |
| The | Graveyard | Alien | From |
| Scary | And | Hairy | Always |
| Screaming | And | Biting | Will |
| Are | So | Eerie | Scream |
| This | Fun | Go | Danced |
| More | Ran | From | Vampire |
| Count | Dracula | It | Are |
| Of | And | A | Are |
| Eat | Frightening | Candy | And |
| The | Coffin | Cauldron | Smoke |
| The | Light | Today | Fangs |

## PHYSICAL GAMES – INDOOR

Note: some of these games may also be played outdoors.

### Brew the Witches Brew

**Objective:** to find all of the ingredients in your witch's brew before the other witches.

76

# Dr. Bonnie

**Rules:** with any word processing program, select five (or more, depending on how many players are in the game) different items to put in your witches brew and print off pictures of these in small ~ 2" squares (e.g. fingernails, mouse tails, fingers). You will need one picture per player of each ingredient. Each player will have a separate ingredient on his or her back. If you had ten players in the game, you would put ten fingernail cards on player A's back, ten-mouse tail cards on player B's back and so on until every player has a different ingredient on their back. For an alternative challenge, assign the same ingredient to two (or more) players.

Make a recipe card for your witch's brew and post it on the wall in plain view of all of the contestants. Give each player a small plastic cauldron or a simple picture of a cauldron and scatter around the room but be sure that each player knows where their cauldron is located. It's probably best to put their names on them to prevent any disputes.

When the host says go, the players view the recipe card and collect the ingredients from each other's backs. They can collect one from their back immediately, or wait to collect it last (there's one for each player, so it will be there). The first to collect all five ingredients and get the ingredients to their cauldron first makes the witches brew and wins! The players are to defend their backs, but at the same time, they are trying to collect the ingredients – get ready for some chaotic fun!

**Props needed:** ingredient squares, witches cauldrons for each player (real plastic or pictures) and the recipe card for the brew.
**Playing time:** ~ 10 minutes.


## Knights of the Round Circle

**Objective:** is to win the prize in the middle.
**Rules:** arrange your players in a circle and have them link arms at the elbow, facing outward from the middle of the circle. Place a prize – it can be absolutely anything the players will want - in the center of the circle. When you say go, the first person to get the prize in the middle gets to keep it and will be declared the winner. Note – the players are not allowed to unlink their arms at any time during the game, or they are out, the game is frozen (everybody freezes in place), the chain is re-linked, and circle is reset. Cheaters do not return to the circle.
**Props needed:** a prize. Depending on your group will depend on what prize to put in the middle of the circle. Kids may want a Halloween toy – adults may want a gift card to iTunes or something else.
**Playing time:** ~ 10 minutes.

### Monster Mouth Mini Golf

**Objective:** is to earn the most points by hitting your golf ball in the monster's mouths.

**Rules:** this is an individual challenge. Prepare the golf course in advance of the game. Using a large box, cut various 'mouse hole' shapes for the monster mouths – depending on the size of your box will determine how many monster mouths will fit. Make the middle mouth the smallest and even leave some 'teeth' poking down to make it more challenging. Mark various point totals with the larger mouth holes being the least points. Paint the box with monster faces above the holes (i.e. their mouths). Mark a 'do not cross' line for the players to stand behind and hand them a golf ball (for younger kids, use practice balls or Ping-Pong balls) and a putter. Note: any time you are using items that can be weapons (such as golf clubs), take extra caution to keep the other players a safe distance. Or, use a plastic golf club for added safety. The players go one at a time and are given five tries to tap their balls into the monster mouth holes that have the largest point totals. Instruct the player not to hit the balls as if they are on a golf tee, but rather as if they are close to the hole. If you believe your players may be too rowdy – bring this activity outside, by all means. Again, keep a safe perimeter for the spectators out of the range of swinging distance.

**Props needed:** a golf club (real or plastic depending on the group's maturity), five golf balls (practice, real or Ping-Pong ball – again, depending on the group's maturity) and a large cardboard box with cut out monster mouths for them to tap their balls into. Also, a starting line that the players do not cross – which is a distance you choose from the cardboard box. A pen/paper to write down scores.

**Playing time:** ~ 10 minutes.

### Monster War

**Objective:** is to shoot as many monsters off the ladder before the timer goes off.

**Rules:** you'll need 12 empty soda cans. Before the game, paint them in various Halloween colors with cute/scary monster faces on the front. Allow drying thoroughly.

Using a ladder with at least four steps, extend it securely on an even surface and place three monsters (cans) on each step, face forward. Using a Nerf gun, test that your bullets are powerful enough to knock the empty cans off the steps and adjust the distance accordingly and make a 'do not cross' line for the players to stand behind. You

# Dr. Bonnie

might need to get a more powerful Nerf gun if it isn't knocking them off. Set a timer for 30 seconds and allow each player a shot at knocking all 12 monsters down from the steps. A point is awarded for all monsters knocked on their side and three points for monsters knocked to the floor. Allow each player to have a turn and then add up their total points. The player with the highest total is the winner. In the event of a tie, set the timer to 10 seconds and allow a shoot off as individual trials.

**Props needed:** 12 empty soda cans, painted as fun monsters. A ladder and a Nerf gun with at least 20 bullets.

**Playing time:** ~ 10 minutes depending on how many players you have in your group.

### Jumping Jack Skellington

**Objective**: not be last to say the word *Skellington* when two cards are duplicated.

**Rules:** Start with one player as the dealer. Shuffle the cards and one at a time; reveal a card by turning it face up in a pile. The moment a card is revealed that was the same as the card previous (not by suit, by number or face card); every player is to say the word Skellington. The last player to say Skellington is penalized and must perform the physical house penalty (i.e. five jumping jacks, run around the house, etc.). The dealer makes the final call on who said it last if it is a close race.

**Props needed:** a deck of cards.

**Playing time:** ~ as long as you wish.

### 1,2,3,4 I Smell an Ogre War

**Objective**: be first to notice another player has the same card as you and to tag the person who does as they run around the circle.

**Rules:** assemble your players in a circle. Deal a card face down in front of each player. When you say go, they are to flip over their cards. If two (or more) players are dealt the same card, the first one to point at the other and say the phrase "1,2,3,4, I smell an Ogre War' causes their opponent to run around the circle two times without being tagged by the one who said the phrase. If the player can run around the circle twice without being tagged, they are safe (if they make it back to their seat). If they make it back to their seat, they get a point and the one who said the phrase loses a point. If they are tagged, they lose a point and the tagger gains a point. If nobody has a match, deal another round until they do.

79

When a match is made, and someone has either made it twice around the table (in either direction) without being tagged &/or was tagged, the dealer's duties are passed to the right. The person with the highest score when you finish playing is declared the winner of the Ogre War and must be referred to as 'General Ogre' for the next hour.

**Props needed:** deck of cards.

**Playing time:** ~ until you get tired of playing.

## Pumpkin Wars

**Objective:** is to be the team with the least amount of stuffed pumpkins on your side of the room.

**Rules:** using painter's tape (or another floor safe tape), split your room into two halves. On the tape, place as many mini stuffed pumpkins as possible – or another safe item like rolled up socks, etc. Divide your group into two teams and put each team against the wall on either side of the room. Set the timer for three minutes and say 'go.' When you say go the teams are to toss the mini pumpkins to the opposing team's side of the room (across the tape). When the timer goes off, the group has to freeze, and the number of pumpkins on either side are counted. The group with the least amount of pumpkins is the winning team.

**Props needed:** mini stuffed pumpkins or another item that won't destroy the house &/or hurt each other when thrown.

**Playing time:** ~ 8 minutes per round with setting up/judging.

## Stump 'n Jump

**Objective**: don't get stumped or you pay the price.

**Rules:** either sit in a circle or just remember the order in which the players will go. The starting player will say the name of a movie title. The next player in line will say the name of another movie with the last letter of the last word in the movie title said by the previous player.

For example, Player A says Home Alon<u>e</u> and then Player B must think of a movie title that starts with the letter 'e' since the last word of the title is 'e' in 'Alon<u>e</u>.' Player B can say 'E.T.' and then Player C must say a movie that begins with the letter 't' and so on until someone is stumped.

Being stumped is subjective but if you want to implement a rule that if the group counts to 3 by saying 1, 1 thousand, 2, 1 thousand, 3 and no answer is given in that time – the player is considered stumped. Or, just play casually and if anybody stalls – call them out and tell them to jump up and down ten times (or more/less depending on the physical fitness of your group). Then, reset with whoever was next in line after the stumped player.

**Props needed:** people who can think clearly enough to think of movies and how to spell them.

**Playing time:** ~ as long as you want.

## The Magical Mouse

**Objective:** is not to be the last person to find the Magical Mouse.

**Rules:** one person is designated the Magical Mouse and the rest are black cats. The Magical Mouse will be allowed to leave the group and hide within designated boundaries. Give this person 15 seconds – counted aloud – to choose a hiding place. Once the Magical Mouse's time is up, the black cats (seekers) set out individually to be the first to find the Magical Mouse. The first one to find the Magical Mouse is declared the winner.

But wait! The Magical Mouse has turned the winning player into a mouse, and they must fit into the hiding place (i.e. enter the mice burrow) with the Magical Mouse. As players discover the mice burrow, they also become mice, and must fit into this hiding place with the group. The last one to find the mice burrow is declared the Magical Mouse for the next round.

**Props needed:** an area big enough for this rendition of the timeless classic hide and seek.

**Playing time:** ~ 10 minutes.

## Rat in a Hoop Challenge

**Objective:** is to throw the most rats through the hula hoop!

**Rules:** Line up the players. One player holds a hula hoop at designated lengths away from the challenging player (e.g. 10, 15, 20 feet from the start line). The first challenging player is handed a stuffed rat toy (or other Halloween-themed stuffed toy) and must throw the rat inside of the hoop for 5 points for the closest hoop, 10 points for the second closest hoop and 15 points for the furthest hoop. The hoop holder moves to a pre-measured/marked spot for each distance. Once the player has had three tries at the various hoop distances, the player will either go to the back of the line for another turn or sit as part of the audience until the next game. The next player in line gets a turn at throwing the rat through the hoop at the various distances, and so on until everyone has had a turn. The host can decide how many turns the players should have before the points are totaled and a winner is declared. The winner is the one with the most points at the conclusion of the game.

In the event of a tie, a 'throw off' will need to be played. The host should hold the hoop further than before, and each player should get one try. If there is still a tie among any players, the host is to back up further and repeat the process until a winner is declared.

**Props needed:** a stuffed toy rat (or other Halloween-themed item) and a hula hoop. It is advisable to mark off areas of the yard/ floor to determine where the hoop holder should stand and where the player should not cross to keep the difficulty of the distances even between players.

**Playing time:** ~ 10 minutes.

## The Bubble Walk Test

**Objective:** is to walk the length of the bubble wrap without popping a bubble.

**Rules:** purchase about 1.5 meters (~5 ft.) of bubble wrap packing material. The players take turns walking the length of the bubble wrap. The first one to walk the length of the wrap without popping a bubble is the winner. If everyone does it without a pop – then change it up to walking on their knees, crab walks, front rolls, etc.

**Props needed:** strips of bubble wrapping material.

**Playing time:** ~ 10 minutes.

## The Disc Test

**Objective:** is to make the longest chain of discs before they drop.

**Rules:** purchase as many orange pool noodles as you wish and slice them into disc shapes using a serrated knife. Feel free to decorate the sides of them with a black permanent marker for a fun Halloween-themed effect. Divide your group into two teams. When you say go, they are to make a horizontal chain of the discs by only touching the outer discs in the chain. They add the discs to the chain at both ends, but they will need to maintain pressure at the ends for the chain to stay intact. No part of the middle may be touched or manipulated by any players – only the two end discs! The team who makes the largest chain of discs without dropping them is declared the winner.

**Props needed:** orange pool noodles cut into ~2 inch discs and some fun Halloween music to play in the background.

**Playing time:** ~ 10 minutes.

# Dr. Bonnie

## Fallen

**Objective:** is to find the demon.

**Rules:** if you've seen the movie Fallen where the demon can jump from living body to living body – this is a game version of that. Everybody will draw from a container that holds the same amount of draw slips as players. The draw strips will say either human or demon. Only one slip will say demon, however. Whoever draws the demon slip will be the first demon and play begins. The demon cannot blink their eyes while they are the demon. So, the other players mingle about and try to find the demon before the demon skips into another body.

      The demon skips into another body by touching another player. It's best not to get caught doing this! Therefore, tell your players not to touch anybody during the game if they are a human or they will lose a point from their main score. Once you've been touched, you are the demon and not allowed to blink until you pass the demon to someone else. The objective for all players is to find the demon by looking at everybody's faces to determine who is not blinking. However if this player touches you before you shout 'I've found the demon' – you are the demon and cannot say a word and must find someone else to pass the demon to. Once the demon is discovered by someone shouting the phrase 'I've found the demon' the round ends and the player who found the demon – without being touched by the demon - is the winner and gets a point. Continue play until the first player reaches a score of three.

**Props needed:** an area big enough to mingle about.

**Playing time:** ~ 10 minutes.

## The Stacking Challenge

**Objective:** is to stack 21 cups in the shortest time.

**Rules:** to stack 21 cups into a pyramid and then un-stack the cups into one stack. Use fewer cups for younger kids.

Each player is timed, and when the host says go, they are to take their single stack of 21 cups and create a pyramid with six on the bottom, five on the next row, four on the next and so on until they get to the one on top. Then, after a quick release of their hand when the pyramid is complete, they take down the pyramid and rebuild the single stack of 21. When they have rebuilt the single stack, the time is called and recorded. The player with the fastest time building a pyramid and taking it down to a single stack is the winner.

**Props needed:** 21 black or orange plastic solo cups and a timer.

**Playing time:** ~ 15 minutes – depends on your number of players being timed.

## The Great Candy Corn Toss

**Objective:** is to toss ten candy corns into your teammate's cauldron first.

**Rules:** divide your group into pairs and arrange the pairs in two lines facing each other, ~ 5 feet between the lines. Mark parallel lines on both sides on the floor with painter's tape and instruct players they must keep their feet behind the tape line at all times. Hand one side of the group a mini plastic cauldron and the other side of the group ten candy corns. When the host says go, the throwers are to toss their candy corns into their partner's cauldron. After they've thrown all ten and if they've missed some, the thrower can retrieve them from the floor and go back to their line and make more attempts. Also, have more available for them to grab from in a container behind the thrower line. The first team to catch ten candy corns in the cauldron wins.

**Props needed:** a cauldron (mini plastic from any party store) for ½ the players and ten candy corns each for the other ½ of players.

**Playing time:** ~ 10 minutes.

## Candy Corn Chaos

**Objective:** is to transfer the most candy corns into a mini cauldron using chopsticks in one minute.

**Rules:** this is an individual challenge. Scatter candy corns onto a table and have a mini plastic cauldron on the side. Hand the player a pair of chopsticks and set the timer for one minute. They have one minute to get as many candy corns in the cauldron as they can. The player who gets the most candy corns in their cauldron is declared the winner.

**Props needed:** a cauldron (mini plastic from any party store), a pair of chopsticks and about 40 candy corns.

**Playing time:** ~ 10 minutes.

## Ring around the Witches Hat

**Objective:** earn the most points by tossing hoops on the witch hats.

**Rules:** using witch's hats from a costume shop or witch hats made from construction paper, place the hats at varied distances from the start line and designate a point value for each hat based on how far it is. For example, if the furthest hat is 6 feet away, make it 20 points, 5 feet, 15 points, 4 feet, 10 points, 3 feet, 5 points, 2 feet, 1 point. Hand each player three hoops and allow them to toss the hoop on their choice of hat to get the most points. They may want to strategize and go for the lower points/sure thing or reach for the stars and get all three on the big money hats. The player with the most points wins.

**Props needed:** five to seven witch hats marked with point values and three hoops. Purchase small plastic hoops in a toy store or simply make some out of a coat hanger and paper mache. You'll need wire cutters and some strength to re-twist the ends of the hanger into a circle.

**Playing time:** ~ 10 minutes.

## The Cemetery Watchman

**Rules:** to be the last zombie in the cemetery.

**Props needed:** elect one player to be the watchman (or watchwoman), and the rest of the players are zombies in the cemetery. When you say go, the zombies will collapse to the ground and get into whatever position they wish. They are to play dead. The watchman's job is to find a zombie that moves, and if they move, the watchman calls them out of the game; they get up, and move to the side.

Moving constitutes any movement of a body part besides the act of breathing (the players are allowed to continue to breathe – or it won't be that fun!) However, blinking is moving.

The timer is set for whatever amount of time you'd like for the watchman to have between two to five minutes. Now – the zombies may move when the watchman has their back turned to them. They can do anything they want as long as the watchman doesn't see them move. They must re-freeze when the watchman can see them or they are out. When the timer is done, the winner(s) is declared. If the watchman catches everybody before the time is out – the watchman wins and earns five points. On the other hand, any zombie still 'dead' in the game is also declared a winner when the time is up and gets one point. Pick a new watchman to play another round and so forth until your group is ready for a new game.

**Props needed:** none needed.

**Playing time:** ~ 10 minutes.

## The Raven and the Rat

**Objective**: to eliminate your opponents by being the one who can grab the lowest item with your mouth while standing on one foot.

**Rules:** this is an individual challenge. The challenging player is the raven and the object in front of them is the 'rat' that they will swoop down and catch with their 'beak' – aka mouth. Use various items as the 'rat' such as a paper bag, cereal box, or another item that can stand up on its own and be 'lowered' each round by either folding it down or cutting off an inch at a time.

Each player will take a turn as 'the raven' while standing in front of the 'rat' (e.g. paper bag, cereal box, etc.), they are to stand on one foot and use only their mouth to pick up the 'rat' and move to a standing position – while remaining on one foot. The player is allowed to remove their shoes if they wish before engaging in the challenge. If their second foot touches the ground before they fully return to a standing position with the rat in their mouth, they are out of the game. Hopping a few times to get balance is alright, as long as their second foot does not touch the ground. Putting an item inside the bag or box is optional – it will add weight to the 'rat' which might help the rat stay in place in front of the player. Try it out before you start the game to see which is best for you.

Once every player in the game has had a turn, the players that are out are to take a seat. You are to lower the bag or box by ~ 1 inch (2.54 cm) by folding the paper bag/box or cutting it. The players give it another try with the lowered rat and so on until you are left with one player. Eventually, it will get low enough to eliminate your players unless you are playing with a group of highly trained ninjas – in that case, just end the game with Mouse-Cat-Witch tiebreaker (see tiebreaking section).

Note: be a fair host - if you are playing a game with a bunch of ladies in fancy cocktail dresses – this may not be the game for you! It wouldn't be fair for the ladies to have to do this challenge with a dress while the gents have pants!

**Props needed:** a paper bag, cereal box or anything about a foot high that can be lowered. If you are cutting the bag/box, you'll need a pair of scissors.

**Playing time:** ~ 20 minutes.

## Ultimate Popcorn Bail Out Challenge

**Objective**: to move every piece of your team's popcorn from start to finish using a wooden spoon.

**Rules:** you will need a container for each team with the same amount of popcorn inside of each container at the start line. The other container is located at the finish line. When the host says go, one member of each group is to scoop as much popcorn as possible into their spoon and transport it into the container at the finish line. If any popcorn is dropped during the transport, the team member has to bend down and pick it up, place it back on his/her spoon - before moving on towards the finish line. Once a team member has dropped their popcorn load into the container at the finish line, they are to come back to the start line and hand off the wooden spoon to the next player in line. This will repeat until every piece of popcorn is transported into the finish line container. The team that transports all of their popcorn first – wins!

*If any popcorn is stepped on and 'crushed' during the challenge, the crushed pieces must be picked up and transported into the finish line container!

**Props needed:** 2 containers for each team, a start line, a finish line (~ 5-10 feet away), a wooden spoon for each team, and an equal amount of popcorn for each team.

**Playing time:** ~10 minutes.

## Marshmallow Madness

**Objective**: to move the most marshmallows from one place to another with chopsticks in two minutes.

**Rules:** set up two containers of any kind (e.g. bowls, box, plate, etc.) and put them as far apart as you wish (e.g. on either side of a table, next to each other, across the room, etc.). This is an individual challenge, and each player will do a timed trial. The person who moves the most marshmallows and earns the most points – wins!

Getting started: when a player is ready to do their trial, hand them a pair of chopsticks. Place the marshmallows in a container designated point A. Put the second container in the second spot and designate it point B. Point B's container will start off empty, as that is the one you will count the marshmallows from when the timer goes off.

Set the timer for two minutes. Using only one hand, they are to move the marshmallows from point 'A' to point 'B' (the two locations you decided upon) using only chopsticks – and nothing else. When the timer goes off, they are to stop immediately. After this point, the players are not allowed to put any more marshmallows inside of the point B container. Count the marshmallows and write down the score (or keep it on a digital notepad). Repeat the trial for each player.

**Alternate rules:** buy three different sizes of marshmallow: mini, regular and jumbo and assign five, two and one point accordingly and mix them up in the container for point A. The player can elect to go for the big point mini marshmallows or take the easy route with the one point jumbos – it's just an additional layer of the game, if you wish to play it that way. Declare the winner by adding up the total points.

**Break a tie:** if there is a tie, host another round – but this time, blindfold the players. Move the containers closer together so they don't have to move far with a blindfold, however. The marshmallows are so light, the challenge becomes more difficult to determine if you have picked them up – so even if you put the containers side-by-side – it will still be a challenge. They can only use one hand and must use the chopsticks to handle the marshmallows. You should have a winner after the second round. If not, solve it by a hilarious Mouse-Cat-Witch tiebreaker.

**Props needed:** bags of various sized marshmallows, two containers (buckets, bowls, etc.). A pair of chopsticks. Maybe have a backup pair just in case. Blindfold.

**Playing time:** ~10-15 minutes.

## The Careful Cotton Carry

**Objective**: to carry the most cotton balls from A to B while blindfolded during three trips.

**Rules:** Place cotton balls all over the floor in about a 3' by 4' area or inside of a large bowl. Blindfold one player, spin them around two times and hand him/her a ladle or a small plastic shovel. The player is to scoop up as many cotton balls as s/he can with the ladle/shovel and then transfer them into a bowl about 5 feet away. (Cotton balls are so light; the player won't tell how many they have.) The player can only use the ladle/shovel to get the cotton balls– they cannot touch the cotton balls with their hands or check to see if they got any into their ladle/shovel. He or she can touch the rim of the bowl with the hand not holding the ladle/shovel and then transfer the cotton balls (if any) with the other hand holding the ladle/shovel. Keeping the blindfold on, s/he can do this three times back and forth – total of three trips. S/he is never allowed to check the inside of the bowl. After three trips, s/he removes the blindfold and the cotton balls are counted. The balls are put back and the next player has a turn and so on until all players have had a turn. A prize or a certificate for the winner of the most transferred cotton balls can be awarded.

**Props needed:** a few packages of cotton balls, a ladle or small plastic shovel, and a large bowl. Blindfold.

**Playing time:** ~ 20 minutes.

## PHYSICAL GAMES – OUTDOOR

### Chaotic Cracker Smasher
**Objective:** is to be the last one with an intact cracker!
**Rules:** cut 10" pieces of dental floss or an equivalent thread. Thread the piece of floss through one or two holes of two saltine crackers. Tie one of these 'saltine necklaces' to each player - through a belt loop preferably. If the player doesn't have a belt loop, grab a piece of their shirt and tie it around the bundled up shirt material. Get a newspaper (or two) and roll up equal amounts of paper for each player. Everyone should go outside as this is about to make a big mess!

Start the game and each player is to swat at each other's crackers and knock them off of their floss until someone is the last one left with an intact cracker. The last one with an intact cracker wins! In the case of a tie - a re-match between the players that tied should take place. Prizes are optional.
**Props needed:** dental floss (or equivalent), saltine crackers, and newspapers.
**Playing time:** ~ 10 minutes.

### Sleeping Vampires
**Objective:** is to slay the vampire before you get bitten.
**Rules:** line up the players (e.g. vampire hunters) behind a starting line and designate one player as the vampire a distance away. As long as the vampire is awake and looking at the players, they may not move a muscle, or the vampire will bite them (in the story, not really) and they are out of the game. For the vampire to get the players out, he or she must raise their cape in front of their eyes and 'go to sleep.' While the vampire is asleep, the vampire hunters can make their way toward the vampire. However, once the vampire awakens, the players must freeze instantly, or they are out. Anybody moving when the vampire is looking has been bitten and must exit the playing area. The vampire continues to go to sleep and wake up in hopes of getting everybody out before they slay (i.e. touch) him/her. The first vampire hunter to slay the vampire is declared the winner. If the vampire gets everybody out before they are slayed – they are declared the winner. Play can continue with a new player as the vampire.
**Props needed:** a vampire cape and an area for playing with a start line.
**Playing time:** ~ 10 minutes.

## Capture the Bat

**Objective:** is to capture the enemy team's vampire bat!

**Rules:** divide your group into 2-4 teams and give each a large rubber vampire bat (or other Halloween-themed item). Establish boundaries of the playing field before the game. Within the boundaries, mark territories for each team by using markers of any kind (e.g. tape, balloons, string, landmarks, etc.). The territories should be as far apart as possible (e.g. the four corners of a backyard). Leave a space in the middle that is a common battleground. Each team is to hide their bat within their designated territory and guard it as they wish. Give each player an inflated Halloween-themed balloon (pick a color per team) and they are to hold onto it by the knotted end with one hand during the challenge. The balloon signifies their life-force and also shows which team they are on.

When you say go, the teams are to find and capture the opposing team's bat. When a team acquires an opposing team's bat, every member of that team is 'slain' and immediately out of the game. They must all leave the playing field, and play resumes between the remaining teams. If a player's balloon is popped or lost at any time, they are 'slain' and out of the game. They are to leave the playing field.

If an invading player is caught by an opposing team member on the opposing team's territory, two things may happen.

1.  The opposing team member may 'tag' them by a gentle touch on the arm and by shouting the word 'dungeon.' The invading player freezes in place (they're in the dungeon) until tagged by someone who shouts the word 'escape' (they break them out). While a player is frozen, their balloon may not be touched by anybody until they are unfrozen by someone. If the frozen player is the last member of their team, the opposing team can leave them in the dungeon or switch their balloon with a balloon of their team's color and they become an ally. (Have some extra balloons available on the side lines in case of this scenario).

2.  The second option that a defending player has is when a player invades, they may choose to attack and pop the invader's balloon instead of putting them in the dungeon. However, the invading player may still search for the opposing team's bat until their balloon is popped. When a player's balloon is popped &/or knocked out of their hand, they are 'slain' and out of the game. They must cease the bat search, and exit the playing field immediately. Note: the opposing team

# Dr. Bonnie

member may not touch the player while attacking the balloon - only the balloon may be touched. Yes, tall players will have an advantage, as they can hold their balloons in the air over their head, so spread out your tallest players as captains of each team to make it fair. If an attacker touches the invading player, the invading player is tagged and in the dungeon (whether or not the attacker shouted dungeon), and the invading player must freeze. The invading player is also not allowed to touch their attacker. They may only defend themselves by running away. On the other hand, the invading player may pose a counter attack on the opposing player's balloon. Take pics if this happens, please – we all want to see this scuffle.

**General rules:**

- If a player is frozen and their balloon is popped by anybody, the host must freeze everybody in the game while they give the player a new balloon. The player who illegally popped their balloon is slain and out of the game.
- A player's balloon can be popped in any territory, as long as they are not frozen.
- A player may sit on another player's shoulders to defend against taller invaders.
- This should not be a highly-physical game. This game is more about strategy. Any player who uses excessive force should be removed from the game.
- The players may not hide their balloons in their clothing, etc. – they must hold on to the balloon with the same hand the entire challenge. If they pop their balloon themselves, they fall on their own sword and must leave the playing field.
- Popping balloons is done by squeezing the balloon itself or using fingernails on the latex. No weapons of any kind may be used to pop balloons, only hands.
- For extra fun, play this at night with glow sticks in the balloons, but make sure the area is safe, and there's enough lighting for the players to see where they are going.

**Props needed:** a balloon color-coded for each team – one for each player (with a few extras of each in case of allies). A Halloween-themed item for each team to hide/protect.

**Playing time:** ~ 10 minutes.

# The Halloween Party Host Handbook

## Crazy Witch Hunt

**Objective:** is to be the last one standing in the field.

**Rules:** divide your group into two teams - one team will only have three players (the crazy witches) and the rest will go on a second team (the little children lost in a forest). Place a pumpkin in the middle of the field. Designate boundaries for your players before you start the game. When you say go, set a timer for three minutes. The little children team will scatter and try to hide from the crazy witches. When they are 'tagged' by a witch they are to go to a designated place called the witch's cottage. Rope this area off with orange streamers, helium-filled balloons, etc. These players must stay there for the duration of the game – unless, they want to make a run for the pumpkin. If they choose to make a run for the pumpkin, and they make it to the pumpkin without being tagged by a crazy witch, they are safe – albeit, they need to keep a hand/foot on the pumpkin to remain safe throughout the round. A crazy witch can tag them at any time if they are not touching the pumpkin. If they are tagged by a crazy witch on a run for the pumpkin &/or if they take their hand/foot off the pumpkin after they are declared safe, they are out of the game and must go to the witch's cauldron where they are an ingredient in the witch's brew (another designated area for players who are out of the game). The crazy witches may not try to physically remove a player from the safe pumpkin.

When the timer goes off, points are assessed for each player. The crazy witches get a point for each player in the cottage, and three points for each player in the cauldron. Each player that is still on the field and has not been tagged by a crazy witch gets three points. Each player that is touching the pumpkin gets one point. Play as many rounds as you wish, switching the players into the crazy witch roles. The first player to 20 points is the winner, but be sure each player gets a turn to be on the crazy witch team for the point system to be fair.

**Props needed:** a large pumpkin to place in the center of the field and two areas clearly designated as the cottage and cauldron.

**Playing time:** ~ 15-20 minutes – depending on how many rounds you play.

## Brave Bone Collectors

**Objective:** to be the team that finds the bones to your skeleton the fastest.

**Rules:** purchase two bags of detached skeleton bones making up a full skeleton at any Halloween/party store. Assemble them on any surface, snap a picture, and print this picture for each team. Hide both skeletons in a backyard area or other designated area – but whatever you do – tell your teams the boundaries. When the host says go, the teams set out searching for the bones. When a player finds a bone, they must run back to home base to assemble the bone in their skeleton. If the bone is not needed for their team's skeleton because the bone(s) have already been found, they can re-hide it within the boundaries wherever they wish. However, please note, the other team may be watching so it would be smart to know what you are looking for and not touch a bone you don't need! The first team to assemble their skeleton resembling the picture wins.

**Props needed:** two bags of bones of a skeleton, a printed copy of the skeleton arranged correctly, and a large area.

**Playing time:** ~ 15 minutes.

## The Ghost Chain

**Objective:** to be the last to become a link on the ghost chain.

**Rules:** designate one player as the ghost and the rest of the players are links on the ghost's chain that have escaped. The ghost is to tag the other players (e.g. the links), and when a player is tagged, they must hold hands with the ghost and help the ghost tag other players. When another player is tagged, they hold hands with the last player tagged and so forth. The chain will grow until there is one player left and they are declared the winner.

**Props needed:** a large enough area to run around and tag players.

**Playing time:** ~10 minutes.

## Fun with Funyuns

**Objective**: to get as many Funyun snack chips to stick to your teammate's shaving cream (or whipped cream) covered head!

**Rules:** separate your players into 2 teams. With masking tape, tape two 'x's on the floor a designated length (e.g. 5 feet, 10 feet, etc.) from two corresponding 'do not cross' lines on the floor (for two teams). Have each team designate one member as the Funyun Head. The Funyun Head will put on a shower cap and have the top of their head covered with shaving cream. The Funyun Heads will stand on the designated 'x' and their respective team members stand behind the corresponding 'do not cross' line. When the host says go, the team members toss Funyun snack chips (or other chips that you choose) onto the Funyun Head team member's shaving cream covered head. The team that gets the most Funyun snack chips to stick and stay on their Funyun Head's head...wins! The host will call 'time' after 3 minutes, and everyone is to stop immediately. The Funyun Heads are to 'freeze' until the chips are counted. Any Funyun that drops off of the Funyun Head's head that was sticking to their head when the time was called should be counted.

**Props needed:** Masking tape, Funyun snack chips (or other chips of your choosing), shaving cream (or whipped cream), any timer, plastic shower caps, goggles for the Funyun Heads, and a big cleanable area ☺.

**Playing time:** ~ 15-20 minutes.

## Shaving the Balloon Bedlam

**Objective**: to be the first team to lather and shave your balloon without popping it.

**Rules:** separate your players into teams of three. Draw a large beard on an overly inflated balloon on the side opposite the knot. It should take up 'most' of the balloon's surface. One person will hold the knot of the balloon between their teeth for the duration of the challenge. Another person will lather the balloon within the beard outline with whipped cream. The third person will carefully 'shave' the whipped cream off the beard without popping the balloon with any fake razor you choose to use. Have them use a credit card, side of a spoon, etc. – just make sure it is a safe item as when and if the balloon pops, realize this player is holding and using this item in front of the balloon holder's face, and when it pops, they can have a reaction to it. The first person who can remove the whipped cream from the balloon without popping it wins.

**Props needed:** balloon for each team, whipped cream, an item to use as the razor for shaving the balloon.

**Playing time:** ~ 10 minutes.

## Pumpkins in the Circle

**Objective**: for your pumpkin to remain in the orange circle.

**Rules:** on the driveway or sidewalk (or any patch of concrete), use sidewalk chalk and draw an orange circle. Then, draw a lane ~ 5 feet long and a start line. Each player is given a mini pumpkin, and they take turns rolling their pumpkin down the lane in hopes it will stop on the orange circle. Players may bump existing pumpkins off the circle. The player who has their pumpkin closest to the orange circle is the winner.

**Props needed:** sidewalk chalk, a mini pumpkin for each player.

**Playing time:** ~ 10 minutes.

# Dr. Bonnie

## Jack O'Lantern Piñata Bash

**Objective**: to get the candy out of the piñata.

**Making the piñata:** no need to purchase a piñata when they are easy to DIY. Blow up a round, large balloon and cut some newspaper into strips about 2" by 8". In a mixing bowl, make the paste by mixing 2 cups of white flour and 2 cups of water with a dash of salt. Stir the mix until it is smooth and the consistency of cake batter. Dip the newspaper strips into the paste and slide onto your balloon, smoothing them out as much as possible. Continue to do this until the balloon is covered, but leave space about the diameter of a golf ball where the balloon is tied (you will later cut this to pop & remove the balloon and add the candy here).

Create several layers of paper mache on the balloon and then allow drying. Drying may take a few days (this will vary depending on the environment the balloon is left in for drying). When the balloon is dry, paint it orange and allow the paint to dry for at least 24 hours. Then, it is time to add the crepe paper. Add in horizontal rows, only gluing the top of each strip. Fringe the lower part of each strip and glue the next strip down 1.5" underneath until the balloon is completely covered. Then, add Jack O'Lantern's eyes and mouth out of black construction paper and attach with a dab of glue.

Since you already have a hole where the balloon knot is located, cut the balloon knot and pull out of the piñata. Add the candy through this hole, making the hole bigger with scissors if needed. Punch out two smaller holes next to the candy hole and tie a string or ribbon through to hang the piñata on a tree branch.

**Rules:** this is an individual challenge. Blindfold the first player and hand them a bat. Ensure all players are out of the way and cannot be hit with the bat once the player starts swinging. Gently guide the blindfolded player toward the piñata and allow them to swing at it a total of 1-5 times (you decide – more for younger kids). Then, move to the next player in line and so forth until someone hits it hard enough for the candy to fall to the ground. Then, the players can scramble to pick it up from the ground. Note: tell the blindfolded player when they have busted the piñata, so they don't continue to swing while the players are hunting candy on the ground.

**Props needed:** For a DIY Piñata: balloon, crepe paper (streamers) of various colors with slits in ¾ of the way, 2 cups of water, 2 cups of flour, pinch of salt, newspaper strips (~ 2" by 8"), glue (Elmer's is fine), fishing wire/string/ribbon to hang the piñata, candy to fill it, black construction paper.

<u>For the game:</u> blindfold, bat (your choice of what kind).
**Playing time:** ~ 10 minutes.

## Monkey Feet Fandango

**Objective**: to be the team who can pass the banana to the end of the line and peel it the fastest...with their feet!

**Rules:** divide your players into two-three teams with no less than four players on each team.

Each team is to sit in a straight line - parallel to each other with each member sitting on the floor - facing front - behind each team member. When the host says go, the first person in line will grab a banana with their feet and pass it to the person behind them - to their feet. Once the player's foot touches the banana, they must make monkey noises until the banana is passed to the next player. It is suggested to do a 'back roll' to pass the banana, but any method that you wish to pass is fine as long as it is feet to feet. Hands are not allowed during this challenge! Once the banana gets to the last person in line, the last person is to peel the banana with their feet only – again, no hands are allowed. The first to peel the banana completely wins! Other team members can help peel as long as they only use their feet! Watch out because too many monkeys can spoil the banana!

Optional: once the banana is peeled, it is removed from the peel completely and passed back up the line to the first person in line. If the banana is in pieces, all pieces must reach the first person in line with the exception of 'residue' on the floor/ground – just leave the residue. Once the first person in the team receives the peeled banana (or all banana *pieces*) the team wins! Place a tarp on the floor or do this game outside, as it would make a mess going back up the line!

**Props needed:** enough bananas for as many teams as you will have and a tarp (optional). A camera for goodness sake, this will be hilarious!

**Playing time:** ~ 20 minutes.

## Melt Mr. Freeze

**Objective**: to be the team who can melt their ice cubes the fastest.

**Rules:** divide your players into two teams. Each team is given a tray of ice. They can devise any plan to melt the ice, without using any electrical devices, that is. They can only use their bodies/clothes. The first team to melt their tray wins.

**Props needed:** a tray of ice for each team.

**Playing time:** ~ 10 minutes.

# Dr. Bonnie

## ARTS & CRAFTS GAMES

### Create a Monster Challenge

**Objective**: make the most awesome monster out of the assorted items provided.

**Rules:** have all of the craft items available on a table (listed below). Instruct the players to create a unique monster of any kind using the materials listed below. The host will give a prize to the best monster of the night.

**Props needed:** an assortment of colors of construction paper. An assortment of colors of felt pieces. An assortment of colors of loose sequins and/or buttons. A box of raisins. Collect an assortment of green leaves (depends on the season). A box of non-toxic markers and crayons. Green, brown, white and black yarn. Any other sort of craft item you can find.

**Playing time:** ~ 20 minutes. Allow the monsters to dry during the party.

### Make Me a Necklace

**Objective**: is to be the first to make a beautiful necklace out of very, very strange items.

**Rules:** Give each player a 24" length piece of yarn with two respective 'knots' on either side about 3-4 inches in to designate the beading length. The yarn on either side of the knots is used to tie the necklace and the knots should be tight & small enough not to prevent the items from being beaded onto the necklace. Place each 'item' into a bowl in a line - either on a table or the floor. It is optimal if the bowls can be reached from either side. Space out the bowls as far apart as possible. When you say go, the players are to start 'beading' their necklaces with the items provided. The first one to make a complete beaded necklace and tie it securely around their neck is the winner. Additional Guidelines: no two items can be identical that touch each other and no piece of the yarn besides the yarn that is tied on the other side of the knot - can show.

**Props needed:** Knitting yarn, any items with a hole in the middle (e.g. bolts, cheerios, olives, lifesavers, etc.).

**Playing time:** ~ 10 minutes.

### Bat Wing Challenge

**Objective**: is to make the most fashionable bat wings out of duct tape and newspaper!

**Rules:** split your group into at least three teams of three. Designate one team member as the 'batty' runway model. Give each team one roll of duct tape (or another tape) and two or three newspapers. They are to design and create the most awesome pair of wearable bat wings for the runway show in the given time (~10-15 minutes). The sky is the limit on how they want to create the wings, but they can only use newspaper and duct tape and they must be wearable (have straps the arms can slip into). They cannot duct tape anything to the model's skin - the newspaper is the only thing that can touch the duct tape! (You don't want to deal with removing duct tape off your players!) Find a good area to make your 'catwalk' - line it off with streamers or tape of any kind and play a fun model song (e.g. Ru Paul's Supermodel) in the background to get the models moving! When the time is called, the runway models are to line up at the beginning of the runway, strut their stuff and 'sell those bat wings' to the judge(s)! Either the host can be the sole judge or the players can vote via a secret ballot - and tell them they cannot vote for their creation!

**Props needed:** duct tape, scissors, newspapers, a mapped out 'runway' and a modeling song!

**Playing time:** ~ 30 minutes.

## RELAY RACES

### Mummy Relay Extravaganza

**Objective**: is to beat the other team(s) across the finish line.

**Rules:** divide your group into two or more teams. Make sure you have a roll of toilet paper for ½ of your players and plenty of candy corn. Each team will need to divide into the mummies and the wrappers (split evenly). Rope off (or just put pieces of tape at either end of the racing lanes) as many racing lanes as you have teams. Make them as long as you wish. Designate one end as the 'start/finish' and the other end as the mummification end. The wrappers will wait at the mummification end of the racing lane with the toilet paper. The host says go, and one mummy from each team races to the other side of the racing lane towards their wrapper. The racing mummies must balance a piece of candy corn on their nose during the race. If at any time the candy corn drops to the ground, the mummy must go back to the start and put a new candy corn on their nose and start over. The mummies cannot use their hands in any way once they set off down the racing lane.

# Dr. Bonnie

Once a mummy gets to the mummification end of the racing lane, the wrapper will wrap an entire roll of toilet tissue around the mummy. They must wrap at least two times around each limb and the head - in addition to the body (torso). No toilet paper can be left behind. The mummy will race back to the start/finish line (no candy corn on the way back) and tag the next mummy in line. The process will repeat until all mummies have made it past the finish line. This is a picture opportunity – don't let it pass by without being a paparazzo.

**Props needed:** enough rolls of toilet tissue for each mummy (~8-10) and candy corn for each mummy (with some extra in case).

**Playing time:** ~ 10-15 minutes.

## Scary Skeleton Relay

**Objective**: is to put your skeleton back together fist!

**Rules:** divide your group into two or more teams. Print out pictures of skeleton bones and cut them out for each team. You will also need a clear wall for the players to tape their skeleton pieces on. Designate a start line a good ways from the wall with a line of painter's tape for each team. The teams line up. When the host says go, they choose one piece of the skeleton, race to the wall and tape it where they believe it should go. The player races back to the start line and tags the next player in line and so forth until the skeleton is correctly pieced together on the wall. If there is an incorrect piece – such as someone puts the femur (leg bone) where the humerus (arm bone) should be – then, the next player in line is allowed to race to fix **one pair of** bones, but they may not touch anything else or bring a new bone to the skeleton. The first team to have the correct skeleton on the wall is the winning team.

**Props needed:** a printed skeleton for each team, painter's tape to attach the pieces to the wall (or large cardboard) and a starting line/wall.

**Playing time:** ~ 10-15 minutes.

## Let's Get Jiggy

**Objective**: is to be the first team to put your puzzle together.

**Rules:** divide your group into two teams. Purchase two 'easy' 20 piece jigsaw puzzles – the same ones for each team to keep it fair. Arrange a table at the end of each relay lane and a bucket with the pieces at the starting line. When the host says go, the first player in line will grab a piece of the puzzle and race to their table and place it where it goes. They are only allowed to touch their piece – they cannot move/arrange a piece that is already on the table. A player may only move existing pieces on the table if they shout 'fix it' before they race to the table and if so – they may not bring a new piece to the table. The 'fixer' can move as many pieces as they wish when they are at the table but realize, no further pieces are being put on the table until they race back to the start line and tag the next player.

The first one to get all of the pieces on the table and put the puzzle together correctly is the winner.

**Props needed:** a 20 piece jigsaw puzzle and a relay race lane for each team with a table for the puzzle at the end of each lane.

**Playing time:** ~ 10-15 minutes.

## The Manic Mad Scientist Sponge Off

**Objective**: is to fill your beaker to the fill line first.

**Rules:** divide your group into two teams and make relay lanes with floor-safe tape – designating a start/finish line with lanes to race. Line up your players behind the start line and give them a bucket of water and a sponge. At the finish line end of the lane, place a beaker, graduated cylinder, or flask that has a fill line marked with tape. When the host says go, the players soak up as much water with their sponge as possible and race to the other end of the lane. They transfer the water in the sponge into their container and race back to tag the next player, handing off the sponge. The process continues until the first team reaches the fill line in their container and completes the mad scientists' experiment. They are declared the winning team.

**Props needed:** a sponge for each team, a bucket of water for each team and a container to be filled at the end of each relay lane.

**Playing time:** ~ 10-15 minutes.

## The Heads will Roll

**Objective**: is to get your final player across the finish line without losing your head.

**Rules:** divide your group into two teams and have them line up at the starting line (create a starting line with painter's tape.) Also, make a finish line however far from the start that you wish. You will need two smooth plates without ridges about 8 -10 inches in diameter. Make these out of paper mache and paint them in a Halloween theme.

You will also need large foam/plastic skulls from any Halloween/party store – or make these out of paper mache.

When the host says go, the first player in line must rush to the finish line, cross it, and race back while holding the plate with one hand

# Dr. Bonnie

and not dropping the skull. If, at any time, the skull drops to the floor or a player has to use a second hand or another body part from preventing it from dropping to the floor – they must start over at the start line. When the first player successfully makes it back to the start line, they hand off the plate and skull to the next person in line until the final person's turn. The winning team is the one who gets their final player across the finish line successfully.

*The final player doesn't need to return to the starting line.

**Props needed:** a skull and smooth plate for two teams and relay lanes marked with start/finish.

**Playing time:** ~ 10-15 minutes.

## Newspaper Mayhem

**Objective**: is to get your final player across the finish line by only stepping on two sheets of newspaper.

**Rules:** divide your group into two teams and have them line up at the starting line (create a starting line with painter's tape.) Also, make a finish line however far from the start that you wish. Line up your teams behind the starting line. Give each team two sheets of newspaper. They race to the finish line and back by only stepping on the newspaper sheets. If they rip their sheet, they must wait for the host to get them a new one, as ripped sheets do not count across the finish line. The safest strategy is to place the newspaper in front of them, step onto it, grab the one behind and place it in front, and so forth. They must cross the finish line and race back to tag the next player in line, handing off their newspapers. The final player only has to make it one leg of the race and cross the finish line. The first team to have their final player cross the finish line with two intact newspapers is declared the winning team.

**Props needed:** newspaper sheets (2) for each team with some backup sheets for ripped sheets during the challenge. You can switch the newspaper to any Halloween cut outs that are as large as a foot, such as pumpkins. Relay lanes marked with start/finish.

**Playing time:** ~ 10-15 minutes.

## The Great Broom Off

**Objective**: is to whisk all of your mini pumpkins across the finish line using a broom.

**Rules:** divide your group into two teams. Create two relay lanes by designating a start line and finish line. Line each relay lane with helium-filled balloons attached to painted rocks or cans with tissue

101

paper around them for cute décor. Give the starting players a witch's hat and a broom. Use a regular house broom or purchase a witch's broom from a costume shop. Hand each player a mini pumpkin. The first player in each line will put their mini pumpkin on the ground and get into position. The host will blow a whistle or simply scream go and the players will push their mini pumpkin with the broom across the finish line. While on the other side of the finish line, they slip the broom in between their legs and ride on their broom back to the next player where they hand off the broom and hat. The player must put on the hat before they start to push their mini pumpkin across the finish line. The first team to have all pumpkins cross the finish line, wins. If you do not have even teams, the first player on the short team may go to the end of the line and play twice.

**Props needed:** two brooms, two witch hats, and a mini pumpkin for each player in the game. Also, a place big enough for two relay lanes. It's best to play this on a smooth surface – it may be more difficult to push pumpkins in the grass.

**Playing time:** ~ 10-15 minutes.

## The Zany Halloween Relay Race

**Objective**: to cross the finish line first after completing all obstacles.

**Rules:** divide your group into two teams. Make ten stations each a distance away from the start line. The stations should have two players (one from each team) accomplishing the same task at the same time, so make sure there are enough materials and room to accomplish this. The stations can be anything : a Barbie dressing station, a red solo cup stacking station, puzzle solving, pumpkin scooping (scooping out the inside of a pumpkin to get a certain weight of 'innards' in a cup, flower petal peeling, beading, Ping-Pong tossing into cups, playing card sorting (sort them into suits), etc.

Once you have your stations created, make the teams line up behind a starting line. When the host says go, the first player from each team will rush to one of the stations (of their choice) and accomplish the task at hand (i.e. put the clothes on the Barbie). When the task is completed, they rush back and tag the next player in their line who will, in turn, choose a different station to accomplish the task. The game continues until the first player from a team crosses the start/finish line with all tasks completed.

Note: each person from a team must accomplish a task in the order in which they are in line. Nobody can go twice unless it is because they have one less player than the other team.

# Dr. Bonnie

**Props needed:** a start/finish line and ~ ten stations a distance from the start/finish line with 'tasks' to perform. Having a couple of judges on hand will be a good idea to determine if the tasks are appropriately completed. If you have ten stations, this will be good for 20 players in your game. If you have only ten players total (five on each team), then only make five stations, etc.

**Playing time:** ~ 10-15 minutes.

## The Chaotic Costume Relay

**Objective**: the first team to cross the finish line wearing the entire costume provided in your lane.

**Rules:** divide your group into two teams. If your players are wearing elaborate costumes, this game might not be possible. However, if they are not wearing elaborate costumes – this is a way to dress them up for the occasion! The host will place an over-sized assembly of costume pieces at the 'finish' line of each lane. When the host says go, the first player in line races to the finish line, picks up one item of their costume, puts it on (putting it on entails the clothing item is fastened with at least one button/snap/tie, and it must stay on without any assistance with the players arms/hands – so you cannot simply pick it up and race back &/or hold it in your armpit or against your body, etc.). The player races back to the start line, removes the item, and transfers it to the next player in line. This continues with the second player racing to the finish line, picking up a second article of clothing, putting it on and racing back, transferring both articles to the next player and so forth until the final player accepts the entire costume from a player and races across the finish line wearing the entire ensemble.

**Props needed:** a start/finish line and relay lanes. An entire costume of your choice for each relay lane (e.g. oversized pants, oversized shirt, sunglasses, gloves, socks, shoes, handbag). You'll need one item for each player in line – minus one since the final player is simply transferred the costume.

**Playing time:** ~ 10-15 minutes.

## The Slithery Snake Pillowcase Race

**Objective**: the first team to cross the finish line by making a snake with two players and slithering down the relay lane to the finish line.

**Rules:** divide your group into two teams and hand each team a pillowcase – it's best to have a King-sized one so it will be long enough to stay on the players' legs. Two players from each team will go at a time. They each put one leg into the pillowcase and lie on the floor.

103

When the host says go, they 'slither' down the lane with their legs inside of the pillowcase – they may each need to hold on to it with a hand. If the pillowcase comes off the players' legs during the race, they must dash back to the starting line and start over. When a slithery snake pair crosses the finish line, one of the players races the pillowcase back to the next pair, and they repeat the process until the final pair crosses the line. In the case of an uneven number, one player from the first pair in the team may join the final single player in the race to the finish. The first team who gets all players across the finish line is the winning team.

**Props needed:** a start/finish line and relay lanes. A pillowcase for each team.

**Playing time:** ~ 10-15 minutes.

## Vampires & Wounded Werewolves Relay

**Objective**: the first team to transfer your werewolves across the finish line.

**Rules:** divide your group into two teams and line them up behind a starting line. Designate a 'vampire' for each team and place them second in line. The vampire will grab the player's legs in front of them (the wounded werewolf). The wounded werewolf should do a handstand and kick their legs up to help the vampire grab them. When the host says go, the vampire will assist their wounded ally down the relay lane, holding their legs, as the wolves use their arms to race as fast as they can towards the finish line (a wheelbarrow). The vampire will rush back and retrieve the next 'wounded werewolf' by the legs and so forth until the vampire has transferred all of their wolves across the finish line.

**Props needed:** a start/finish line and relay lanes.

**Playing time:** ~ 10-15 minutes.

## Jell-O'Tastic Relay Race

**Objective**: is to be the fastest team to transport the most Jell-O cubes to an empty bowl while suffering various vertical challenges.

**Rules:** divide your players into equal teams. It's no big deal to have an 'odd number team' as the players rotate - the odd team will just have one extra player to rotate - no worries!

Fill a bowl with Jell-O cubes and place in front of each team. Place a rounded plastic toothpick by an empty bowl about 10 feet away in front of each team. When you say go, the first player on each team will run and grab the toothpick, come back to the Jell-O cube bowl, carefully stab a Jell-O cube and then transport it to the empty bowl. The players are not to ever touch the Jell-O cubes! If at any time, the Jell-O cube falls off the toothpick - or any piece of it falls off the toothpick - the player must return to the bowl to get a new cube. (Make sure you make plenty of cubes!) After the player has transported a cube, s/he must rush back to their team, tag the next player in line, and hand them the toothpick (carefully)!

Here's where the difficultly comes into play: Each racer must get 'lower' than the team member in front of them did when they raced until someone has to lie down and scoot along the floor to the other side. Then, the next racer can start over by standing up. For example - the first player can walk, the second player can bend their knees slightly, the third player can walk on their knees, the next racer can sit down and scoot across the floor (or crawl) and then the next racer can lie down on the floor and scoot to the other side. Once each player gets to the 'empty' bowl side, they can stand up to put their cube into the bowl on a table - if it is on the floor - then there's no need to stand up until the Jell-O cube is in the bowl. If at any time the host (or other judges) notice that a team member is not transporting their Jell-O cube 'lower' than the team member before them, they must go back to the starting point and start their turn over.

The host will decide the time limit and set the timer (~5-10 minutes), but have enough Jell-O cubes for your time limit!

**Props needed:** plastic toothpicks, Jell-O cubes (use an ice tray to make them). A pair of kneepads for each team is suggested for the players who have to walk on their knees, but this is optional. Instead of kneepads, have some long tube socks available, and the players who will have to walk on their knees can tie these around their knees before their turn. Note: Jell-O can stain, so do this challenge on a stain-proof surface or put protection down.

**Playing time:** ~15 minutes.

## FOOD GAMES

### Crazy Candy Bar Caper

**Objective**: is to guess the most melted confections correctly!

**Rules:** Purchase five to eight different types of chocolate candy bars. Put each on a separate plate and melt each candy bar in the microwave and stir thoroughly. Break up any cookies, caramel, etc., inside, and try to make it as uniform of a mixture as possible. Designate each candy bar with a number make an answer key to

reference when you score the players' answer sheets. For each contestant, line the numbered plates in a row and have them sample the melted candy bar (have plenty of mini spoons/spatulas available for tasting). They write down their guess for each melted chocolate bar on their answer sheet. They only have one guess and they may not resample. The player that guesses the most melted candy bars wins! In the event of a tie, a guess off can take place - melt two candy bars together and see if any of the tied players guess it correctly. If it's still a tie, make three melted candy bars and so on...until you get a winner!
**Props needed:** five to eight types of candy bars, melted on small plates. Small sampling spoons, pens/pencils and candy guess sheets.
**Playing time:** ~5-10 minutes.

## Crazy Candy Bar Caper Volume II
**Objective**: is to guess the most melted confections correctly!
**Rules:** Purchase 7-9 different types of chocolate candy bars. Break off a third from each and put them in a pile on a microwave safe plate. Put in the microwave until they are somewhat unrecognizable; stir gently, but leave in 'clumps.' Place the platter in the center of a table and have the players guess the candy bars that have been melted together. They may sample the concoction, but only 3 times (have plenty of sampling spoons). They write down their guess for what is contained in the melted pile of candy bars on their answer sheet. The player that guesses the most correct melted candy bars wins!
If you get a tie – go to a Mouse-Cat-Witch tiebreaker (see directions under tiebreakers).
**Props needed:** 5-8 types of candy bars, melted on a platter. Pens/pencils and candy guess sheets.
**Playing time:** ~5-10 minutes.

## I Vant to Suck Your Jell-O Blood
**Objective**: is to eat the red (strawberry, etc.) Jell-O through a straw the fastest.
**Rules:** have one container of Jell-O and a straw for each player. When you say go, the players suck the Jell-O through the straw as fast as they can. The first one to empty their container wins.  As a fun alternative, make this challenge more difficult and have each player wear a plastic pair of vampire teeth. Take pictures, please!
**Props needed:** a small container of Jell-O for each player and a wide straw.
**Playing time:** ~5-10 minutes.

# Dr. Bonnie

## Trickin' & Treatin'

**Objective**: not to have to drink the 'trick' beverage.

**Rules:** Using six labeled orange solo cups with numbers in front of them on place cards (standing paper tents), pour four tasty beverages in a sample size (e.g. soda, milkshake) and two disgusting beverage samples (e.g. sour cream and water, soy sauce and pickle juice) Each player gets a turn rolling a dice, and they have to drink the corresponding numbered beverage sample. By the look on their face – you'll know if it was the trick-or-treat! Warning: don't play this with players who have weak stomachs. Bad outcome!

**Props needed:** someone to create tasty treats and yucky trick beverage samples.

**Playing time:** ~ 10 minutes.

## The Great Colorful Candy Hunt

**Objective**: is to choose to hunt a candy color with (hopefully) the biggest point value and find as many candies of that color during the hunt.

**Rules:** purchase many mini cauldrons (~15-20+) and fill with colorful candies such as M&Ms, Skittles, etc. Before the game, assign a point value to each color but do not announce the point values to the guests. Instruct your players to remain within your defined boundaries and give each team a small-medium sized cauldron to collect their candies (or a Halloween treat bag). Set the timer for five minutes and allow your teams to choose one color and whatever color they choose – they must stick with that color for the game, and they must not tell another team what color they are hunting for.

When the host says go, the teams set out to find as many candies in the cauldrons in their team's color. They collect them, return the other color candies to the cauldron, and search for the next cauldron, etc. until the timer goes off. Then, they return immediately to home base for judging.

The host/judge will then reveal the point value of each color (i.e. red=1, blue=2, yellow=3, etc.). Then, count the number of candies each team has collected, noting their color choice. Again, each team can only collect one color – any other color in their cauldron (or treat bag) is a point deduction for that color's point value. This should deter the teams from trying to sabotage by removing candies of the different colors.

Another note: if two (or more) teams end up going for the same color, it's just another layer of the game to get lucky and be the only

# The Halloween Party Host Handbook

one to select your color - as well as selecting the color with the highest point total, and finding the most candies.

**Props needed:** about 15-20+cauldrons filled with about five candies from each color. Put a few more of the lower point candies to try to even out the point advantage of the higher point candies.

**Playing time:** ~10 minutes.

## Dangling Donuts

**Objective**: is to eat your donut the fastest!

**Rules:** using string, hang a donut for each player from a secure spot such as a tree branch, door jamb, etc. When the host says go, the players eat the donut without using their hands. However, if a piece of a donut drops from the string, they are allowed to catch it/pick it up with their mouth.

**Props needed:** a donut for each player, string, a place to hang the donuts. A very clean floor &/or sanitary drop cloth for the donuts to land on.

**Playing time:** ~5-10 minutes.

## Cookie Monsters

**Objective**: is to be the first to eat your cookie.

**Rules:** place a cookie on each player's forehead. When you say go, the players do anything possible using only their face to get the cookie into their mouth. If it drops to the floor, they are out. If they touch it with their hands, they are out. The first player to get the cookie into their mouth and eat it is the winner.

**Props needed:** a cookie for each player.

**Playing time:** ~5-10 minutes.

## Save the Worms

**Objective**: is to find the most gummy worms in your whipped cream plate.

**Rules:** this is a tournament-style challenge. Set the timer for 30 seconds and place two plates in front of each contestant: one with gummy worms and whipped cream piled on top, and the other a clean plate. When you say go, they fish out the worms with their mouth (no hands) and place on the clean plate. The player who fishes out the most worms at the end of 30 seconds, wins, and moves on to the next round to face the winner of that round. This continues until you've got a final winner.

# Dr. Bonnie

**Props needed:** plenty of gummy worms (or bears, but those aren't as Halloween-themed). You'll need ~ 10 for each player, each round of the tournament. Whipped cream and paper plates (2 per player). It is acceptable to use worms with the same player if they progress to the next round as long as it is within two hours or one hour in 85F weather. For returning players, reset the plate and add of whipped cream. Don't allow a player to use someone else's worms they've had in their mouth.
**Playing time:** ~5-10 minutes.

## Crazy Chef'tastic Challenge

**Objective**: is to be the team who makes the best Halloween-inspired dish given the ingredients.
**Rules:** divide your group into teams of four. Make a wide array of ingredients available and decide if you will allow baking and if so, choose a temperature and preheat your oven(s). When you say go, set the timer for 20-30 minutes. The team is to plan out the most creative Halloween inspired edible dish before the time runs out.
**Props needed:** an assortment of ingredients. If you allow baking, preheat an oven at ~ 350F before the challenge and have baking dishes, mixing bowls, measuring cups, spoons, knives, etc. available for each team. When time is called the judge will be presented with the dish and will judge on presentation (10 points), taste (10 points), and creativity (10 points).
**Playing time:** ~30 minutes.

## Trick-or-Treat Relay

**Objective**: is for your team to eat your bag of 'goodies' the fastest and come back across the start/finish line first.
**Rules:** place random items on a table that are secured in Halloween treat bags and taped shut. Divide your teams into two groups and line your players behind the start/finish line. When the host says go, the players race down their lane by doing a crab walk (or other style of walk, crawl, or slither the host selects.) When they reach the end of the lane at the table, they choose one of the bags, open it, and eat the item inside. Once the item is eaten, they can crab walk (or whatever you decided to do) back to the start/finish line and tag the next player. Game continues until all items are eaten and the final player races back across the start/finish line.
**Props needed:** random items in sealed bags. Have some of them easy items, such as a marshmallow crème on a plastic spoon, and other

items maybe a bit gross – like a spoonful of mayonnaise or mustard. Important note: please check for food allergies of your players before gameplay. Also, don't use food that the players are likely to choke on such as hotdogs, carrots, apples, grapes, peanut M&Ms, etc.
**Playing time:** ~10-15 minutes.

## SCAVENGER HUNT GAMES

### Eerie Eyeball Hunters
**Objective:** to be the one who finds the most Ping-Pong balls (e.g. eyeballs) in a set amount of time.
**Rules:** cook plenty of spaghetti noodles and assemble them into large buckets for as many teams as you will have. Rinse the noodles thoroughly with cold water and allow cooling before placing into the bucket. Allow the noodles to remain a little wet, as you don't want them to dry and become sticky. Draw eyeballs on the Ping-Pong balls and bury as many balls in the noodle bucket as you can. As an alternative, assign a point value to the balls.

Set the timer for 30 seconds and when the host says go; each player will hunt for Ping-Pong balls without spilling any noodles from the bucket! For each spilled noodle, they lose a corresponding Ping-Pong ball that they have collected. (This prevents players from dumping the bucket and collecting them that way which is a huge mess!) The player with the highest point total wins! In the event of a tie, have a 10 second timed faceoff of the eyeball hunting challenge between the players that tied until you get a winner.
**Props needed:** Ping-Pong balls, markers, cooked spaghetti noodles, buckets for each team.
**Playing time:** ~ 15 minutes.

### Find the Golden Spider
**Objective:** to be the one who can rack up the most points by hunting for spiders (not real ones, of course).
**Rules:** purchase small plastic spiders from any party store in the Halloween aisle (or online). Spray paint one (or more) a metallic gold. Hide the spiders in a designated location around your home, backyard, office, school, etc., and when the host says go, the players hunt for the spiders. When the time is called (~5-10 minutes), the players come back for judging. Each spider is worth five points, and the golden spider is worth 20 points. The player with the most points wins.

# Dr. Bonnie

**Props needed:** plastic spiders, gold paint, and an area for hunting. Also, get silver and bronze paint and make a 15 point and 10 point spider if you want to add more point options.
**Playing time:** ~ 15 minutes.

## Tie a Black Ribbon

**Objective:** to be the team who can locate as many envelopes containing various lengths of black ribbon and tie them together to make the longest strand.
**Rules:** purchase black satin ribbon and cut it into various lengths (long enough to be tied together). Place in orange envelopes and hide within your boundaries – hiding the longer pieces in more difficult spots. When you say go, set the timer for five minutes, and the two teams hunt for the envelopes and collect as many as they can before the first timer goes off. When the timer goes off, the teams have 10 seconds to come back to home base for phase two of the challenge. When the teams are ready, the host says go, and they open each envelope and tie their ribbons together. The team with the longest ribbon strand is declared the winner!
**Props needed:** black ribbon cut into various lengths and orange envelopes. A timer.
**Playing time:** ~ 15 minutes.

## Halloween City Hunt

**Objective:** to be the team who can race about town to get the most Halloween-themed pictures in the designated time limit.
**Rules:** give each team a list of Halloween-themed items (e.g. spider, witch, black cat, skeleton).

When the host says go, the team is to race about town (or the neighborhood if you so choose) and snap a picture of their team posing with this item. The items (i.e. bats, spiders) do not have to be real – they can be pictures, cut-outs, etc. The teams are not allowed to get two pictures, however, from the same location. A location is defined as having a parking lot. Therefore, if two stores share a parking lot, they are considered the same location. The first team back to home base with all pictures wins.

Alternatively, the host can also set a time limit (~30-45 minutes) and have the players meet at home base at this time – with a five-point penalty for any team that is late. In this case, have the winner be the team who gets the 'most' pictures of items on the list. It is important to have a rule that no speeding is allowed – that way, your teams will remain safe and not out breaking the law and putting themselves in danger. It's more about strategy than speed.

**Props needed:** cameras for each team (smartphones are suggested) and a car for each team if you play the about town hunt.

**Playing time:** ~ 1 hour.

## PUMPKIN BASED GAMES

### The Great Halloween Pumpkin Hunt

**Objective**: to find the most pumpkins in the 'pumpkin patch.'

**Rules:** purchase miniature pumpkins of a variety of colors. Hide them in any boundary of your choosing and give a point value to each color (e.g. white pumpkins are one point, orange pumpkins are five points, yellow pumpkins are ten points). When you say go, each hunter is to search the pumpkin patch and whoever collects the most pumpkins, wins!

**Props needed:** miniature pumpkins (you may substitute real pumpkins with cut-out pumpkins from orange and black construction paper).

**Playing time:** ~ 15 minutes.

### The Great Pumpkin Hunt

**Objective**: to find a pumpkin, so you don't suffer the penalty (e.g. eating something gross, doing jumping jacks).

**Rules:** the first person who is 'it' is safe from having to suffer the penalty. This player is to hide mini pumpkins in a designated area (e.g. backyard). They hide for as many players are hunting – minus one. When the person who is 'it' says go, the hunters hunt for their pumpkin. When they find a pumpkin, they come back to home base (e.g. back patio). The person who fails to find a pumpkin must suffer your penalty.

**Props needed:** a mini pumpkin for the number of players in the hunt (minus one, as you want someone not to find a pumpkin each round).

**Playing time:** ~ 10 minutes.

### Pumpkin and Ghosts Bowling

**Objective**: to obtain the highest score by knocking down the most pins.

**Rules:** Using ten painted 2L soda bottles (paint them to look like fun monsters), set up a bowling lane and put the bottles at one end and a start line at the other end. (*Note, the bowling pins can also be made out of paper towel rolls with googly eyes.*) Hand your player a rounded pumpkin at the start end of the lane and have them bowl the pumpkin down the lane and knock over as many ghosts as they can. This game is great for kids.

**Preparing pins:** take some 2L empty soda bottles and put a bit of sand inside the bottle to give weight. Paint the outside of the bottle white and allow drying. Add the eyes and mouth with black paint to make them spooky ghosts or other fun monster faces. Allow thorough drying before you play.

**Props needed:** ten painted 2L soda bottles (white and black paint &/or any colors for the monster faces) as the bowling pins, sand, and a rounded pumpkin (smaller) as the bowling ball.

**Playing time:** ~ 10 minutes.

## Pumpkin Neck Pass Challenge

**Objective**: to be the team who gets their pumpkin to the end of the line and to a designated location the fastest.

**Rules:** this game is an oldie but goodie. Divide your group into teams of six-ten players each. Give the player first in line a mini pumpkin and instruct them to hold it against their chest with their chin (they place it against their neck). When you say go, they pass the mini pumpkin to the next player in their line until the last person has the pumpkin and runs to a designated finish place/line with the pumpkin still being held by their chin. If they drop their mini pumpkin, they must go back to their start position, reposition it and then race to the finish again. The first team that has their final player cross the finish line with their pumpkin will be declared the winning team.

**Props needed:** a mini pumpkin and a finish location (e.g. a chair about 10 feet away from the players).

**Playing time:** ~ 5-10 minutes.

## How much do the Pumpkin's Weigh?

**Objective**: to guess the correct weight of the pumpkins and put them in order from small to large.

**Rules:** The host is to arrange an assortment of pumpkins on a table for the players to view. They are allowed to pick each one of them up to determine how much they believe they weigh. On a sheet of paper, they write the order from less weight to most weight and a guess of the exact weight besides each guess. When every player has written down their choices, the host will weigh the pumpkins on a scale in front of the group. The one who was the closest and had them in the correct order will be declared the winner!

**Props needed:** an assortment of pumpkins and a scale to weigh them. If you use small pumpkins, make sure your scale will measure them – you may need to get a kitchen scale.
**Playing time:** ~ 15 minutes.

## The Great Pumpkin Carve-Off

**Objective**: to carve the most awesome face into a pumpkin!
**Rules:** give each player a marker, a piece of paper and a medium sized (or small) pumpkin and a pumpkin carving knife. *Do not play this game if the players have had cocktails as accidents can happen with a knife - alcohol combo! So if your players will be consuming cocktails - either play this game before the cocktails or skip it☺.

Set the timer for 15 minutes and instruct the players to design and carve the best face into their pumpkin. Tell them to plan out their design on the paper and then draw the outline on the pumpkin before they start carving.

When everyone is done with their creations, line them up on the table for judging! You can also slip in an LED light into each creation and turn off the lights to see which looks best in the dark. The host should appoint the winner, or everyone should vote via secret ballot with the host being a tie-breaker.
**Props needed:** pumpkins, carving knives, paper and markers for each player. LED lights for each pumpkin (optional).
**Playing time:** ~20 minutes.

## The Great Pumpkin Drop:

**Objective:** to get as many mini pumpkins in your team's witch's cauldron before the timer runs out!
**Rules:** divide your players into as many groups as you wish. Give each team a plastic witch's cauldron in the center of the room and a pile of mini pumpkins of a designated color (there are white, orange, yellow varieties available, or you can paint them). The cauldrons should touch and cluster together in the center of the room. Each cauldron should be marked clearly for each team (use tape and a marker or adhere a fun Halloween item to the front to designate the teams).

Each team should have a start line designated with tape an equal distance away from the cauldrons. Make sure the teams are spaced appropriately and their cauldrons in the center are facing them. For example, if you have two teams playing, place their start lines at opposing ends of the room. With four teams, use the four corners, etc.

# Dr. Bonnie

*As an alternative cool effect, if you are playing in a large room or outdoors, add a center cauldron that is not assigned to a team. Add some dry ice and a flashlight with a red piece of saran wrap on top to make an eerie red smoke on top of the cauldrons. Place a piece of mesh on top of this cauldron to prevent any pumpkins from going inside. If anyone's pumpkin lands on the mesh, this pumpkin is out of play.

Set the timer for ~three minutes (or whatever time you choose). When the host says go, every member of the team will bend down and pick up a pumpkin and place it between their knees. They may use their hands to place it between their knees, but they may not use their hands after they leave the start line.

Each person races to their center cauldron with the pumpkin in between their knees and drops their pumpkin into the correct cauldron. If they get a pumpkin into another team's cauldron, they receive 2 points for it whereas each pumpkin placed into the correct cauldron is 1 point. If at any time they drop their pumpkin from between their knees, they must go back to the starting line and start over. The teams are not allowed to retrieve a pumpkin from the cauldron. Once a pumpkin lands in a cauldron, it is final. Anyone that spills a cauldron's pumpkins will receive a five-point penalty for their team for each cauldron knocked over.

The host notifies everyone when the timer goes off, and everybody must freeze. No additional pumpkins can enter a cauldron after the time is called. The team with the most points wins!

**Props needed:** ~20 mini pumpkins for each team and a large plastic witch's cauldron for each team. A timer.

**Playing time:** ~ 20 minutes.

## Pass the Mini Pumpkin

**Objective**: to be the first team to pass the mini pumpkin through their line to the last player.

**Rules:** divide your group into two (or more) teams. Give each team leader a mini pumpkin. When the host says go, each team is to pass the mini pumpkin in any way possible without using their hands. The teams can strategize before the host says go and as long as they do not use their hands, anything goes. The winning team is the one who gets their pumpkin to the final player in line. All players must pass the mini pumpkin – a team may not bypass anybody.

**Props needed:** mini pumpkins for each team.

**Playing time:** ~ 5-10 minutes.

### Pumpkin Duels

**Objective**: not to allow anybody to knock your mini pumpkin off your spoon.

**Rules:** this is an individual challenge played tournament-style. Make a roped-off circle with helium-filled balloons, crepe paper, etc. This is the duel ring. Hand the two opponents a plastic spoon and a mini pumpkin. Instruct them to be the first to knock the pumpkin off their opponent's spoon. Warn the contestants that they are not to physically harm each other in any way; they are only to go after the pumpkins on the spoon. The first one to knock their opponent's pumpkin off the spoon is the winner and will move to the next round and so forth until a winner is declared.

**Props needed:** two mini pumpkins and two plastic spoons (and backups in case something happens during the rounds).

**Playing time:** ~ 5-10 minutes - depending on how many rounds you have to play to determine a winner.

### Wrecking Ball Pumpkins

**Objective**: to be the first to push your pumpkin on the floor across the finish line by using only a pumpkin in a pantyhose leg tied to your waist, dangling between your legs.

**Rules:** Play this game via a tournament and only have a set number of players each round and winner plays winner, etc.

Use a pair of pantyhose for each player in the game. Slip a mini pumpkin inside of the leg of a pair of pantyhose (preferably black hose since it's Halloween) and tie the pantyhose using the other leg around their waist with the pumpkin in the pantyhose leg (e.g. the wrecking ball) dangling from the back of their waist and reaching ~ ½" off the ground. Line up the players at the start line and designate a finish line whatever distance you wish (you might try to play a practice round to determine difficulty on your given floor surface).

A second pumpkin is placed on the floor in front of each participant. Make sure it is the appropriate size where the mini pumpkin wrecking ball can actually move it. When the host says go, the players make any bodily movement necessary to swing their dangling pumpkin between their legs to push their pumpkin on the floor across the finish line. They are not allowed to touch the floor pumpkin with anything besides the 'wrecking ball' pumpkin. The first player who gets their floor pumpkin across the finish line is the winner.

# Dr. Bonnie

**Props needed:** mini pumpkins for each player, pantyhose for each player and a floor pumpkin for each player. If you play in rounds for a tournament-style game, you don't need the items for each player – you'll just need a set up for the number of players playing each round. **Playing time:** ~ 15 minutes.

## Pumpkin Ring Toss:

**Objective**: to toss the most rings on the pumpkin stem!

**Rules:** locate a tall, oval pumpkin with a large stem. Increase the stem with paper mache. Allow the paper mache to dry and then paint the stem to match the original. Using hoops (any hoop – DIY or purchased), allow your players to stand behind the line and have three attempts at a toss around the pumpkin stem. Halloween candies can be the prizes for the winners.

**Props needed:** a large, oval pumpkin with a large stem, embroidery hoops (or others), Halloween candy for prizes.

**Playing time:** ~5 minutes.

## Pumpkin Juice Bottle Feeding Challenge

**Objective**: to drink your pumpkin juice the fastest out of a baby's bottle.

**Rules:** this is an individual challenge. Each participant will have a baby bottle (or at least a clean nipple portion for each person). It's best to use the toddler bottles, as the newborn bottles will take too long as the hole in the nipple is too small. The host is to pour the same amount of pumpkin juice (or other Halloween inspired beverage) into each bottle. When the host says go, the contestants suck on their bottles to see who can finish their juice the quickest. The first player done is the winner.

**Props needed:** a baby bottle with pumpkin juice inside for each player.

**Playing time:** ~5 minutes.

## Pumpkin Penny Toss:

**Objective**: to toss the most pennies inside of your team's pumpkin.

**Rules:** scoop out a large pumpkin and make a wide opening at the top. Create a 'do not cross' line with floor-safe tape, placing the pumpkin a far enough distance for difficulty for your age group (do a couple of trials to determine difficulty). This is a great opportunity for you to use your jar of pennies before you take them to the bank! Hand the team a container of pennies and start the time for 30 seconds. Taking turns, they toss pennies one at a time into their pumpkin. The team who gets the most pennies into the pumpkin at the call of time is declared the winner. Host this challenge simultaneously or make it a timed trial.

**Props needed:** a large pumpkin carved out with the top removed to make an opening for the pennies to enter. Jar of pennies for each team. Timer.

**Playing time:** ~5 minutes.

## SPOOKY GAMES

### Forbidden Words

**Objective**: to be the team to guess the most phrases correctly.

**Rules:** divide the players into two teams. The teams will alternate sending a representative to the front to face the host (who is seated on the floor with their back to the group). The host will set the time for one minute and show a phrase on a card to the team rep. The team rep then has to say words – one at a time – in hopes their team can guess the word. None of the words the rep says may have any part of the phrase in it. If they say part of the phrase, the phrase is skipped, and no point is given. At the end of the time, the host records the points, and the next team sends a rep. This continues until everybody has had a turn. Then, the combined total points are calculated for each team.

**Props needed:** phrases on paper cards – at least one for each player with some to spare for people who say the forbidden words.

**Playing time:** ~20-30 minutes.

**Some examples of Halloween-themed phrases:**

| HAPPY HALLOWEEN | ALL HALLOW'S EVE | TRICK-OR-TREAT | HOCUS POCUS |
|---|---|---|---|
| WITCHY WOMAN | DOUBLE, DOUBLE, TOIL AND TROUBLE | PUMPKIN PATCH | COSTUME PARTY |
| JEEPERS CREEPERS | ENTER AT YOUR OWN RISK | ZOMBIE CROSSING | CANDY CORN |
| BOBBING FOR APPLES | FRIGHT NIGHT | TALES OF THE CRYPT | OCTOBER 31$^{ST}$ |
| JACK O'LANTERN | FRANKENSTEIN'S BRIDE | SKELETONS IN THE CLOSET | WITCH'S BREW |
| GHOSTLY GREETINGS | GHOULS JUST WANNA HAVE FUN | HAPPY HAUNTING! | SCAREDY CAT |
| THE SCREAM ZONE | BLOOD DONORS NEEDED | GHOST TOWN | GOT CANDY? |
| BITE. DRINK. BE SCARY | BATS IN THE BELFRY | A HAUNTING WE WILL GO | MONSTER MASH |

# Dr. Bonnie

| THE WITCHING HOUR | MISCHIEF & MAYHEM | EYE OF NEWT | ARSENIC & LACE |
|---|---|---|---|

## Mortifying Movie Challenge

**Objective**: to match the movie prop with the movie the fastest.

**Rules:** divide your players into three to four teams (you'll want about five-ten players on each team). In the adjacent room, you'll have movies printed out on a piece of paper (simply print the title or print a picture of the movie poster) and taped to a wall. Movie props are placed in a pile on the other side of the room. When you say go, you'll set a timer and the team will match the appropriate movie props to the movies on the wall. For example, for Friday the 13$^{th}$, you'll have a hockey mask (see examples below). When the team has matched them all correctly, stop the timer and then reset the props into a pile for the next team. The team with the fastest time is the winning team.

**Props needed:** printed movie posters (posters don't need to be poster size) of ~10-15 movies and associated movie props. Painter's tape to adhere the printed sheets to the wall. A timer (a smartphone has a timer).

**Playing time:** ~20 minutes.

## Some example movies with associated props are below:

| Nightmare on Elm Street | Freddy's glove with knives (a toy prop, of course) |
|---|---|
| Friday the 13$^{th}$ | Hockey mask |
| Poltergeist | Picture of a static'd television |
| Rosemary's Baby | A baby carriage |
| Texas Chainsaw Massacre | Chainsaw (a toy prop, of course) |
| Shaun of the Dead | A cricket bat |
| Halloween | Michael Myers (William Shatner) mask |
| Saw | Tricycle (using a picture is acceptable) |
| The Ring | VHS tape |
| Blair Witch Project | Twigs (assemble them into the figures used in the movie) |
| Silence of the Lambs | Hannibal's mask |
| Paranormal Activity | Video camera (although, being a potentially rough challenge, it may be best to have a toy one or picture) |
| Ouija | Ouija board |
| They Live | Sunglasses |

# The Halloween Party Host Handbook

## Creepy Chalk Outlines

**Objective**: to guess the owner of the most chalk outlines.

**Rules:** on a long sidewalk, escort your players (one at a time) outside and have them lie down on the sidewalk in any position they wish. Draw an outline of their body with chalk. Important – don't keep the same order on the sidewalk as you bring players outside. Switch it up so they can't figure out whose outline belongs to who as you bring them outside. Blindfold them to ensure they can't see the outlines as they are being created but guide them to where they need to lie down. After you draw an outline, draw a letter/symbol/number inside the outline and make a key to keep track of the correct answers. Again, it's not suggested to write numbers in order in case players are keeping track of the order they went out to make their outline. When everybody has an outline created, allow the group to come outside together and guess via ballot which outline belongs to whom. Then, score the ballots to find your winner. In case of tie, go to a Mouse-Cat-Witch tiebreaker (see the tie-breaking section).

**Props needed:** a large sidewalk, sidewalk chalk, answer key, answer sheets, and a writing utensil for each player.

**Playing time:** ~20-25 minutes.

## Murder in a Dark Alley

**Objective**: to catch the murderer.

**Rules:** first, play some spooky music. Using strips of paper, write one slip that says *homicide detective* and one that says *serial killer.* The remaining slips will say *suspect*. Place the strips in a bowl, allowing each player to draw one and not reveal which they drew. Tell the players not to tell which cards they have.

Using an open space that is safe to be in the dark (i.e. no sharp corners or pointed objects for your players to bump into), turn off the lights. The serial killer will now start to claim victims by poking the players in the shoulder three consecutive times. The victims, at that time, fake their death in any manner they wish – as long as they are not the homicide detective. They can moan, scream, wail, and then collapse to the ground. Once someone physically discovers a murder victim (while still in the dark), they scream *someone's been murdered,* and the lights are turned on immediately.

If the serial killer tries to kill the homicide detective, the homicide detective will say *turn on the lights, there's a killer among us,* and lights are turned back on immediately – even if no victims have been claimed. The homicide detective cannot die in the game.

120

# Dr. Bonnie

Instruct the players to be very careful as they are walking around in the dark as not to step on a victim and hurt them. Have your players remove shoes before starting the game, if possible.

Then, the homicide detective is to solve the crime (murder &/or just an attempted murder of the homicide detective) by interrogating everybody. They can ask where everybody was standing, what the 'pokes' felt like – small finger, large finger, angle, how much force. Yes, in this game, victims can talk. The detective can ask each suspect/victim who they think did it, and so forth.

**Props needed:** a darkened, safe room and slips for the players to draw that say homicide detective, serial killer, and suspect. Assign glow sticks to the players for added safety in getting around in the dark.

**Playing time:** ~15 minutes.

## The Undead Memory Game

**Objective**: to remember the scariest items from the memory tray after seeing it only one time.

**Rules:** put random scary-themed items on a tray or arrange them on a table (e.g. skulls, ghosts, spiders). Find these small items at any party store in the Halloween aisle. Allow each player to view the items for one minute before you cover the items with a tablecloth/towel/sheet. At this time allow the players to write down as many items as they can remember. The winner is the one who can remember the most items! In case of tie, go to a Mouse-Cat-Witch tiebreaker (see the tie-breaking section).

**Props needed:** 10-15 random scary items, pen/paper for each player.

**Playing time:** ~ 5-10 minutes.

## Guess the Halloween Flick

**Objective**: to earn the most points by having your team guess the title of the horror/Halloween-themed movie you are acting a scene from.

**Rules:** divide your players into two teams. One at a time, the players send a player to be an actor who stands in front of the group and performs a 30-second scene from any horror movie. They are allowed to speak, but may not use any part of the movie title in their words, and they must at least attempt at 'quoting' the movie as closely as possible. They are not allowed to simply describe the movie. Each team who can correctly guess the movie title after the 30-second monolog gets a point. The first team to five points wins. Digital devices are not allowed – this is a test of memory.

# The Halloween Party Host Handbook

**Props needed:** none.
**Playing time:** ~ 20 minutes.

## Zombie Movie Challenge

**Objective**: to be the team that answers the most correct zombie movies according to the synopses given!

**Rules:** pair the players into groups of two or three. Give the teams ten minutes (or more) to fill in the correct movie next to the movie description on the movie challenge sheet. When the time is up, and/or the players are finished, collect the answer sheets and score them using the 'zombie movie answer key.' As an alternative, open it up to spooky movies in the horror genre and not just zombies.

**Props needed:** you will need to create a 'zombie movie challenge' sheet and give a pen/pencil to each team. Also, create an answer key.

**Playing time:** ~15 minutes.

**Some example movies are below (just look up their synopsis on the movie's IMDB.com page to make your game sheets):**

| White Zombie (1932) | Night of the Living Dead (1968) | Dawn of The Dead (1978) | Zombie (1980) | The Return of the Living Dead (1985) |
|---|---|---|---|---|
| 28 Days Later (2002) | Dawn of the Dead (2004) | Shaun of the Dead (2004) | Land of the Dead (2005) | Fido (2006) |
| Dead Land: The Rising (2006) | Planet Terror (2007) | Deadgirl (2008) | Dance of the Dead (2008) | The Horde (2009) |
| Zombieland (2009) | Exit Humanity (2011) | The Battery (2012) | Maggie (2015) | Scout's Guide to the Zombie Apocalypse (2015) |

## What Spooky Thing Am I?

**Objective**: to be the first one to guess the 'spooky thing' on your forehead!

**Rules:** Create squares of paper with a spooky thing printed/drawn on them. Affix tape to the back of each square and affix a random spooky thing sheet onto their forehead. Do not show the players the item that is being affixed to their forehead, and make sure there are not any mirrors or highly reflective surfaces in the party room during this game. When all of the players have a sheet attached to their forehead, the game begins. The players are allowed to ask each person one and only one yes/no question (e.g. 'am I a person?' or 'am I blue in color?'). No lying is allowed, so all players must answer the questions truthfully.

If a player has asked every player at the party a yes/no question and still cannot guess the thing on their forehead, s/he may start the cycle over. They continue until they make a correct guess. There is one winner and one loser in this game. The winner is the first to guess the spooky thing, and the loser is the last one standing without a correct guess. You can, however, elect only to declare a winner and not single-out a loser. You know your group best – if they are ultra-competitive adults, declaring a loser may be a fun bonus. For kids/non-competitive adults, end it as soon as a winner is declared.

**Props needed:** spooky things on paper squares and a way to affix them to your players' foreheads.

**Playing time:** ~15 minutes.

## Horror Quote Challenge

**Objective**: to get the most horror movie quotes correct.

**Rules:** before your party, make a list of horror movie quotes. There are two ways to play this challenge.

1. Gather your players and stand in front of the group. Say each quote and the first player to shout the correct answer, gets the point. The player with the most points at the end of your list wins.
2. Do as above and say each movie quote one by one to the group. Give them a pen and paper and allow them secretly to make their guesses. Score their answer sheets to determine the winner. In the event of a tie, host a Mouse-Cat-Witch tie-breaker (see the tie-breaking section for details).

**Props needed:** a list of horror movie quotes (grab these off IMDB.com), and pen/paper for each player if you play with the second option.

**Playing time:** ~ 10-15 minutes.

## Push 'Em Up

**Objective**: when anybody dies in a slasher film, don't be the last to put your hand on your forehead, or you have to do five push-ups.

**Rules:** play a cheesy horror flick, with the volume on low because it's not necessarily what this is about. Move on with the party mingling and fun and play this game in the background. The players causally watch for a victim being murdered in the movie. The moment the victim dies, the players put their right palm on their forehead without saying a word. The last player to notice has to drop and give five push-ups – or whatever house penalty you choose.

**Props needed:** a cheesy flick and moderately physical players.

**Playing time:** ~ as long as you wish.

## Frightening Film Festival

**Objective**: to make the most creative and interesting zombie-themed movie (*to be done in advance of the party).

**Rules:** before the party, invite your players to create a five-minute zombie-themed movie. They prepare a script, direct the film, edit the film, and put it on Vimeo, YouTube or another video sharing site. Instruct them to post as 'private' if you don't want your videos shared with the world. Obviously, you know if your friends will pull this off – but if they can – it is a real 'scream!' At any time during the party, take a break and watch the films and allow the players to vote for the best film!

**Props needed:** your players will need to prepare a film in advance of the party and post their five-minute zombie-themed film on a video sharing site. You will need a device to play the videos to the players.

**Playing time:** ~ depends on the number of films you will watch.

## Zombie Charade Challenge

**Objective**: to earn a point by being the player that is first to guess the charade correctly! The winner is the player with the highest point total!

**Rules:** one player draws a charade topic from a hat and acts it out for the rest of the group. The first one to guess the correct charade topic gets a point. The next player will draw a topic from the hat and act it out until one of the other players guesses it correctly, and this will repeat until all of the topics are guessed correctly.

The actor of the charade may not speak, point to an object, or acknowledge the other players until they give a correct guess. They are not allowed simply to point to someone in costume – they must 'act out' their charade topic. ***This game may also be played in teams.

**Zombie penalty:** if a player blurts out an incorrect guess, they must run a designated distance (i.e. around the room) as a zombie (i.e. arms extended in front of their torso and moaning) before they can return to their seat and guess again.

Either type or write the charade topics on equally-sized pieces of paper fold them and put them inside of a plastic pumpkin, a witch's hat or another container.

# Dr. Bonnie

**Example charade topics are as follows:**

| | | | |
|---|---|---|---|
| Graveyard Dirt | Survivor | Horror Movie | Cannibal |
| Coffin Nail | Monster | Tombstone | Frankenstein |
| Undead | Dusk | Midnight | Apocalypse |
| Coffin Nail | Crowbar | Nocturnal | Walkers |
| Brains | Night Of The Living Dead | Tales From The Crypt | Dawn Of The Dead |
| Nightmare | Sarcophagus | Walking Dead | Morgue |
| Zombie Land | Toxin | Ghoul | Katana Sword |
| Virus | Crossbow | Map | Grave |

**Props needed:** paper, pen, hat to place the charade topics.
**Playing time:** 30 minutes.

## Ew, What Is It? The Great Halloween Guess Game

**Objective:** to guess what Halloween item is in the containers!

**Rules:** using any container such as a cardboard box, decorate the outside in a fun Halloween theme so you cannot see inside. Create a hole wide enough to get a hand inside to feel the item. If you are using containers that you cannot cut into, purchase some felt and make a slit for a hand to get through and secure the felt with a rubber band around the rim of the container or glue to the rim of the container.

Choose 10 of the following items (or more/less) and put each of them into an individual box. Allow the players to one at a time put their hand in the container and before withdrawing their hand; they must make a guess as to what Halloween item is in the box. The objective is not to guess the real item, but rather what the item simulates. For example – the player must say fingers or more specifically dead man's fingers when they stick their hand into the lil' smokie sausage box. Have plenty of baby wipes available for the players to clean their hands.

**Props needed:** containers for the food (empty cereal boxes, etc.) Random food items, baby wipes.

**Examples of random food items are below:**

| | | | |
|---|---|---|---|
| Soft Flour Tortilla Strips (Add A Few Drops Of Oil) – **Witch's Skin** | Dried Corn Kernels– **Dead Man's Teeth** | Little Smokie Sausages – **Dead Man's Fingers** | Pretzel Sticks - **Petrified Rat Tails** |
| Cooked Spaghetti Noodles (add a few drops of oil) - **worms or zombie veins** | Peeled, Hard-Boiled Eggs – **Baby Hearts** | Fake Spider Webbing – **Spider Webs** | Cornflake Cereal – **Scabs** |
| Broken Sunflower Seeds or Almond Slices – **Witch's Fingernails** | Tongue-Shaped Cured Ham – **Dead Man's Tongue** | Cooked Large Egg Noodles– **Tape Worms** | Cornhusk Silk – **Dead Man's Hair** |
| Steel Wool Pad (tease off pieces of it)– **Witch's Hair** | Cooked Rice (add a few drops of oil) – **maggots** | Candy Corn - **Vampire Fangs** | Peeled Grapes – **Zombie Eyeballs** |

**Playing time:** ~ 10-15 minutes.

## The Pandora Box Challenge

**Objective**: to choose the good box - not one of the bad ones.

**Rules:** set up five Styrofoam boxes (i.e. coolers) and label each of them as Pandora's Box, cutting a hole just large enough to get a hand through. Decorate them in any way you choose, but make them all the same so the players can't tell the difference between them. Do not allow them to see inside the hole. Make a shield in front so the players can't view the hole until after they have selected their box. In one Styrofoam box, you'll put something 'good.' In the other four boxes, you'll put undesirable things. Have hand wipes ready.

**Examples of things to put in the boxes:**

| GOOD THINGS | BAD THINGS |
|---|---|
| Satin fabric | Fake blood and cooked spaghetti noodles |
| Feathers | Ice / ice cold water |
| Candy | Durian fruit (it smells awful, so it would be hilarious. However, it could make your party area stink) |
| Faux fur | Earthworms (can pick these up at a bait store) |

# Dr. Bonnie

These are only suggestions – think up anything you wish that is desirable/undesirable. However, just have safety in mind. Also, if you have anything that stains or is hard to get off the hand, have a way for your players to clean their hand and not stain the room or their costume! Also, dirt from the Earthworms can harbor germs.

Each player, one at a time, will come up to the boxes and select which box they will put their hand in the bottom of for one minute. They have to put their hand in the bottom of the box. After each player takes the challenge, have someone hold a curtain in front for you to mix up the boxes and repeat the challenge.

**Props needed:** five Styrofoam boxes with lids (coolers), items to put inside the boxes, decorations for the outside of the boxes.

**Playing time:** one minute per player that accepts the challenge plus time for them to choose a box (~ 15 minutes).

### Witch's Wart Mayhem

**Objective:** to get your wart closest to the real witch's wart!

**Rules:** print off a picture of a witch's face (at least an 8" by 10" picture). Give each player a pea sized portion of Play-doh (green preferred). Put the blindfold on the player, spin them around a few times and then gently direct them towards the witch's face. With one hand, they put the wart on her face. They cannot feel around the paper and when the Play-doh hits the paper (or wall), that is where it must stay! Closest to the bulls-eye wins.

**Props needed:** a printed witch face, blindfold, green Play-doh and possibly a ruler if it is close to determine the winner.

**Playing time:** ~ 20 minutes.

## GAMES FOR THE DURATION OF THE PARTY

### Stick and Win

**Objective**: to have the least amount of stickers stuck on you at the end of the party.

**Rules:** hand each player a sheet of stickers (~ 8-20 stickers). Once the party commences, the players sneak stickers onto the other players. Make sure not to use stickers that will leave a residue on clothing!

At the end of the party, call time and count the number of stickers on each player. The one with the least amount of stickers is the winner! As an alternative to gameplay, assign a set of specific

127

(hopefully Halloween themed) stickers to each player. The player with the most stickers that are on the other players when the host calls time, wins.

**Props needed:** a set of Halloween stickers for each player.
**Playing time:** ~ game duration.

### Follow the Ice King/Queen

**Objective**: not to be the last one to freeze or you do five push-ups.
**Rules:** designate one player as the Ice King or Ice Queen. During the game, this player – at any time – can freeze (stop moving). When players notice this player is frozen, they are to follow suit and freeze. The last one to notice that is standing in a room of frozen people – has to do five push-ups (or another fun penalty as you wish). If it is a tie – they both do the penalty. No arguments! Whoever suffered the penalty is the new Ice King/ Queen and play continues until you wish to stop.
**Props needed:** people who can pay attention.
**Playing time:** ~ until you get tired of playing.

### How Many Candy Corns are in the Jar?

**Objective**: to guess how many candy corns are in a jar.
**Rules:** in a clean jar, put a designated amount of candy corns. Seal the jar with the lid and decorate the lid in a festive Halloween style and tie ribbons around the lid for a fun effect. As your players arrive at the party, have each player write on a ballot their best guess of how many candy corns are in the jar. At the end of the night, reveal the number of (pre-counted) candy corns in the jar. Present an award/prize (e.g. the jar of candy) to the winner!
**Props needed:** a clear jar with a decorated lid; candy corns; a ballot for each player with a pen.
**Playing time:** ~ game duration.

### The Ultimate Bag of Destiny

**Objective**: not to be the one who has to pull a dare slip from the bag of destiny.
**Rules:** before the party, assemble a bag of dares. The dares can be anything and will vary according to your group – this game can be played with kids to adult – make adjustments accordingly.
**Some examples of dares are:**

| |
|---|
| Eat a teaspoon of mayonnaise |
| Go outside and run in circles for one minute while shouting: this is Halloween |

# Dr. Bonnie

| |
|---|
| Name all of Snow White's dwarves. If you miss one, you have to write the name(s) you forgot on your forehead – use nontoxic marker to do this |
| Make a post on social media that says 'I am a real witch/warlock. Just thought you should know that' |
| Allow the group to film you singing your favorite song while doing a headstand (put your feet against a wall for support if needed) |
| Do a solo dance to 1 minute of the song 'Monster Mash' |
| Wrap the top of your head with toilet paper as a mummy and wear it for 10 minutes |
| Draw a mustache on your face worthy of a snooty Frenchman. If you have a mustache, draw in 'angry eyebrows' – use nontoxic marker to do this |

To start the game, secretly hand a player the chip clip (or clothespin). This challenge is a background game in your party – no rush. Whenever they feel like they will not be caught, the player holding the clip/pin may slip it on to another player's backside on their costume/clothing. After they've secured the clip onto someone, the player shouts *'destiny's coming,'* and everybody in the group counts down aloud from four. If the clipped player doesn't find the clip by the time the group gets to zero, they must draw a slip from the bag of destiny and complete the dare. If the player discovers the clip in time, nothing happens, and the game resumes with this new player having a chance at slipping the clip onto another player.

If a player is caught while trying to attach the clip to another player, the clip is confiscated by the intended victim and play resumes.

Never 'force' anybody to perform a dare, as that is not only psychologically harmful to a person to be peer pressured into doing something they do not want to do, but also it leads to bad feelings about you and your party. Let them off the hook if they are apprehensive!

**Props needed:** a small chip clip or clothespin. It would be nice to decorate the clip in a Halloween theme. Slips of dares put into any drawstring bag (Halloween-themed bag is preferred).

**Playing time:** ~ game duration or when the dare slips are used up.

## Shhh, Don't say that!

**Objective**: to have the most candy at the end of the party.

**Rules:** the players are handed a bag full of candy at the start of the party, and they are instructed not to eat it during the game. Write the players' names on their bags so they don't get them mixed up. Choose at least three buzz words that the players are not allowed to say during the party. If a player catches another player saying one of the buzz words, they get a piece of candy from the violator's bag. This continues the rest of the party and the player with the most candy wins – and gets to keep it!

**Props needed:** a bag full of candy for each player (five to ten pieces of wrapped candy is a good amount.

**Playing time:** ~ game duration.

### Hat's Off to You

**Objective**: not to be the last one to take your hat off.

**Rules:** if your players have elaborate costumes with headpieces, this game may be challenging. Nevertheless, make paper hats, crowns, etc. – whatever can be worn on the head is fine. Designate a player to be the leader. Whenever the leader feels like it, they can remove their hat. Once they remove their hat, the other players (who are paying attention to them) are to remove their hat until the final person realizes they are the last one with their hat on. The loser then has to perform a 20-second interpretive dance performance to any song the leader chooses.

Please note: a player may not remove their hat for any reason unless the leader has removed their hat. If a player removes their hat while the leader has their hat on – they suffer the same penalty as the loser. The loser becomes the new leader, and everybody puts their hats back on.

**Props needed:** a paper hat for each player.

**Playing time:** ~ game duration.

### Predictable Friends Bingo

**Objective**: to make predictions about what people will do and be the first to 'bingo' at the party. (This game can only be played with guests who are familiar with each other.)

**Rules:** this is an individual challenge that will continue throughout the night. Hand each player an empty bingo card (three across, three down is fine) and a pen (not pencil). The players write in 9 things (within the bingo spaces) that are predicted actions that other people at the party will do during the party. For example, they can put things like Scot will trip and fall, Billy will have two pieces of cake, Vera will cackle like a witch, etc. When a player has filled in their bingo card, the player has it checked and approved by the host. Give them a sheet of star stickers. During the party, as they see one of their predictions come true, they can place a sticker on the prediction. Tell them not to cover it completely, so they can remember which one it was. It is good to use stickers that can be removed without taking the paper up with them in case you need to verify the bingo item was done correctly.

# Dr. Bonnie

The first person to get three across –horizontal, vertical or diagonal – is to call bingo and they are declared the winner.

**Props needed:** an empty 3" by 3" box bingo card for each player. A sheet of star stickers (or other themed stickers that can be removed from paper without damaging the paper). As an alternative, give them a highlighter to use and the players can highlight each bingo square as the game progresses.

**Playing time:** ~ game duration.

## MENTAL STRATEGY GAMES

### Eyewitness Testimony

**Objective**: to remember the most details about what you just witnessed.

**Rules:** divide your group into pairs. The host explains there has been a burglary (or other crime that you choose) reported in this area and for everybody to remain seated, stay calm and vigilant. They should keep their eyes and ears open and look for a suspicious person.

The host is to be the 'burglar' and after giving the scenario above, they excuse themselves into an adjacent room – warning everybody to remain seated. The host will dress up in an assortment of clothes – the sillier, the better. Use many different accessories (e.g. sunglasses, hat, fake beard, rolled-up newspaper, purse).

Then, from the doorway (without them seeing you) announce to the players of the game that the suspect was last seen running away from the scene. Then, run into/around the room and back out to the adjacent room to remove the silly items you put on.

Return to the room with the other players and explain they are all eyewitnesses, and they will need to leave an accurate account of what they saw as far as the suspect's description is concerned. The players then write down anything that they can remember about the suspect's appearance. The team with the most accurate list wins.

**Props needed:** an assortment of clothes and props for the burglar placed in an adjacent room. Pens and paper for the eyewitnesses. Slip of paper for each player.

**Playing time:** ~20 minutes.

### Pumpkin Patch Pandemonium

**Objective**: to avoid making a mistake or you do five push-ups.

**Rules:** have the players sit in a circle. Starting with the person who has a birthday closest to Halloween, the player says the word *pumpkin.* The next person to their right will say the number one. The next person will say *patch.* The next person will say two. The next person will start over with *pumpkin.* The next person will say three (and continue in order, alternating the words *pumpkin* and *patch*) and so on until someone messes up. When someone messes up &/or pauses too long to think about it - they must do the push-up penalty (or other penalty you choose).

**Props needed:** none needed.

**Playing time:** ~ until you get tired of playing.

## Bumbling Numbers

**Objective**: not to mess up when you reach a 'binkie boo,' or you have to do the penalty.

**Rules:** put your players in a specific order for this game. The first player starts with saying one, the next player continues with two, the next person says 'binkie boo' since it is a number divisible by three. Then next player says four, and so on. Each time a person gets to a number divisible by three, they have to say 'binkie boo' and if they fail to do so – they suffer the penalty (e.g. do five push-ups).

**Props needed:** people who can pay attention and divide by three.

**Playing time:** ~ until you get tired of playing.

## Let's Make A Halloween Deal:

**Objective**: to be the member of the audience who makes out with the big prize!

**Rules:** you've probably seen the show 'Let's Make a Deal.' Let's put a Halloween spin on it for your players. Assemble them in an audience and you are the game show host. Before the party, prepare some fun boxes with assorted 'booby prizes' such as cooked spaghetti (call it zombie brains) and then others with 'great prizes such as a gift certificate to a store or maybe just an upgraded piece of Halloween candy. Randomly select players from the audience and offer them a prize of a candy bar (or other small Halloween token prize that's good enough to want). Then, offer them to trade with what is inside of a random mystery box, and so on, until you've given away all of the prizes. The players will enjoy watching the stress of it all!

**Props needed:** gag prizes, good prizes, Halloween candy for the starter prizes and random containers/boxes to hide the gag and good prizes inside of.

**Playing time:** ~20 minutes.

# Dr. Bonnie

## Let's Describe Halloween

**Objective**: to be the last one to remember the Halloween words in the correct order.

**Rules:** it is best for your group to sit in a circle for this challenge. With the youngest player going first, s/he says *I think that_____describes Halloween best.* This player fills in the blank with any word they believe describes the spirit of Halloween. Play continues with the player on their right who will add to the growing chain of words by saying *I think that_____, and_____describe Halloween best.* A player should be designated as the judge, and they will write down the growing chain on a piece of paper. They will check everybody's answer as the game progresses and call a person out of the game when they are wrong. A player is out when they either forget what word was next or get one wrong in the chain. The last player to recite the long list of Halloween words wins.

**Props needed:** a sheet of paper and pen for the judge.

**Playing time:** ~20 minutes.

## Direct the Sketch Artist

**Objective**: to be the pair who gets the most points by guessing what you are drawing.

**Rules:** divide your group into pairs and have the players sit in a line, back-to-back with their partners. The first directors will be on the right and sketch artists on the left.

Directors will pull a slip from the container, and it will contain a Halloween-themed word. When the host says go, they will direct their partner how to draw this item, and they will draw it on their pad in front of them. The first person to guess the item they are drawing gets a point. This continues until the directors have directed five drawings, then the roles reverse – the directors become the sketch artists and vice versa. Continue five more times and the team with the most points is declared the winner. In the event of a tie, the tied teams will elect a rep to participate in Mouse-Cat-Witch tiebreaker (see directions under the tiebreaker section).

Examples of Halloween words are pumpkin, moon, star, mouse, cat, rat, witch, skeleton, etc. Realize that some words will be easier to draw than others, so picking the right slip is the luck portion of the game.

**Props needed:** a pad of paper for half the # of players and Halloween words on slips of paper – you'll need five per player/10 per team.

**Playing time:** ~20 minutes.

## Picture the Pieces

**Objective**: to be the first team to guess the Halloween legend in the puzzle.

**Rules:** each team is handed a 'puzzle' of a Halloween legend (e.g. Count Dracula, Frankenstein).

With this game, it will not make a difference if the teams are equal or not. An extra brain on a team could be a good thing or a really bad thing and cause more chaos and arguments, so it's luck of the draw - fair enough. Cut the pictures you print into equal puzzle pieces (put them on top of each other while you cut so they are equal) and place these puzzle pieces into an envelope for each team. When the host says go, each team is to put the puzzle pieces together as fast as they can to guess the legend in the puzzle. The first team to guess the puzzle correctly wins.

**Props needed:** two copies of printed pictures of any Halloween legend (e.g. Swamp Thing, Bride of Frankenstein) cut into puzzle pieces and placed inside of an envelope for each team.

**Playing time:** ~20 minutes.

# GAMES TO PLAY IN A CIRCLE

## The Perfect Dance

**Objective**: is to perform the perfect dance.

**Rules:** have your players sit in a circle. One at a time, each player will stand up and make up a four-count dance move of their choice. The next player in the circle will stand up and perform the previous player's dance move and then add a four-count dance move of their choice. This will continue until everyone has had a chance to add a four-count dance move around the circle. Then, go around the circle once more so each player can practice the 'perfect dance.' It is all right at this time for the players to make mistakes and be corrected from the group. Then, when everyone is ready, have the players sit as an audience, play a great Halloween song and allow each player to perform the 'perfect dance' to music in front of the group.

An alternative way to play is to allow the players to perform in groups of two or three. Some may not want to perform at all, and this is fine - don't try to force it as some people are just shy. The host is the judge, or the players can vote via a secret ballot for the winner - the winner is the one who performed the 'perfect dance' the very best!

For lasting memories, have the group perform the dance together and get it on video!

# Dr. Bonnie

**Props needed:** any Halloween dance song.
**Playing time:** ~ 30 minutes.

## Rhythm Busters

**Objective**: to be the most rhythmic person in the room.
**Rules:** your players are to be seated in a circle. Designate each player as a Halloween character and give them a gesture as a symbol of their character. For example, if they are Count Dracula, they can say mwah *ha ha* and make a gesture as if they are pulling their cape in front of their face. It must be something done verbally and with the hands/face as a combo. Another example is black cat – the player will hiss and show their claws with one hand.

Once you have everybody in the circle set with a character and a corresponding gesture, play will begin with the person whose birthday is closest to Halloween. The player claps their hands, pats their knee, does their gesture and then does someone else's gesture in the circle of their choice in a rhythmic pattern like in music one, two, three, four.

Play continues until someone messes up the rhythm by stalling, stumbling or simply going blank. They are asked to leave the circle and play continues until one player is left and is declared the winner.
**Props needed:** rhythmic talent, decent memory, and a quick mind.
**Playing time:** ~10 minutes.

## Matchmakers

**Objective**: to make a match with the challenge number or you get a point. The player with the lowest point total is the winner.
**Rules:** seat your players in a circle. The game begins with a roll of a die – this is the challenge number. The player to the right rolls two dice and must match the challenge number with at least one of the dice. If they have a match, the challenge passes to the player on their right and they roll to match the challenge number, and so forth until someone is unable to match the number. This person gets a point (points are bad in this game). The player with the lowest point total when you finish playing is the winner. You can say (before the game) the first player to reach 5 points ends the game.

**Example**: Player A rolls a single die and rolls a four, making four the challenge number. Player B (on his right) will roll two dice. If Player B rolls a four on one die *or* the two dice add up to four, play passes to the right and Player C (D, E, F, etc.) will roll the dice until someone fails to match the number.

If any player rolls double fours – he can select another player to earn the point, and the round resets with a new challenge number. The player to his right rolls for the new challenge number.
**Props needed:** two dice.
**Playing time:** ~ until you get tired of playing or until you reach your set point total (i.e. 5, 10 points).

## Pumpkin Pass Panic

**Objective**: to be the last one in the circle – not holding the pumpkin when the music goes off.
**Rules:** have the players sit in a circle and hand the player with an October birthday (closest to Halloween) the mini pumpkin. Start the music and the players are to spend as much time as they wish passing the pumpkin to the player to their right. At any time, a player can shout 'Zombie' and switch the direction of the pass to the player on their left and then the passing continues in that direction until another player shouts the word Zombie – and so forth.

When the host turns the music off randomly, whoever is holding the pumpkin is out, leaves the circle, and must pass it to the player on their right (no matter what direction it was going when the music turned off), as the game resets and play continues to the right. The players scoot in and tighten the circle each time a player is out. The last player in the circle who isn't holding the pumpkin when the music goes off wins.
**Props needed:** mini pumpkin.
**Playing time:** ~ 10 minutes.

## Let Me Take a Selfie

**Objective**: not to be the one in the selfie when the camera's timer goes off and takes the pic.
**Rules:** your players are to sit in a circle. Using a smartphone or other camera that an auto timer can be set, set the timer for 10 seconds and each player must (carefully) pass the phone while pointing it directly at their face, holding it with two hands. Eventually, the timer will go off and whoever the camera is pointing to takes the selfie and gets a point. The person with the least selfies and least points is declared the winner!
**Props needed:** a camera with an auto-timer (smartphone is great).
**Playing time:** ~10 minutes.

# Dr. Bonnie

## Pumpkin Panic

**Objective**: not be the first team that gets four of one type of card.

**Rules:** this game is best played with six to eight players. If you have more players at your party, create multiple circles and play the game simultaneously. Then, further divide players into pairs and sit them on opposing sides of their circle. Hand each circle a deck of cards. Deal 6 cards in the center of the circle and then, each player is dealt four cards. The teams decide upon a secret signal that will be used to signal their partner to end the game in the event they draw four of a kind. Starting with the player whose birthday is closest to Halloween, they are allowed to choose one of the cards from the middle or draw one from the pile that is face-down next to the face-up discard pile. They must place a card into the discard pile each turn – a player may not keep more than four cards in their hand at any time. Play continues around the circle with players drawing and discarding one card. If a card is taken from the center, the next player is to draw one from the face-down pile and place it face-up in the missing card's spot. This player may choose the new face-up card or draw a new one. When the face-down pile is exhausted, the discard pile can be reshuffled – along with the face-up cards in the middle. The six cards in the center are re-dealt, and the draw pile is placed back into position. The players may not draw a card from the discard pile at any time.

When a player draws a four of a kind, the player secretly signals their partner with their secret symbol. When their partner sees the signal, they shout the phrase *Pumpkin Panic* and their teammate reveals their hand of four of a kind, ending the round. However, if a player from an opposing team sees this signal before their partner seeing it, they can shout *Halloween Havoc* and force the player that has the four of a kind to lose two of their cards to the discard pile, and they must draw the next two cards from the draw pile. If any player shouts *Halloween Havoc* when a player hasn't truly given the secret signal &/or doesn't have a four of a kind, they are no longer eligible to shout *Halloween Havoc* and call out a player for using a signal for the remainder of the round. If a player mistakenly believes their partner has signaled them and shouts *Pumpkin Panic* and their partner does not have a four of a kind, their partner must re-draw all four cards by placing their entire hand in the discard pile and re-drawing four cards from the draw pile.

**Props needed:** a deck of cards for every six to eight players.

**Playing time:** ~10 minutes or as long as you wish to play.

## Yeah, Baby, You're So Beautiful

**Objective**: not to smile when the photographer in the middle asks you to smile for them.

**Rules:** your players are to sit in a circle. One player is designated as the photographer and is to stand in the middle of the circle. They choose any player they wish and pretend to be a photographer by pretending to snap photos, etc. The photographer is to say the following words: *Yeah, baby, you're so beautiful, but I need a smile.* If the player smiles, they are the new photographer. If they keep a straight face, the photographer must move on to their next model. After the photographer has tried to make five models smile unsuccessfully, he or she can pick a new photographer. Gameplay continues until you're tired of it.

**Props needed:** people who are ready to laugh...or able to hold it in, actually.

**Playing time:** ~10 minutes.

## Monster in the Middle

**Objective**: not to be the monster in the middle!

**Rules:** the monster in the middle shouts: twin switch for everybody who is:_____. The blank can be absolutely anything – wearing green, has a cat, has a sister, drives a white car, etc. Those matching the description are to stand up immediately and switch with another player who also fits the description. The person in the middle must fight for one of the open seats and the last person standing without a seat is the monster in the middle. It's similar to musical chairs but without the music. The person who had to be the monster in the middle the least after the end of gameplay is the winner! During a twin switch, a person cannot re-sit in a chair.

**Props needed:** chairs for each player besides the monster in the middle.

**Playing time:** ~15 minutes.

## Have a Seat in Dracula's Throne

**Objective**: to sit in each other's lap while connected in a circle.

**Rules:** this is a group challenge. The players are to stand in a circle with their shoulders touching. Then, tell them to turn to their right, facing the back of the player to their right. Then, the player places their right hand on the player in front's right shoulder. The objective is to each sit in the lap of the player behind them without falling and making

# Dr. Bonnie

chaos happen in the circle. The players win as a group if they all can sit down in each other's lap without falling. If you have enough players, make two circles and let them compete!

**Props needed:** none needed.
**Playing time:** ~15 minutes.

## Ha Ha Ha Ha Ha!

**Objective**: not to be the comic in the middle.
**Rules:** the players are to sit in a circle with one player designated as the comic in the middle. Set as many Halloween related props as you wish in the center of the circle for the comic to use. Set the timer for one minute (two if you wish) and the comic's goal is to make at least one person laugh by doing anything s/he desires – s/he can tell jokes, use props, etc., but the comic may not touch any of the players in the circle.

Whoever laughs has to be the next comic. If nobody laughs, the comic gets to choose the next comic from the players in the circle. Laughing is anything audible – if you can hear so much as a loud breath – it's a laugh.

**Props needed:** Halloween props of any kind such as a rubber bat, plastic snake, mini pumpkin, etc.
**Playing time:** as long as they want to play.

## Black Cat & Her Kittens

**Objective**: not to get caught being a kitten.
**Rules:** on slips of paper, write the word 'kitten' on half the slips and the other half, write 'human.' Fold the papers and slip into any container. Designate the youngest player as the mother cat and instruct them to go into the center of the circle. The players are to draw a slip of paper and without telling anybody what they drew, get into random positions within the circle surrounding the mother cat. Therefore, the humans and kittens will make a circle, and the mother cat will get in the center of the circle. When the host says go, the kittens will meow without being caught by the mother cat. Each kitten must meow twice per minute – you cannot remain silent if you are a kitten. The mother cat will identify her kittens one by one. If s/he is incorrect, she loses a point immediately, the round is over, and the players draw cards again. The mother cat gets a point for each kitten s/he correctly identifies. Any kitten that is not discovered by the mother cat gets a point. The mother cat will alternate until

everybody has had a turn being the mother cat. The game is over once everybody has had a turn, and points are totaled.

**Props needed:** a writing instrument and slips of paper equal to the number of players (minus one for the mother cat) with either kitten or human written on them in equal proportions.

**Playing time:** ~ 15 minutes.

## Scream King/Queen Contest

**Objective:** to have the best B-movie scream.

**Rules:** this is an individual challenge. Sit your players in a circle and hope the neighbors understand. One at a time, the players are to perform their best B-movie slasher film scream. After everybody in the group has had a turn, allow the players to vote via secret ballot and instruct them not to vote for themselves. Whoever gets the most votes is the Scream Queen/King.

**Props needed:** a pen and paper for each player to vote for the best screamer.

**Playing time:** ~8 minutes.

## Poetic Justice:

**Objective:** to be the best poet at the party!

**Rules:** this is an individual challenge. Whatever your party theme is, you are to instruct your players to create the best poem about the theme of the party. Give your players a set time limit to write their poems and a pen/paper. When the time is up, each player will recite his or her poem in front of the group. Play a low jazz beat in the background for ambiance. The host will judge the winner, or the players can vote via secret ballot. Get your video camera ready, as this will be awesome to watch later!

**Props needed:** a pen and paper for each player, optional low jazz style beat as ambiance.

**Playing time:** ~ 30 minutes.

## Scary Story Tellers

**Objective**: to come up with the scariest story to scare your friends!

**Rules:** each person in the group is to get into a circle in a darkened room or at night during a camping trip by the campfire. One by one, each person is to take the flashlight and put it underneath their chin for a scary effect. They draw a story starter and have two minutes to tell the scariest story s/he can create without preparation. Continue until everybody gets a turn!

**Props needed:** the story starters, a dark area, and a flashlight!

# Dr. Bonnie

**Playing time:** ~20 minutes.

**Examples of story starters are:**

| | | | | |
|---|---|---|---|---|
| It was twilight and the vampire awoke in his coffin... | The werewolf howled at the moon as the young boy hid behind a tree... | The door slowly creaked open... | The lightning bolt struck the roof of the old farmhouse.... | The witches cackled as they stirred the brew in the cauldron... |
| The four boys were lost deep in the forest. They heard a low growl... | The guard left the security shack to find the source of groaning in the graveyard... | In a crowded movie theater, a skeleton appeared... | A bold knock at the door echoed throughout the house. It was 3 AM... | She walked into the hallway and swore she saw a ghostly apparition... |

## The Spooky Tale

**Objective**: to come up with an awesome ghost story with your friends.

**Rules:** have your players sit in a circle and turn off the lights. Hand the starting player (the oldest one in the group) a flashlight to start the game. The player says two sentences of the story and passes the flashlight to the player on their right. The next player adds two sentences and so forth until each player has contributed three times. Make sure the last person (the one on the left of the starter) knows to give the story a great ending!

**Props needed:** a dark area and a flashlight.

**Playing time:** ~20 minutes.

## Catch Me If You Can!

**Objective**: a group game where the detective attempts to guess who the murderer is before everyone in the group is murdered.

**Rules:** you will need to create slips for each player in your game. There must be one *detective* and *murderer* strip, and the rest are *citizen* strips. Create your strips, fold, and put into a hat (or any container) and each player draws one strip and secretly reads their role in the game. Have the exact number of strips as players. A signal is chosen by the group (e.g. pointing a finger, a wink, sticking out the tongue) before the game commences. The detective goes to the middle of the circle where s/he must guess the identity of the murderer before the murderer kills everyone. The murderer kills victims by secretly using the signal. If any player detects the signal coming from the murderer, s/he must 'die' in an overly dramatic manner and cannot disclose who the murderer is. The detective only has three guesses to guess the murderer (more or less guesses can be done if the group agrees before the game commences). If the detective fails to guess in three guesses, the murderer wins the game. If a five-minute timer runs out and the murderer isn't caught, the murderer wins. If all the players die besides the detective, the murderer wins. The game starts over by players drawing new roles out of the hat. This is repeated until nobody is willing to continue ☺.

**Props needed:** the same amount as there are players in the game of the draw slips. A hat or container to draw the slips from.

## Moving Down the Line

**Objective**: to avoid pulling an ace from the line of cards – or you have to suffer the penalty.

**Rules:** deal ten cards face down in a line in the center of the circle. Starting with the first player, they flip over the first card in line. If it is an ace – they have to suffer the penalty (e.g. eating a gross bite of food, doing push-ups). If it is a queen, they can choose another player to suffer the penalty. If it is a king, everybody in the game has to suffer the penalty besides the player that pulled the king. If it is a number two to ten, nothing happens, and the next player gets to pull the next card in line. Play continues around the circle until all ten cards have been revealed. If you're having fun, deal again!

**Props needed:** a deck of cards.

**Playing time:** ~ until you get tired of playing.

## Roll 'Em Low

**Objective**: not to have the highest score via dice rolls.

**Rules:** pick a starting player who will roll four dice. They keep the lowest number and slide it in front of them (or to the side, so they don't change it). They roll the remaining three dice and keep the lowest numbered one. They do this again for the next two rolls (obviously, the last one will stick). The score keeper will add up their score and write it down. The play passes to the next player in the circle and so forth until everybody has had a turn. The player with the lowest total is the winner. In the event of a tie – they must do a Mouse-Cat-Witch tiebreaker (see tiebreaker rules for details).

**Props needed:** four dice.

**Playing time:** ~ as long as you want.

## BALLOON GAMES

### Balloon Belly Relay

**Objective**: to be the first team to get your balloon across the finish line after all of your team has crossed it carrying a balloon as their belly.

**Rules:** divide the group into two teams. Give each team a balloon and start the game. Within each team, the members take turns either taping a balloon to their belly with scotch tape or they can slip it underneath their shirt/costume – either way as long as it doesn't fall off during the race. Have judges available for this game!

Create a start line and a finish line about ten feet away. This is relay style, and each team should line up in a single-file line behind the start line. When you blow the whistle, the first team members grab a balloon and create their balloon belly by slipping it securely under their shirt or taping it to their belly (no help is allowed from their team members unless you decide to allow them to get help before you start) and then, they 'crab walk' across the racing path with their bellies intact. If a player's belly falls off at any time – the player starts over at the start line (with a new balloon if it pops). Once they cross the finish line, they can remove their balloon belly and race back to the start line, handing it off to their teammate who is next in line. This continues until the last team member crosses the finish line.

**Props needed:** two balloons for each team but have extra balloons on hand in case one more pops during the challenge (this is likely to happen).

**Playing time:** ~20 minutes.

### Balloon Truth or Dare:

**Objective**: to pick the easiest dare balloon and accomplish the task without blinking an eye!

**Rules:** write funny dares on small, folded slips of paper and slip into balloons before filling with helium. Use black and orange balloons for Halloween. Tie a long ribbon (lime green, purple, orange, &/or black) onto each balloon and allow the balloon to float to the ceiling. Make the ribbon long enough for your players to reach. One by one, as they pick a balloon, the player sits on it until it pops, gets the dare slip, and fulfills the dare. If they refuse to do the dare, they have to tell a 'truth' that nobody knows about them. (This is a great way for a group to get to know one another!)

**Props needed:** balloons, ribbons, dare cards and the corresponding items to go along with the dares (e.g. if the dare says to eat a jalapeno covered in whipped cream – have those items available).

**Playing time:** ~20 minutes.

## First to Create a Jack O'Lantern, Wins

**Objective**: to make your Jack O'Lantern first.

**Rules:** this is an individual challenge. Hand each player an orange balloon and a black permanent marker. When the host says go, the first one to blow up the balloon and draw a Jack O'Lantern face including two eyes and a mouth (which must be filled in completely), wins. Have a balloon available on display to show the approximate size requirement, and instruct the players they must at least get their Jack O'Lantern to that size. The first one to create their balloon Jack O'Lantern is the winner.

**Props needed:** orange balloon for each player and a permanent marker.

**Playing time:** ~10 minutes.

## Balloon Bedlam

**Objective**: to keep the most balloons off the ground at one time.

**Rules:** clear out a large space in the room or outside. Blow up at least 15 balloons (just to be sure you have enough in case they pop, etc.) This is an individual challenge, and each player will go separately.

Line up the balloons to your right (or left if you are left-handed). When you are ready, hit one balloon into the air in the middle of the space. After successfully keeping it in the air by hitting it above the head two times, add another balloon for the player to keep in the air. Continue to add balloons in this manner until a balloon hits the ground. There must be two hits above their head on each balloon before you add another one to the challenge.

For example, the player starts with an orange balloon. They hit it twice in the air before adding the black balloon. When they add the black balloon, they'll hit the orange, black, orange, and then black before adding the purple balloon and so forth. If, at any time, one of the balloons hits the ground, the player is out, and the score (# of balloons) is tallied. The balloon that failed the challenge is not counted toward the total. Take the top four players who could keep the most balloons in the air for two rounds of hits to go to the next round. If there is a tie, allow the players in a tie to go a second time. If there is still a tie after the tied players have attempted the challenge twice, decide it with Mouse-Cat-Witch tie-breaker (see the tie-breaking section for details).

You may not grab the balloons with your armpits, hands or rest on your palm to keep them in the air. However, if you want to attempt to rest any of them on your head, shoulders, etc. – you may do so but remember, you may not add a balloon to your collection until you've hit each balloon above your head two times (meaning, two rounds). It's not the time you keep them in the air, but the total amount you can keep off the ground for two rounds.

**Props needed:** balloons (at least 15).

**Playing time:** ~20 minutes depending on the number of players in your group.

## The Great Jack O'Lantern Round Up

**Objective**: to gather the most Jack O'Lanterns and put them in your bag/box within the time.

**Rules:** blow up a good number of orange balloons and draw Jack O'Lantern faces on them with black marker. Scatter them in your yard and give each team a container to put their collected balloons into (large box, plastic bag(s), etc.). Divide your group into two teams and when you say go and set the timer for two minutes, the players collect balloons and bring them back to their container before the timer goes out. The players keep their hands behind their back, however, as they collect their balloons. They must strategize to determine the best method to bring them back to their home base container. The team who collects the most balloon Jack O'Lanterns inside of their container is the winning team.

**Props needed:** at least 30 balloons and a container for each team. It's preferred if you use orange balloons and draw Jack O'Lantern faces on them for a fun Halloween theme – or you can use a simple orange and black theme.

**Playing time:** ~10 minutes.

## Boisterous Balloon Pop

**Objective**: to pop your three balloons the fastest.

**Rules:** give each player three balloons. When you say go, the first two people to pop all three of their balloons will move on to the final round. They can only use their body to pop the balloon. They are not allowed to use any external object – even if it is clothing (i.e. a high heel on a shoe). They can use their hands, sit on it, and use any part of their body to pop it.

**Props needed:** balloons – three for each player (and have a few extra in case of a pop before the start).

**Playing time:** ~10 minutes.

## Killer Bees Knees

**Objective**: to transfer your team's balloon to the final person in the line using only knees.

**Rules:** divide your group into two teams of bees and have them stand in a line. Hand the first player a balloon (e.g. pollen) and ask them to place it between their knees. When you say go, the player transfers the balloon to the next player using only their knees – with the player accepting the balloon only using their knees. Play continues until the final player grabs it with their knees and races to an object that you decide is the hive (that is equal distance from both ends of the line) – such as a chair, etc. If the balloon drops to the ground, the team must start over at the starting player. If the balloon pops, they get a new balloon and start over with the starting player.

**Props needed:** balloons – one for each team and a designated hive to finish the race (and have a few extra in case of a pop before the start).

**Playing time:** ~10 minutes.

## Boisterous Balloon Pop Relay

**Objective**: to pop your team's balloons the fastest by racing down the relay lanes.

**Rules:** set up two relay lanes with start/finish lines. At the finish line side, have a balloon for each player on the team (put them in a trash bag to keep them together). Line up the players at the start line and when you say go, the first player will race to the end of the lane, grab a balloon, pop it in any way possible (but without weapons). Once it is popped, they can race back and tag the next player. The team who pops their final balloon first is the winning team. Note: each player who races down to the finish line may only pop one balloon.

**Props needed:** a balloon for each player and a container to put them in at the end of each relay lane.

**Playing time:** ~15 minutes.

# Dr. Bonnie

## Swattin' Fly Relay

**Objective**: to hit all of your flies (balloons) down the relay lane using a fly swatter.

**Rules:** set up two relay lanes with start/finish lines. At the start line, hand each player on the team a black balloon (a fly). Line up the players at the start line and when you say go, the first player will race to the end of the lane, swatting their fly with their flyswatter until they cross the finish line. If their balloon drops, they must pick it up and start over at the start line. Once their fly crosses the finish line, they race back and tag the next player by handing them the swatter. The team who gets all flies across the finish line first is the winning team. Note: each player who races down to the finish line may only swat one fly.

**Props needed:** a (black) balloon for each player and a fly swatter.

**Playing time:** ~15 minutes.

## Vivacious Balloon Volley

**Objective**: not to be the one who allows the balloon to touch the ground.

**Rules:** this is a challenge for two players. They stand on opposite sides of the room, and each player is given a different color balloon (or at least mark them). The host will give the boundary, and the players are not to go outside of the boundary &/or hit their balloons outside of the boundary. When you say go, the player hits their balloon into the air above their head. Each time the balloon is hit by a player, they are responsible for keeping the opposite balloon in the air.

For example, player A starts with a black balloon and player B has an orange balloon. The host says go and both hit their balloons into the air. Player A will lunge to keep the black balloon in the air and player B will assure the orange balloon doesn't hit the ground. Once either player has hit their balloon into the air above their head, they will switch again – and so on until the first balloon hits the ground. If either player hits the balloon onto a ledge of any kind that doesn't allow the balloon to come down – the opponent automatically wins the round. If either player either steps outside of the boundary or hits their balloon outside of the boundary, the opponent wins the round.

**Major rule →** the player must hit the balloon above their head for the hit to count or the opposing player wins the round.

If, for any reason, there is a tie, start the challenge over. If it keeps being a draw, which is very unlikely, call it at any time and make them do a Mouse-Cat-Witch tie-breaker (see the tie-breaking section).

# The Halloween Party Host Handbook

**Props needed:** at least 15 inflated balloons. Not helium-filled balloons, just use air. Depending on the number of people you have in your party, you might want to have more balloons on hand.
**Playing time:** ~20 minutes.

## Quick Thinker Balloon Challenge

**Objective**: to be the team to keep your balloon in the air the longest by saying words within a theme in alphabetical order.
**Rules:** divide the groups into two teams. Give each team a balloon and start the game. *as an alternative, time each team and allow them to go separately to avoid chaos.

Within each team, the members take turns hitting the balloon into the air – in a specified order - to avoid it touching the ground. The host is to pick a theme such as Halloween. The team members designate a specific order in which they will come up with words in alphabetical order of this theme. They have to stick with this order during the entire challenge (i.e. player 1, 2, 3, 4 – then, start over with player 1, 2…).

For example, if you choose animals as your theme, player one will shout armadillo and hit the balloon, player two will shout baboon and hit the balloon, player three will shout cat and hit the balloon.

When it is a team member's turn, they must say their word before hitting the balloon to keep it in the air. If at any time a team member goes out of order, fails to shout a word in the correct alphabetical order, or shouts a word out of the designated theme, the game is over for that team and the host records what letter they were on when they got out &/or how many times through the alphabet they went. If you have two teams going simultaneously, the other team automatically wins – even if they haven't gotten as far in the alphabet (as long as they started at the same time). You can do separate trials or play simultaneously. The team that makes it through the most letters of the alphabet without making a mistake wins!

If you are not doing simultaneous trials, have a separate theme for the second team – as they will have heard the answers from team one. In this case, make the themes equally difficult – farm animals and zoo animals would be nearly difficult yet similar themes. If you are sticking with Halloween – have one team do Halloween candy and the other Halloween costumes. Alternatively, have the second team waiting outside where they cannot hear the words being used by team one – this way, they can keep the same theme. If at any time a team's balloon hits a surface of any kind that is below the level of the team member, the team's trial is over. It is acceptable if the balloon hits a high part of a wall or ceiling but a table below the level of a player is not acceptable. Pay attention while judging this game!

**Props needed:** two differently colored balloons with a few balloon backups in case of an accidental popping.

**Playing time:** ~20 minutes.

## Balloon Blower Challenge!

**Objective**: to be the team that keeps your balloon in the air the longest by only your breath.

**Rules:** divide the groups into two teams. Give each team a balloon and start the game. Within each team, the members take turns blowing their balloon into the air to avoid it touching the ground. No hands can ever touch the balloon or the team is disqualified and the other team automatically wins! The team must alternate the 'blowers' and stay in the same order or they are disqualified. The first team that does not alternate the 'blowers', uses their hands, or allows their balloon to touch the ground is the losing team. Have judges available for this game!

For an additional challenge, require the team members to shout out a Halloween-related word in alphabetical order before blowing on the balloon to keep it in the air (i.e. off the ground). The alphabetical order will remain within teams and the blowers cannot receive help from team members in coming up with the Halloween-related term for their assigned letter of the alphabet. Any team going out of alphabetical order or not shouting a Halloween-themed term before blowing on the balloon is immediately disqualified and the other team wins the point. First team to five points - wins!

**Props needed:** two differently colored balloons (i.e. orange and black).

**Playing time:** ~ 10 minutes.

## The Boisterous Balloon Battle

**Objective**: to be the team with the last remaining balloon intact.

**Rules:** divide your group into two (or more) teams. Tie a specified color balloon to each player's ankle (i.e. orange for one team and black for another). When the host says go, each team is to pop the balloons of the opposing team. Once a team member's balloon has been popped, they are out of the game and must sit down and cheer their remaining team members on until the game is over. The winning team is the one who has the last balloon intact!

**Props needed:** color-coded balloons (i.e. orange and black) for each player.
**Playing time:** ~ 5-10 minutes.

## Alien Antennae Challenge
**Objective**: to be the first team who stuffs ten balloons in the pantyhose that one team member is wearing as a headpiece.
**Rules:** divide your group into two (or more) teams. Hand each team a pair of nude XL pantyhose and ten un-inflated balloons. When you say go, they must blow up the balloons and stuff them into the legs of the pantyhose that one team member is wearing around their head *Remove it each time you stuff a balloon inside, but it must be put back on their head each time. When they get five balloons stuffed into each leg of the pantyhose, they must scream 'extraterrestrial in the house' to end the game. Please, take pictures.
**Props needed:** ten balloons (i.e. orange and black) for each team and a pair of nude XL pantyhose.
**Playing time:** ~ 10 minutes.

## Hot Air - On the Mark
**Objective**: to hit the target with your wild 'n crazy released balloon.
**Rules:** this is an individual challenge. Give each player a balloon and ask them to blow it up as much as they wish, but do not tie it off and make a knot (they just hold the air inside). Make a fun target in advance of the party – it can be anything (e.g. witch face, pumpkin cut-out, Halloween-themed bull's-eye) and place on the wall/floor. You may do a test run and see where your balloon lands the most and place the target there. One at a time, the players are allowed to stand wherever they wish – as long as it is behind the throw line that you designate with floor-safe tape. (That way, they don't move up too close to the target). They are allowed to release their balloon and try to land on the target/hit the target. The player with the closest hit to the center of the target wins.
**Props needed:** balloon for each player and a target.
**Playing time:** ~ 5-10 minutes.

## Don't Let It Drop
**Objective**: to be the player with the last remaining balloon in the air.
**Rules:** this is an individual challenge. Give each player a balloon and allow them to mark their balloon before you start. When the host says go, the player keeps their balloon in the air. Players may be offensive

and try to hit other players' balloons to the ground &/or pop them, but they must keep their balloon in the air by tapping it, blowing on it, hitting it with their head or an object – any means necessary to keep it in the air by hitting it once with anything. The final player to have their balloon floating in the air is the winner. Get ready for chaos.

**Props needed:** balloons (orange) for each player and a black marker to label them – or simply hand each player a different color.

**Playing time:** ~ 5-10 minutes.

## Balloon Hunger Games

**Objective**: to be the last one with an intact balloon.

**Rules:** this is an individual challenge. Tie as many helium-filled balloons to your player as you wish. However, check safety when tying them to limbs, etc. It is best to make a Velcro piece to wear around the ankle (or a large sweatband) to tie the balloons on instead of tying them directly to the body – to avoid injury or damage to their clothing.

When the host says go, the players are to pop the opposing players' balloons with their hands (don't give them weapons). The last player to have an intact balloon still attached is the winner. If the balloon dislodges from the player and floats to the ceiling and is out of reach, it is out of play and counts as a popped balloon. If the balloon dislodges from a player and can be retrieved, any player may retrieve the balloon and tie it to their Velcro strap/sweatband (or another item it can be tied to) and it is in play. However, if a player has been called out, they may not retrieve any floating balloons.

The players are not allowed to harm each other physically. Players may hide with their balloons still tied to them – if they can do so within the given boundaries.

**Props needed:** balloons (i.e. orange, helium-filled is preferred) for each player tied with ribbon to them in any manner which will avoid injury/damage to clothing. You can have more than one per player.

**Playing time:** ~ 5-10 minutes.

## Greedy Balloon Challenge

**Objective**: to pick up and hold for three seconds as many balloons as possible.

**Rules:** this is an individual challenge. Blow up ~20 balloons and place on the floor. Set a timer for one minute and allow each player to attempt to pick up and hold as many balloons as they can. When the timer goes off, count to three and as many balloons that are in the player's possession is their recorded score. Possession means 'controlled' by the player – hitting them into the air is not in possession. The players are allowed to put them in their clothes. Popped balloons are not added in the final count.

**Props needed:** ~ 20 inflated balloons and a timer.

**Playing time:** ~ 10-15+ minutes – depending on how many individuals you will time.

## TOILET TISSUE GAMES

### Creepy Disguise Challenge

**Objective**: to make the most creative disguise out of one roll of toilet tissue!

**Rules:** pair the players into groups of two or three. Give the teams ten minutes (or more) to create the most unique disguise by using one roll of toilet tissue. Scotch tape is allowed and should be available to all teams as they need it. The teams can mummify (easy and predictable) or make weird, intricate things out of the tissue to completely disguise one of their group members.

When the time is up, and/or the players are finished creating their disguises, one at a time the disguised players are to model their disguises. The host judges or the players vote via a ballot for the best and most creative disguise. In the case of a tie via ballot, the host will be the tie-breaker.

**Props needed:** one roll of toilet tissue per team.

**Playing time:** ~ 15 minutes.

### Transylvanian Vampire Cape Challenge

**Objective:** to make the best vampire cape out of one roll of toilet tissue!

**Rules:** pair the players into groups of two or three. Give the teams ten minutes (or more) to create the most unique and awesome vampire cape by using one roll of toilet tissue. Scotch tape is allowed and should be available to all teams as they need it.

When the time is up, and/or the players are finished creating their capes, one at a time, the vampire models are to model their capes. Play a fun song in the background so the vampire models can get into the groove during their runway walk! The host judges or the players vote via a ballot for the best and most creative cape. In the case of a tie via ballot, the host will be the tie-breaker.

**Props needed:** one roll of toilet tissue per two/three players.

**Playing time:** ~ 15-20 minutes.

# Dr. Bonnie

### Unravel | Wind

**Objective:** to unroll and re-roll a roll of toilet tissue the fastest.

**Rules:** pair the players into groups of two and hand each team a toilet paper roll. When you say go, they are to unwind the toilet paper roll. When they get to the cardboard, they must hold it up and say 'out of paper' and allow the host/judge to acknowledge them before they wind the toilet tissue back on the roll. The first one to successful wind the toilet paper back on the roll is the winning team. In the event of a tie, resort to a Mouse-Cat-Witch tiebreaker (see tiebreaker section for details).

**Props needed:** one roll of 2-ply (strong) toilet paper per two players.

**Playing time:** ~ 10 minutes.

### Break the Line of Communication

**Objective:** to be the final pair with an intact 'line of communication' with toilet tissue.

**Rules:** pair the players and hand them a 5' sheet of toilet tissue. They are to each hold on to an end of it with one hand (they can choose which hand but must stick to their choice during the game). They are not allowed to hold on to their end by grabbing more than three sheets, and may not make adjustments during the challenge. When the host says go, the teams must break the toilet tissue held by their opponents. When a team's toilet tissue is broken, they are out of the game and must leave the field. The last pair to have an intact toilet tissue is declared the winning team. If you wish to continue, give the pair a point for the round and keep playing until a team gets to five. Or, switch up the pairs and make the points an individual challenge, and the first person to five will be the winner.

**Props needed:** 5' sheets of toilet tissue per pair.

**Playing time:** ~ 10 minutes.

### Toilet Paper Press Relay

**Objective:** to be the first to have your final players cross the start/finish while pressing together five rolls of toilet tissue.

**Rules:** prepare relay race lanes for teams of eight players (make it six or ten each, but it must be an even number). Have half of each team stand on either side of the lane at the start/finish line (make one with floor-safe tape on either side of your lanes). On the starting side, give the first two players in line five rolls of toilet tissue. They are to hold them by horizontally pressing them together. During the race, they are only allowed to touch the end roll of toilet paper on either side. When the host says go, they race to their teammates on the other side of the lane, cross the finish/start line and transfer their toilet paper rolls to the next two players in line. If, at any time during the race down the lane, the middle toilet paper rolls drop, they must pick them up and go back to their start line and start their leg of the race over. The first team to have their final players cross the start/finish line is declared the winning team.

**Props needed:** five rolls of toilet tissue for each team.

**Playing time:** ~ 10 minutes.

## Toilet Tissue Towers

**Objective:** to create the highest tower out of toilet tissue rolls (&/or paper towel rolls).

**Rules:** pair the players into teams of up to four players (too many cooks will spoil the food). Give each team plenty of toilet tissue (~20-25 rolls –have some extra in case) &/or paper towel rolls to make their tower. Set the timer for one minute and allow the teams to build the highest tower they can. When the timer goes off, everybody must step away from their tower and if it falls, they are out. Hopefully, someone will have the highest tower, if not; host another round for a tie-breaker.

**Props needed:** 20-25 toilet paper rolls per team and/or paper towel rolls (provide about half the amount if you add these – they are taller, but can be less stable).

**Playing time:** ~ 10 minutes.

## 360 Spin Challenge

**Objective:** to score the best time un-wrapping a roll of toilet tissue by spinning in 360 turns.

**Rules:** this is an individual challenge. Hand each player a roll of toilet tissue. The host (or another player) is to slide their index fingers into both ends of the roll and support it vertically to allow the tissue to flow properly off the roll. The contestant will grab the end of the roll and when the host shouts go and starts the timer, they will spin, wrapping themselves in the toilet paper as quickly as possible until the roll is completely unraveled and wound around them. The timer stops and time is recorded. Repeat this process for each player and the best time wins. In the event of a tie, you've got plenty of unraveled toilet tissue, so when you say go; the player to successful wind a roll back onto the cardboard center is declared the winner. Note: it won't look like it did before – it will be about five times larger and messy but if it's wound, it counts.

**Props needed:** one roll of toilet tissue for each player and a timer. Pen and paper to record scores.

**Playing time:** ~ 15 minutes.

### Bridge and Tunnel Relay

**Objective:** to get your toilet paper roll to the end of your line and back by passing it over the bridge (over their head) and in the tunnel (between their legs) without breaking the tissue.

**Rules:** divide your group into teams of six. Hand the starting player a roll of toilet paper and have everybody stand in a straight line facing the backside of the player in front of them. When the host says go, the roll must be passed to the player in front of them either over their head (the bridge) or between their legs (the tunnel). The bridge and tunnel must alternate with each pass. If the tissue breaks - it needs to be repaired with Scotch tape before the team can proceed. The first team to make it to the end player and back to the starting player with an intact line of toilet paper will be the winner.

**Props needed:** one roll of toilet tissue for every team of six players. You can adjust the number of players in each team, but if you make the line much longer, have an extra roll handy in case they run out of a roll. Also, have Scotch tape available for each team.

**Playing time:** ~ 15 minutes.

## PING-PONG BALL GAMES

### Twerk 'Til Ya Lose It All

**Objective**: to be the quickest to lose the Ping-Pong balls in your box.

**Rules:** Using an empty Kleenex box (or another box you engineer to be about the same size with the same size opening). You might have to increase the size of the opening where it is just wide enough for a Ping-Pong ball, and they don't all fall out immediately. Run a piece of rope/fabric through it big enough to tie around your players' waist with the box in the back on their lower back to bum/booty/gluteal area – whatever you call it. Now, set a timer and play the #1 dance song. The player is to use their best dance moves to shake out the Ping-Pong balls from their box. When they've danced the final ball out of the box – mark the time. If attempted with all the players at once, you've got to rig a box/belt set up with Ping-Pong balls inside for everybody. You

can easily host this as a timed trial for each player who wants to participate. Get ready for everybody to video this one! It is hysterical.
**Props needed:** a box of any kind that has an opening for Ping-Pong balls to be shaken out of (not to fall out of) and a rope/piece of fabric weaved through so you can fasten the box to the player's bum.
**Playing time:** ~15 minutes.

## Ping-Pong Ball Droppers

**Objective**: to get as many Ping-Pong balls in your team's bucket before the timer runs out!

**Rules:** divide your players into as many groups as you wish. Give each team a bucket in the center of the room and a pile of Ping-Pong balls of a designated color (use markers on them to write a symbol, etc.) The buckets should touch and cluster together in the center of the room. Each bucket should be of the team's color or marked clearly (use tape and a marker to put the same symbol as the Ping-Pong ball). Each team should have a start line designated with tape an equal distance away from the buckets. Make sure the teams are spaced appropriately and their buckets in the center are facing them. For example, if you have two teams playing, place their start lines at opposing ends of the room. With four teams, use the four corners, etc.

Set the timer for ~ three minutes (or whatever time you choose). When the host says go, every member of the team will pick up a Ping-Pong ball and place it between their knees. They may use their hands to place it between their knees, but they may not use their hands after they leave the start line.

Each person races to their center bucket with the Ping-Pong ball in between their knees and drops their Ping-Pong ball into the correct bucket. If they get a ball into another team's bucket, the team that the bucket belongs to will receive two points for it whereas each Ping-Pong ball placed into the correct bucket is 1 point. If at any time a player drops their Ping-Pong ball from between their knees, they must go back to the starting line and start over. The teams are not allowed to retrieve any Ping-Pong ball from a bucket. Once a Ping-Pong ball lands in a bucket, it is final. Anyone that spills a bucket's Ping-Pong balls will receive a five-point penalty for their team for each bucket knocked over.

When the timer goes off, the players freeze. No additional Ping-Pong balls may enter a bucket after the time is up. The team with the most points wins!

# Dr. Bonnie

**Props needed:** ~10-20 Ping-Pong balls for each team and a bucket for each team, any timer.
**Playing time:** ~ 10-15 minutes.

## Ping-Pong Pandemonium Relay

**Objective**: is to be the first team to bounce a Ping-Pong ball into cups down the line and back.
**Rules:** divide your group into two or more teams and ask that they sit in parallel lines, spaced about 3-4 feet away from each other. Everybody is to sit on the floor with their legs crossed holding an orange or black solo plastic cup (or whatever cup you choose). The first player in each team is handed a Ping-Pong ball. When the host says go, the first player bounces the Ping-Pong ball into the next team member's cup. The player can move the cup, but cannot move otherwise. The ball has to bounce once. If the ball doesn't bounce, it needs to be re-bounced. If either player moves anything besides the cup – they need to reset and start over with the bounce of the Ping-Pong ball towards the cup. Once the Ping-Pong ball is caught in the player's cup, they swivel around to the next player (their bum may never move from the original spot) and bounce the Ping-Pong ball towards the next player in line's cup and so on until it gets to the final player. Then, you come back the other direction. When it gets to the starting player's cup, the game is over, and the team wins.
**Props needed:** a cup for each player in the game and a Ping-Pong ball for each team.
**Playing time:** ~ 10-15 minutes.

## Spoon the Ping-Pong Relay

**Objective**: is to be the first team to transfer the Ping-Pong ball to the end of the line via spoon to spoon without dropping it to the floor.
**Rules:** divide your group into two teams and hand each player a spoon (plastic ones are fine). Line up the two teams into lines and hand the Ping-Pong ball to the starting player for each team and instruct them to put the ball on their spoon. The Ping-Pong balls are not allowed to have any human contact until they reach the last player's spoon.

The host says go and the first player will transfer their Ping-Pong ball to the next player's spoon without dropping it. If it drops, they must start over. Play continues and the Ping-Pong ball is transferred from spoon to spoon until it reaches the final player's spoon without dropping. The team who gets their ball to the final player's spoon is the winning team.

At any time, if the ball drops from a spoon &/or a player touches it by any manner with a body part, they must go back to the starting player and start over completely.

**Props needed:** a spoon for each player in the game and a Ping-Pong ball for each team.

**Playing time:** ~ 10-15 minutes.

## Ping-Pong Obstacle Course

**Objective**: is to do a timed trial through the obstacle course the fastest while holding a spoon in your mouth that is holding a Ping-Pong ball.

**Rules:** this is an individual challenge. Each player will be timed as they navigate through your designated obstacles course and cross the finish line while holding a spoon in their mouth that is holding a Ping-Pong ball. If, at any time, the ball drops, they go back to the start line and their time never stops until they cross the finish line.

**Props needed:** make the obstacle course with anything you wish. If you have pylons, make a course where they must weave through them. If you have a bean bag chair, have them have to walk over it – use couch pillows (if they are sturdy and won't get damaged), etc. The sky is the limit but just be very clear what they must do and demonstrate before the first person goes through. The player with the quickest time is the winner. Also, you'll need a spoon for each player (as they will hold these in their mouths, it's best to give them a fresh disposable one), and a Ping-Pong ball.

**Playing time:** ~ 25 minutes (really depends on the number of players).

## Take Out the Witch...and Ruin her Potion

**Objective**: is to get the most hits on the witch and land your Ping-Pong ball in the cauldron.

**Rules:** this is an individual challenge. Do an online search for a witch's face and print it out. Tape the witch's face to a wall/door. Before the party, do a trial run and stand a few feet to the left/right of the picture and toss a Ping-Pong ball at her face and see where the Ping-Pong ball lands the most. Mark the spot and place a plastic witch's cauldron there. For added fun, add some dry ice and a glow stick inside (but if so, do not allow your guests to retrieve the balls from the cauldron, as dry ice can damage skin, causing injury).

# Dr. Bonnie

Each player will receive five Ping-Pong balls, and they may stand anywhere they choose. The rule is to hit the witch and cause the ball to land in the cauldron. They have five tries to hit the witch's face (1 point) and land their Ping-Pong ball in the cauldron (3 points). Each player has a total of 20 points possible. The player with the highest point total is the winner. For ties, use the Mouse-Cat-Witch tiebreaker (see tiebreaker instructions for details). For younger kids, show them where to stand to give them the best chance of landing in the cauldron.

**Props needed:** five balls for each player and a cauldron. Also, a witch's picture to tape to the wall with paint-safe tape.

**Playing time:** ~ 15 minutes (really depends on the number of players).

## Straw Your Way to Victory

**Objective**: is to get your bucket of Ping-Pong balls across the finish line the quickest by only using a straw to push them down the lane and across the line.

**Rules:** divide your group into two to three teams. Provide each team with a bucket of Ping-Pong balls – or any amount that you wish – but be sure that there's enough for each player to have a turn. Give each player a plastic straw and have them line up behind the start line. Designate a finish line a distance of your choosing away. In any manner they wish, the players are to use the straw to propel their Ping-Pong ball across the finish line. The Ping-Pong ball may not have any human contact during its journey across the finish line. The player can push the ball with the straw, they can blow through the straw, they can suck in and keep a vacuum, etc. However they wish to use the straw to get it across is allowed. Once a player has their ball across the lane, the next player in line can immediately start with another Ping-Pong ball and so forth until the last ball in their bucket crosses the finish line. If you have more balls than players, they must stay in their original order – meaning once all players in the team have transported a ball across the finish line, the starting player will go and so forth until all balls are across.

**Props needed:** you will need a start line and finish line, a straw for each player and at least a Ping-Pong ball for each player in the game.

**Playing time:** ~ 25 minutes (really depends on the number of players).

## Nose Your Way to Victory

**Objective**: is to get your bucket of Ping-Pong balls across the finish line the quickest by only using your nose to push them down the lane and across the line.

**Rules:** see the rules for Straw Your Way to Victory and exchange the straw for the player's nose. The players must get on 'all fours' and the only contact with the Ping-Pong ball can be the nose.

**Props needed:** you will need a start line and finish line, at least a Ping-Pong ball for each player in the game.

**Playing time:** ~ 25 minutes (really depends on the number of players).

## DANCING GAMES

### So You Think You Can Dance Contest

**Objective**: to be the most awesome dancers at the party!

**Rules:** pair the players into groups of two or three. Create your dance type slips, fold them and place into any container. Each team is to draw a type of dance. Give the teams ten minutes (or more) to create a unique 30-second dance routine in their type of dance that they drew to be performed to any dance song of your choice. Play the song repeatedly in the background so the teams have ample time to practice with the music. If the team doesn't know the style of dance - they can re-draw, trade with someone who does…or just give it their best shot! When the time is up, and/or the players are finished creating their routines, one at a time, the players are to perform their routines for the other players. The host will judge who came up with the best interpretation of the dance style and fit it best with the music. The players can vote via a ballot for the best dance routine (and they cannot vote for themselves). In the case of a tie, the host will be the tie-breaker.

**Props needed:** any music playing source and a dance song (preferably Halloween-themed). There are example dance type strips below – create them, fold them individually and place into any container for your players to draw one for each team.

**Playing time:** ~ 30 minutes.

**Here are some example dance types**:

| Salsa | Jive | Swing | The Robot |
|---|---|---|---|
| Hip Hop | Lyrical | Waltz | 7th Grade Couples' Dance |
| '80s Dance | '70s Disco | African Tribal | Tap Dance |
| Tango | Mambo | Ballet | Paso Doble |

# Dr. Bonnie

### Hilarious Halloween Dance Contest

**Objective**: to be the most radical fun Halloween dancers at the party!

**Rules:** pair the players into groups of two. Give the teams ten minutes (or more) to create a unique 30-second fun Halloween dance routine to be performed to the song 'Monster Mash' or another fun Halloween song of your choice. Play the song repeatedly in the background so the teams have ample time to practice with the music.

When the time is up, and/or the players are finished creating their routines, one at a time, the players are to perform their routines for the other players. The host will judge, or the players will vote via a ballot for the best fun Halloween dance routine. In the case of a tie, the host will be the tie-breaker.

**Props needed:** any music playing source and a fun Halloween song.

**Playing time:** ~ 30 minutes.

### Do the Freeze

**Objective**: to have the best reflexes on the dance floor.

**Rules:** make a dance floor and tell your players to warm up while you ready the Halloween song. When you push play, they are to dance (as best as they can) until the music stops. Dancing constitutes the movement of arms, legs and torso – at a minimum. They must freeze the very second the music ceases to play and anybody that moves at that time is out and must leave the dance floor immediately Dancers are not allowed to freeze until the music stops or they are out. The last person on the dance floor wins.

**Props needed:** any music playing source and a fun Halloween song.

**Playing time:** ~ 10 minutes.

## MUSICAL GAMES

### Scare-Tastic Rap Contest

**Objective:** to be the team that gives the most awesome rap duo performance!

**Rules:** divide the players into groups of two or three. Give the teams ten minutes (or more) to write the most awe-inspiring and hilarious rap lyrics about Halloween. Play a steady rap beat in the background so the groups can get inspired and can practice.

When the time is up, allow each team to perform their rap song in front of the group. Each member of the team must play a role in the duo (or trio). The host will choose the best upcoming rap artist duo at the party!

161

**Props needed:** a cool rap beat (instrumental) to play in the background and during the performances. The Party of 2 Monstrous Halloween Dance Party Mix CD has an instrumental rap song for you to do this challenge. The CD is available on iTunes, and many rap beat songs to choose from on the MyMysteryParty.com site to download instantly upon purchase.

**Playing time:** ~ 15 -20 minutes.

## Halloween Rap Battle

**Objective:** to be the team that outperforms the other groups.

**Rules:** divide the players into groups of two or three. Create slips of Halloween-themed rap topics and allow the teams to draw from a container. Give the teams ten minutes (or more) to write the most hilarious rap lyrics about what they drew on their slip. Play a steady rap beat in the background so the groups can get inspired and can practice.

      When the time is up, allow each team to perform their rap song in front of the group. Each member of the team must play a role in the duo (or trio). The host will choose the best upcoming rap artist duo at the party.

**Props needed:** a cool rap beat (instrumental) to play in the background and during the performances. The Party of 2 Monstrous Halloween Dance Party Mix cd has an instrumental rap song for you to do this challenge. The cd is available on iTunes and MyMysteryParty.com prop emporium at http://mymysteryparty.com/party-props/. There are also many rap tracks to choose from on the MyMysteryParty.com site to download instantly upon purchase.

**Playing time:** ~ 15 -20 minutes.

**Example topics to use that should incite hilarious lyrics:**

| | | | |
|---|---|---|---|
| Troll Boogers | Black Cat Kitty Litter | Bat Guano | Soggy Candy |
| Orange And Black | Graveyard Party | Zombie Attack | Dracula's Dentist |
| Flying Brooms | Headless Horseman | Living Dolls | Bat in my Backpack |
| Lightning in the Pumpkin Patch | Alien Invasion | Monster Toe Jamb | My Dad's a Warlock |

# Dr. Bonnie

## Halloween Song Rally

**Objective**: to be the final player in the game.

**Rules:** the game is an individual one. Sit your players in a circle, or just remember their order if they are scattered about the room. The oldest player in the room will go first and sing a line from any song that has something Halloween in the lyric – pumpkin, monster, night, bat, vampire, scary, creepy, moon, etc. Be flexible with this rule.

The next player in line has to sing a song lyric of their choice that contains at least one of the words included in the previous song lyric, but the Halloween theme doesn't have to continue, or this game may become impossible. If you are extreme music lovers and know many lyrics, keep the Halloween rule in play for the duration.

**For example:** Player 1 sings a lyric from the chorus of 'Bark at the **Moon**' and then player 2 sings 'Bad **Moon** Rising' and then player three sings '**Bad** to the Bone' and so forth until someone is stumped. When someone is stumped, they are out and play continues to the next person who starts fresh with a new lyric that is Halloween-themed.

**Props needed:** brains that know music.

**Playing time:** ~ 10 minutes.

## Ding-Dong, Ping-Pong, We are Ready to Sing our Song

**Objective**: to be the first team to put your song lyrics in order.

**Rules:** before the party, choose two of the most popular songs your group will know. Choose a recognizable verse from each song and write down a line of the lyric on a separate sheet of paper. Depending on how many players you will have at your party will depend if you need to choose more songs. Four to six lines of a verse per song should be the max. Therefore, if you have 20 players coming to your party, choose four songs and use five lines of a verse for each song.

You should have one slip of paper per player and scatter them around the room on brightly-colored paper. For more of a challenge, hide these slips of paper and ask the players to find them first – if you do this, affix some ribbons to the sheets, so they look more like hunt-able items and not just slips of paper randomly in the room. Once each player has found one slip each, they are to locate their teammates by finding matching song lyrics. Once they find their team, they are to put themselves in order and shout the freeze phrase 'Ding-dong, Ping-Pong, we are ready to sing our song.' Everybody is to freeze, and the group is allowed to sing their song – whoever is holding the first lyric starts the song by singing their lyric. The rest of their team members

163

sing the lyrics in order according to what is on their slips of paper. If they are correct (i.e. the lyrics all go together and are sung in the correct order), they are the winning team. If they are not correct, play resumes until another team (or that team) shouts the freeze phrase and attempts the challenge. The first team to sing their verse correctly is the winning team.

**Props needed:** slips of song verse lines.

**Playing time:** ~ 10 minutes.

## TEAM-BUILDING GAMES

### No Mirror Monster Makeup

**Objective:** to be the team that works together to put on the best monster makeup without a mirror!

**Rules:** pair the players into groups of two. Each team is to have a dark–colored lipstick, three colors of eye shadow with applicators, eyeliner, blusher with blush brush, and various colors of lip/eye liners and any other makeup you wish to use. Or, you can get a Halloween makeup kit and give one to each team. Leave mascara out of this. Instruct them to close their eyes while applying the eye shadow as not to get eye shadow inside of their eyes.

Set the timer for two minutes and when the host says go, the team is to work together to put on one team member's monster makeup – they can choose any monster they wish and create the makeup. One team member is to 'talk' a team member into putting on the makeup without a mirror, and the other team member is to apply the makeup to their face according to the instructions by their partner. The team member that is guiding the 'makeup wearer' is not allowed to touch the player's face in any way! Allow each team their two minutes (or do this simultaneously if you have enough 'sets' of makeup). When every team has a monster face ready, the host is to judge the best-applied makeup! If this is a co-ed party, the boys are to be the ones applying their makeup with the girls giving direction.

**Props needed:** a set of makeup and a timer. Optional to have a set of makeup for each team to do the challenge simultaneously.

**Playing time:** ~10-20 minutes.

### Drama Kings & Queens

**Objective**: to be the team that can correctly guess the spooky event that your team member is reacting to.

# Dr. Bonnie

**Rules:** divide your group into two teams. Create your drama slips, fold, and place folded into any container. Each team will select an actor/actress for each turn (you cannot repeat until everybody has acted a scenario on the team). The teams will alternate having one player act out the scenario without speaking a word – this is a silent challenge. The team has one minute to guess the correct reaction before the timer is up. The team with the most correct guesses after three turns each wins. In the event of a tie, a Mouse-Cat-Witch challenge is needed. Select a captain from each team and the two out of three will win. Note: you will need an impartial judge to determine if a guess should be counted as 'correct.'

**Here are some example drama slips:**

| |
|---|
| Stumbling upon a creepy tarantula |
| Being chased by a vampire bat |
| Being bitten by a hungry vampire |
| Being thrown into a boiling pot of witch's brew |
| Being in a cemetery at midnight |
| Being haunted by a ghost |
| Unwrapping a mummy |
| Being awoken by a howling werewolf |
| Watching Frankenstein come to life for the first time |
| Riding on a witch's broom and plummeting towards Earth |
| Running from a zombie |

**Props needed:** strips, container for drawing the strips, a one-minute timer (a smartphone can be used).
**Playing time:** ~ 15-20 minutes.

## Sightless Mona Lisa

**Objective**: to be the team that works together to create the best drawing of an object.
**Rules:** divide the group into pairs. Blindfold one member of each team and give them a pad and pencil. Give their teammate any random object (e.g. stapler, umbrella) after the blindfold is secured.

Set the timer for two minutes and when the host says go, the sighted member holding the object must direct the blindfolded team member how to draw the object without telling them what the object is or allowing them to touch (or hear) the object in any way. All they are allowed to do is give directions on what to do with the pen/pencil (i.e. turn to the right, make a squiggly line, draw a circle). The host is to judge and select the best representation of a team's object. It is optional to have prizes for the winners.

**Props needed:** a pen/pencil and a notepad/sheet of paper for each team and random objects.

**Playing time:** ~20 minutes.

## Find It, STAT

**Objective**: to be the team who can find the text in the newspaper the fastest.

**Rules:** divide the group into as many teams as you wish – but no more than six players per team (as it will be crowded as they stand around the newspaper). Give each team a newspaper – the same one from the same date. In advance of the game, select a specific text, picture, ad, etc., from any part of the paper and read it aloud/describe it to the group. The first team to find that text (ad, picture, etc.), tear it out of their paper, and give it to you will win the point. Continue for at least ten total finds and then declare the winner. Get ready for chaos!

**Props needed:** a newspaper of the same kind for each team.

**Playing time:** ~15-20 minutes.

## The Spider's Web

**Objective**: to get untangled before the timer goes off.

**Rules:** have your players stand in a circle (six players should make each circle). Each player is to grab hands with two different members of the circle (preferably across the circle). The objective is to unravel the web without letting go of anybody's hands once a three-minute timer is started.

**Props needed:** a timer.

**Playing time:** ~5 minutes.

## Writers, Producers, Directors, and Actors

**Objective**: to be the team that writes, produces, directs, and acts out their skit the best!

**Rules:** pair the players into groups of two or three. Give each team a script scenario slip and ask them to create a one to two-minute skit on the scenario given to them. They have to use the two characters given to them, and have to use the skit premise. If there are three (or more) on a team, they can create the role the third person (and others) will play. They should plan the skit and then rehearse the skits quickly. The host should call time, and one-by-one the groups should perform their

166

# Dr. Bonnie

skits in front of the rest of the group. The host of the party will judge and select the group who wrote, produced, directed, and acted out their skits the best. (A prize to the winning group(s) is optional.)
**Props needed:** printed copies of the script scenarios.
**Playing time:** ~20 minutes.

**Example script scenarios:**

| |
|---|
| **Script scenario #1 The Witch and the Mouse**<br>**Characters:** Wanda the Witch and the mouse<br>**Premise:** Wanda lures mice to her cabin, as mice are an important ingredient in many of her potions. The mouse has stumbled upon Wanda the Witch's cabin made of cheese, deep in the forest. |
| **Script scenario #2 Pumpkin Patch Pandemonium**<br>**Characters:** Earl the Pumpkin Patch farmer and Gene the annoying customer<br>**Premise:** After a terrible hail storm, the pumpkins in Earl's Pumpkin Patch are in horrible shape. Earl must sell a partially destroyed pumpkin to Gene – who is particular. |
| **Script scenario #3 The Zombie's Conundrum**<br>**Characters:** Zelda Zombie and Frank the Human<br>**Premise:** Zelda and Frank find themselves stuck in an elevator between floors 12 and 13. Zelda is very hungry. |
| **Script scenario #4 Chaos in Cathy Cat's Litter Box**<br>**Characters:** Cathy the black cat and Mark the mouse<br>**Premise:** Mark doesn't want Cathy to use the litter box for her 'personal use' anymore, as he has made a nice nest for his family there. Cathy is shocked that Mark has the nerve to do this to her. |
| **Script scenario #5 The Skeleton King and Santa Claus**<br>**Characters:** The Skeleton King of Halloween and Santa Claus – King of Christmas.<br>**Premise:** The Skeleton King and Santa Claus both end up in Easter Land – a magical land ruled by Peter Cottontail. Peter is a cruel king and has only agreed to allow one of them to travel home. They must plead their case to King Peter to be the one who can return home. |
| **Script scenario #6 A Horrible Night for a Rat, Bat, and Cat.**<br>**Characters:** Ronda Rat, Brent Bat, and Chris the Cat<br>**Premise:** Characters are seated together at a poorly planned Halloween ball with no food, music played by screeching banshees, and the vampires keep biting everybody. |

## Acid River Challenge

**Objective**: to get all the members of your team across the (hypothetical) acid river.

**Rules:** mark two 'lanes' in an open area. The length of the lanes depends on how difficult you wish to make this challenge, but make sure the lanes are of equal distance. Mark a start line and a finish line on either end of each lane.

The two teams line up at the starting line and the river-crossing player for each team (the one in first position) has the imaginary hazmat suit. In story – the teams must cross the river because an angry troop of gorillas is coming their way. Each team has one acid-resistant suit. However, the suit is weak and can only touch acid long enough for one trip across the river.

When the host says go, a player from each team (wearing their team's imaginary acid-resistant suit) will cross the river. However, whatever part(s) of their body that touch the ground will wear the suit out in that spot. The player crosses the finish line and hypothetically throws the suit back across the river to the next player in line. The next player will cross the river, but they cannot touch the ground with the same body part that the player before them (or any players before them) and so on until everybody has crossed the river safely. The players will need to be creative.

Do not give them further instructions, but for example: one can hop on the left foot, the next player can hop on the right foot, one person can wiggle across on their belly, on their knees, on their elbows & tops of feet (as the other players used the bottom of their feet), they can do handstands, etc. But no matter what – they cannot duplicate any body part, or the player that has duplicated will start over at the starting line.

**Props needed:** no equipment needed. You will just need to mark off the 'river' and put a start and finish line for two lanes – one for each team.

**Playing time:** ~20 minutes.

## Find the Flag

**Objective**: to be the team that captures the other team's flags before your flag is caught.

**Rules:** four teams will select a historical monument/landmark to 'hypothetically' hide their team's flag. This landmark/monument may not be obscure, and it must reside within the country in which this game is being played. Before the game can begin, each team will write the location of their flag on a card and show it secretly to the host. The host will check each of the team's landmarks/monuments to determine if they are viable and not too obscure before the game begins. If the host does not agree with the landmark/monument chosen by the team, they are to select another one until they can get the host to agree with the choice. If the chosen landmark/monument is not listed on any website as a historical monument or landmark, the host has every right not to allow it. The host has the final say and has the duty to ensure the game is fair.

**Starting the game**: when the host says go, the team who has the oldest player in the room will go first and will be designated as team #1. They will decide who goes next (i.e. team #2) and are allowed to ask this team one yes/no question. If the team answers 'yes' to their question, they are allowed to ask another question and so on until they receive an answer of 'no.' The other teams in the room can hear the answers and can use this information, as well. Once team #1 receives an answer of 'no,' the play moves to team #2, and they will decide who team #3 will be. Gameplay continues as before. Once the order of teams is established, it will remain until a reverse is played (see below).

**Smartphone rules**: smartphones may not be used once the game has begun. The host can allow, at any time, a 60-second phone use period in order to look things up. This will prevent the players from being stuck.

**Capturing a flag:** a team that gets continual 'yes' answers will eventually narrow down the landmark/monument and can submit a guess of where the flag is hidden. They must say the words 'we wish to capture your flag' at any time during their turn and the game host must acknowledge them before they submit the guess by saying: 'where is team #___'s flag'. This will prevent someone in the group haphazardly guessing the answer and getting extra guesses &/or being wrong. If the official guess is incorrect, the team will forfeit their next turn. A forfeit means they can still be asked their line of questions from the previous team, but will not, in turn, ask their line of questions to the next team on the following rotation.

On the other hand, if the official guess is correct, the opposing team's flag is captured, and they are eliminated from the game. The team that captured the flag continues by moving to the next team in order and asking questions until they are told 'no.' Then, the gameplay continues until there is one team left. If a team guesses incorrectly two times in a row, their flag is captured, and they are out of the game.

**Reverse play:** each team can reverse play at the start of their turn – one time during the game. This means if it is team #1's turn to ask a question, they have the ability to switch to team #4 instead of team #2. The rotation will remain this direction until a different team calls 'reverse' at the start of their turn.

**Free pass:** if, for any reason, a team wants to pass on their turn to ask questions, they can.

The strategy of this game comes into play with which teams they initially want in order if they are one of the teams allowed to choose who is next, whether or not the teams want to use a free pass, a reverse, and when to guess to capture a flag. As well as overall knowledge of your country's geography and landmarks/monuments!

**Props needed:** a sheet of paper for each team to write their landmark down on – or a smartphone note app can be used – whatever can be shown to the host in secret is fine.

**Playing time:** ~20 minutes.


## Night at the Improv

**Objective**: to get the most improvisation points for your team – you must be creative and think quickly to improvise as many items as possible out of a random prop.

**Rules:** divide the group into teams. If the teams are not equal, the one that is short a player must designate who will go twice before the game begins. This player will go first and last for their team.

The host will assemble a random assortment of items (one for each player in the game). The items can be anything such as a coin, spatula, shoe, dental floss – absolutely any random items will do. The items are to be placed in a bag so nobody can see them.

The teams will take a seat as an audience with the host at the front. The host will call one player from the first team to the front, and when a 30-second timer is started, they will be handed a random item from the bag (designate a player on each team to set the timer for the opposing team each time – they can use a smartphone). This player has 30 seconds to act out as many improvisations (i.e. 'improvs') of this item as they can. It must be a reasonable improv and make sense with the general shape of the item. They are not allowed to communicate verbally what they are acting out – it must be obvious by their actions with the item. For example, if they are handed a shoe – they can act out using it as a telephone, pretend to eat from it as a bowl with an imaginary spoon, etc. The host will give the point when they acknowledge the improv & they will keep track of legitimate improvs for each team. If an improv isn't working out, the improviser should move on, but shouldn't expect a point unless the host verbally gives it during the 30 seconds. If the improviser speaks while improvising, they will not get the point – so remind them to keep their mouths tightly shut when it is their turn.

When the host recognizes the improv, they are to say immediately what it is and tell the improviser to move on. The improviser will move on to their next improv of the item until the timer goes off. To assist their team player on the stage, the members of the improvising player's team can shout out what they believe the improv to be, and the game host can accept their suggestions at their discretion. Or, if they are way off base, it may only serve to confuse the host and waste time. Work as a team, not against your improviser. It is the host's call on each point—they are the judge and jury in this game. No arguing with the game host!

Optional: if you wish to do a bonus round, after all players have taken a turn, allow the teams to elect one player (obviously the player who did the best) to go a final time to rack up as many points as possible with a previously used item from the opposing team. However, the player cannot use any improvs given to the opposing team. For example, if team A was given the shoe and the player got two points for the telephone and bowl – the team B bonus round player cannot improv the shoe as a phone or a bowl – they must act out something different for their points. The team with the most points at the end wins the round.

**Props needed:** a large bag and as many random household/office items as there are players in the game. A timer – a smartphone can be used – set for 30 seconds.

**Playing time:** ~20 minutes.

## How Do You Do? Hey, I Know You! Or Do I?

**Objective**: to guess the most people correctly by only a handshake while you are blindfolded.

**Rules:** blindfold one player, and the other players are to stand in a straight line in any random order - facing the blindfolded person. After the blindfold is secure, everyone is to switch positions and remain completely silent. The host will guide the blindfolded person to the first person in line. They are allowed to shake hands - and only shake hands! The blindfolded person must give a guess who this person is that they just shook hands with. This repeats until the blindfolded player has shaken hands with and guessed every player in line. The host tallies up the number of correct guesses and puts it on the score sheet. Each player takes a turn being the blindfolded person until everyone has had a chance. The highest score - wins! In the event of a tie (or multiple ties) - the host will choose a number and write it down on a piece of paper, and each person will guess a number between one and one hundred. The closest without going over will win the tie-breaker and therefore, the game!

**Props needed:** blindfold, score sheet.

**Playing time:** ~20 minutes.

# VI. Halloween Party Themes

## MURDER MYSTERY PARTY:

Halloween is the #1 time for murder mystery parties. At least one All Hallow's Eve in your lifetime, you must host a murder mystery party! However, be careful as they can be quite addicting!

With a murder mystery party, you invite your friends, family, colleagues to any location to sleuth an intriguing mystery. You can serve light snacks all the way to an elaborate fine-dining menu. There is flexibility built in when hosting a murder mystery. Typically, these are inexpensive home parties but may also be elaborate events in a private dining room of a casual or fine-dining restaurant, a recreation center room, a high-school gymnasium, a park, or even a hotel hospitality suite. All you need is one party area and a restroom – not only for your guests to use but to allow the victim (with murder games) to leave and become the victim. Note: not all murder mystery parties require the victim to leave the room.

There are different kinds of murder mystery formats and most revolve around a dinner. With MyMysteryParty.com's format, dinner is always optional. A pregame is implemented before the party, and there is an optional round. This builds pregame excitement. The guests arrive ready to play the character role you have pre-assigned them and will undergo three rounds of gameplay. There is also a pregame guest site at Your Mystery Party (www.yourmysteryparty.com) that has, depending on the mystery, fun facts about the characters, an exciting video game trailer, the town or location of the mystery, costume suggestions and vendors, and a synopsis of the mystery. Some games even have downloadable news articles that give hints about the storyline. This site will build pregame excitement for your party and has shown to increase party guest attendance to over 90%. Pregame excitement reduces your amount of no-show guests!

When the game begins, you, as the host, will pass out the interactive clue cards to the guests for three rounds, and the characters are instructed to perform certain tasks and discuss their clues. The story line unravels and motives grow with each round until a murder occurs. Obviously, the murder is simply outlined in the storyline, but a designated player will become the *pretend victim* (in murder games) and the investigation will ensue – typically in Round

Two. Don't worry; the victim is never out of the game, in fact, they have the largest role!

The guests will investigate the crime, guess whodunit, and then accuse each other. In the final round (Round Three), they'll find out the solution to the mystery. MyMysteryParty.com also has a wide selection of non-murder mystery games, if you want to avoid the murder style games.

**Here are some of the favorite MyMysteryParty.com games for Halloween:**

**INSANE ASYLUM THEME**

**WEREWOLF, VAMPIRE, SORCERER THEME**

**HAUNTED HOUSE THEME**

**COSTUME BALL THEME**

**HAUNTED HOTEL HORROR THEME**

**WITCHES AND WIZARDS THEME**

**MYSTERIOUS MASQUERADE THEME**

**WITCH COVEN THEME**

**ZOMBIE APOCALYPSE THEME**

# Dr. Bonnie

## PARTY GAME PALOOZA:

Either with or without costumes and in any location - have the primary focus of the night center around Halloween party games. You can't go wrong with party games, and there are many to choose from in the game section of this handbook.

For a Halloween party game extravaganza, decorate your home in spooky décor, ask your guests to dress up in their best Halloween costumes, serve fun party food, and have a slew of games ready to go! Create an itinerary of the night's fun or allow the guests to draw from a hat for the next party game. Have all game props organized and ready – you don't want long lulls in energy while you gather them in between games.

Prizes for the winners are expected, but always optional. Pick up cheap prizes anywhere such as the grocery store, local party store, etc. by going to the Halloween aisle. Give out candy or other cheap confections. Or, make painted skeleton trophies as described in the DIY project section of this handbook.

## HAUNTED PARTIES:

**Home based haunted house:** the haunted house party is an exciting crowd pleaser! If your home/backyard is large enough, a route can be created for your guests to travel through without breaking everything you own. Why not set up a few rooms as a haunted house? Recruit some close friends to play the roles of the various rooms in the haunted house such as an alien invasion room, a Phantom of the Opera room, a serial killer room, a Bride of Frankenstein room. When the guests arrive, have someone dressed as a grim reaper escort them through the show and then into the final party room. Have someone waiting at the front to put the guests in a line in case you have many guests show up at once. The guests should go one-by-one in a home haunted house. If you allow multiple guests at once, there will be more accidents as far as breaking pictures, sheetrock, etc. Remember – you live there!

Once everybody gets into the party room, ask if anyone would like to go through again – why not? You went to a lot of trouble to create the spooky masterpiece! Then, the guests can relax and have fun with party games, dancing or whatever activities you have planned for them next.

**Commercial haunted houses/hayrides**: if you have haunted attractions in your city - haunted houses, haunted hayrides, creepy

175

panic rooms, etc., you have to do it at least once! Get your guests together and make a night out of hitting the haunted hot spots around town as a big group! With this type of party, you *must* disclose what you are planning to do on the invitation. Some guests do not enjoy being scared and will not want to endure a night of peer pressure from the other guests! However, gather your friends who are dying for a night of fright and have an excellent time.

Terror venues are not for everybody, and peer pressure is not okay at a party! In fact, it can cause hard feelings against you as the host. Extend the invite – but don't force it on anyone. Do not peer pressure anybody into doing anything during the night. If they think they want to do it and decide at the last minute to back out – allow them to do so without any ramifications or you may lose a friend.

## NIGHT UNDER THE STARS:

**Halloween camp out:** contact your local campground and reserve a camping site. Nothing is spookier than being in the open nature around a campfire on Halloween night! Tell ghost stories by the fire as you roast marshmallows! If there will not be hay bale seating around the bonfire, bring a chair for each guest.

Adult supervision is essential and mandatory with kids/teens around a campfire, and in the great outdoors in general, so have an acceptable adult-to-child ratio if you have a party with minors at a campsite. Don't let campers venture out into the wilderness alone!

**Don't forget these items when camping:**

| Rope | Pack of matches | Jar of peanut butter | First aid kit |
|---|---|---|---|
| Tarp | Portable spice rack | Lantern, flashlight | Map of the area |
| Compass | Durable shoes / extra socks | Pocket knife – multi-tool is preferred | Trash bags |
| Tents | Extra cold/wet weather gear | Water treatment tablets/filter | Folding chairs |
| Water | Food in ice chests | Folding table | Insect repellent |
| Toiletries | Sleeping bags, pillows | Pans, utensils, plates, cups, etc. | Extra batteries |

**Backyard bash:** Can't rent a campsite? Well, don't do the bonfire but still set up a tent and grab some flashlights to tell ghost stories all night in the backyard! If you have a fire pit (mobile) and can order some hay bales from a tractor supply/farming company – make a circle around the fire or use folding chairs for the guests.

## COSTUME BALL/PARTY:

**Home parties:** it's easy enough to host a costume party (or masquerade party) at your home. Make sure you outline the costume requirements on the invitation, however. Once you've made the costume party official, plan out your events for the night. Maybe host a simple mixer where the guests just chill, talk to each other and listen to music – oh, and eat party food.

**Extravagant events:** if you have the budget, bump up your night to a hotel ballroom and go all out. Rent a hotel ballroom from ~ $2000 to over $20,000 for ~ a five-hour period. This fee will usually cover the food and beverages. Also, expect a 20-24% service fee and a sales tax on top of that. Therefore, if you are quoted $2000, expect your total bill at the end of the night to be ~ $2685+. Get everything in writing in a contract before your event so you know your total costs. Monetary surprises are never good, and hotels are known for tacking on fees (some can be negotiated, but only in advance). The price is highest on Saturday nights and tends to be higher in May to July, as during these months, you compete with weddings. In October, you should be sitting pretty with a lower cost. Make an appointment with the sales representative for the hotel and look at the room you wish to rent in advance – never lease without viewing first.

Make a note of where the electrical outlets are and see what they will do for you regarding a stage and dance floor. Talk to your DJ in detail about the audio-video needs and make certain the hotel can accommodate their needs. The DJ needs to contact the sales representative/coordinator on your behalf to discuss the arrangements and what is provided, etc. Before putting down a deposit, make sure there will be enough seating and food (if they are catering) for your guests, ask about the availability of any décor, and by all means – ask for a complimentary guest suite or two to spend the night and not worry about driving home after the long night of partying. The sales representative/coordinator should throw in a room or two as a bonus but they may not offer unless you ask.

While speaking about hotels, do not lease a hotel suite in hopes of hosting a party there. Most hotels will not allow this and will abruptly evict you from the room when they figure out you've got a shindig going on. Then, you've wasted big money. Ask before planning a party in a suite.

Local country clubs will also lease their ballrooms to members, and most will lease the ballrooms to non-members. The prices vary by the club and the type of ballroom but are typically comparable to the hotel ballrooms, possibly even cheaper. A nice country club ballroom may be rented for ~$5,000 for the night, even if you are not a member. Some may even give you a credit towards a membership if you later decide to become a member with this fee. However, you will not have as many amenities as a hotel does and the ability to get a free suite for the night.

If you host a masquerade style ball, play classical Phantom of the Opera style music for ambiance. Guests have probably attended home costume parties since they were five-years-old but having it at a ballroom is a definite step up and very memorable! There will be excitement in the air of anticipation of what will come next. Teen groups might not appreciate classical music associated with the traditional masquerade ball, but there's nothing set in stone when it comes to teens (or kids), so choose whatever music the teens want to listen to – it's their party, and you want them to have fun. Make sure the DJ is lively and plans to host dance floor games with the group. The more the atmosphere changes, the less likely your teens will become bored and veer towards trouble. Contests for the best costume and dance contests are always big crowd favorites.

## LIMOUSINE PARTY HOP:

Plenty of establishments around town will be hosting Halloween celebrations on Halloween night. Gather up your friends dressed in their best Halloween costumes and rent a limousine and call it a *Crawl'oween Extravaganza!* You can split the cost of transportation as long as you disclose this up front on the invitation! It would be totally acceptable to divide the costs among friends. However, do not, by any means, try to collect funds from your invited guests upon arrival if you haven't mentioned splitting the costs with the invite. Bad party etiquette! That's a bait and switch and you'll forever be labeled as a dreadful party host.

In advance of your party, do an internet search and create the perfect schedule to hit as many of the costume contests and other fun Halloween festivities around town. First, go to dinner in your Halloween costumes! To get the party started, give a detailed itinerary to your limo driver and *party on!*

## SCAVENGER HUNT PARTY:

Scavenger hunt parties are high energy and very challenging events. Do an about town hunt, a neighborhood hunt, or a building hunt. ScavengerPlanet.com (as well as MyMysteryParty.com) has tons of themes of scavenger hunt parties available for download instantly upon purchase as well as boxed sets with the task list sealed so the host can play along. Scavenger hunts are active parties and are extremely memorable events. They are contagious, as once you attend a scavenger hunt party; you and your guests will be itching to do it again!

There are *about town* photo hunts where the guests divide into teams and travel around town looking for items on their task list. The tasks are written to provide memorable pictures – not just pictures of a statue or a random book in the library, but of the team members posed in a specific and hilarious way with the item they found. These scavenger hunt pictures make for great memory books. There are also *on-foot* neighborhood hunts and building hunts available. Cars will not be necessary with these types of hunts.

With kid's parties, you'll need plenty of chaperones to supervise the hunts, as the kids will be super peppy as it is a competition. Scavenger hunts are one of the most enjoyable parties and are relatively inexpensive as compared to other parties. You can download some of the kits for under $20.00 and invite an unlimited amount of players.

# VII. Halloween Inspired Recipes

At your Halloween party, the menu is part of the Halloween décor. Check out our menu suggestions and prepare spooky food, labeling your offerings with clever yet eerie names on gothic-inspired cards.
**Find picture examples on
http://partyhost411.com/halloweenhandbook**

## SNACKIN' APPETIZERS

### Roasted Pumpkin Seeds
**Ingredients:**
Pumpkin seeds
Salt
*As desired, add other flavors to the seeds such as ground cumin, ground cinnamon, ground ginger, sugar, peanut oil, etc. And after they are roasted (see below) sauté in a skillet about 1-2 minutes.
**Directions:**
Do not wash the seeds from carving, but remove extra pulp from them. Place the seeds in a single layer on a cookie sheet. Add salt to taste and bake at 250F until dry, occasionally flipping until a light golden color.

### Black Cat Eyes
**Ingredients:**
Any cracker (bite-sized)
Peanut butter
Banana (cut into slices)
Raisins
**Directions:**
On each cracker, spread a thin layer of peanut butter. Lay the banana slice on top and then gently place a raisin on top of each banana slice to form the pupil of the eye.

### Ghostly Lollipops
**Ingredients:**
Any wrapped lollipops on a stick
Facial tissue (white)
Rubber bands (small, thin)

# Dr. Bonnie

Black and orange ribbon
Black marker
**Directions:**
Lay the facial tissue flat and place the wrapped lollipop in the center with the stick hanging off the tissue. Wrap the tissue around the lollipop and secure at the 'neck' with a rubber band. Tie a thin black &/or orange ribbon over the rubber band. Draw two ghostly eyes and a mouth if you wish with the black marker.

## Skeleton's Guts Meat & Cheese Platter

**Ingredients:**
Any crackers (bite-sized)
Bite-sized meats (ham, prosciutto, salami, and turkey)
Bite-sized cheeses (Gouda, Swiss, American, cheddar)
A plastic skeleton from any party store.
**Directions:**
Wash the skeleton thoroughly with soap and water where it will touch the food and dry thoroughly. Place the skeleton on your buffet table with the torso section on a large platter. Arrange the meats and cheeses inside the rib cage and serve with crackers.

## Deviled Eyeballs

**Ingredients for 12 servings:**
12 hard boiled eggs
¼ cup of mayo
1 tsp. of Worcestershire sauce
Salt and pepper to taste
Pickled relish to taste
(For eye décor: olive (black or green) and red food coloring, small paintbrush)
**Directions:**
Cut hard boiled eggs in half lengthwise. Remove the yolk and mix the yolk with the ingredients above (besides the olives). Spoon in the mixture into the egg cups and use the olive (either black or green) as the iris of the eye. Using food coloring (red), paint red squiggly lines for the capillaries.

## Scary Spider Eggs

**Ingredients for 12 servings:**
12 hard boiled eggs
½ cup of mayonnaise (olive oil based)

Salt and pepper to taste
1 tsp. white vinegar
Crumbled bacon (not too crunchy)
Whole black olives
**Directions:**
Cut hard boiled eggs in half lengthwise. Remove the yolk and mix the yolk with the ingredients above (besides the olives). Spoon in the mixture into the egg cups and place one whole olive in the center as the spider's body (abdomen). Add a smaller rounded piece of olive as the thorax/head of the spider. Take another olive and slice into halves longwise. Then, slice thin segments and place four curved slices on each side of the olive spider as legs. Note: for a more realistic spider, have the legs coming out of the thorax part of the spider.

## Witch's Dip
**Ingredients for ~ 10 servings:**
1 package of ranch flavored cream cheese (10.5 oz.)
1 package of chopped spinach, thawed (10 oz.)
8 slices of bacon, minced
2-3 drops of green food coloring
Crackers for dipping
**Directions:**
Mix the cream cheese, spinach, bacon and food coloring and place into a serving bowl. Serve with veggies or crackers. Makes ~ 2.5 cups.

## Scary Stuffed Mushrooms
**Ingredients for ~12 servings:**
1/2 cup garlic bread crumbs
1 teaspoon Worcestershire sauce
1 package of large whole mushrooms with the stems removed and diced
1/2 cup of cooked, crumbled sausage
1 egg
2 tablespoons butter
**Directions:**
Cut the stems from the mushrooms and carefully scoop out the tops without breaking them apart and dice the stems.
Place the mushroom caps with the scooped side up on a baking sheet. Combine the remaining ingredients with the diced stems and mix thoroughly.

# Dr. Bonnie

Fill the mushroom caps with the mixture (save a little bit of the breadcrumbs for the top) and sprinkle with breadcrumbs and drizzle melted butter over the top. Cook at 350 degrees until lightly browned (~ 20-30 minutes). *substitute the sausage for diced lobster if desired.

## Mummy Dogs

**Ingredients for 10 servings:**
10 hot dogs or ~ 25 cocktail wieners
Refrigerated crescent roll dough (1 can)
Sliced American cheese
Mustard and ketchup for dipping

**Directions:**
Quarter your cheese slices for the hot dogs or slice in half and quarter for cocktail wieners.
Place a strip of cheese lengthwise on your hotdog. Open the dough and cut into thin strips. Wrap your hotdog (or cocktail wiener) with the dough strips like mummy gauze, leaving space for the 'face' of the mummy. Put on a baking sheet (use cooking spray to prevent sticking) with the cheese side down. Cook per the instructions of the dough, checking to see when it turns a golden brown. Remove and allow cooling. Draw two eyes with mustard on the face and serve with dipping sauces.

## Mummy Jalapeno Poppers

**Ingredients for 10 servings:**
10 jalapeno peppers with the center removed (pulp, seeds) – sliced lengthwise
Refrigerated crescent roll dough (1 can)
8 oz. cream cheese
8 oz. pepper jack cheese
1 finely chopped green onion
Salt, pepper to taste
2 beaten eggs
Black olive

**Directions:**
After slicing your jalapenos, wash them and dry with a paper towel. Mix the cheeses with the onion and salt, pepper and fill the jalapenos with the cheese mixture. Open the dough and cut into thin strips. Wrap your cheese-filled jalapenos with the dough strips like mummy gauze, leaving space for the 'face' of the mummy. Put on a baking sheet (use cooking spray to prevent sticking) with the face side up. Cook per the instructions of the dough, checking to see when it turns a golden

brown. Remove and allow cooling. Using a piping bag (use a plastic food bag and cut the corner), add two circles for the eyes and top with a small piece of black olive on each for the iris/pupil. Or, for bigger eyes, affix a sliced green olive with pimento center with a dab of cream cheese.

## Frankenstein Guacamole
**Ingredients for ~ 12 servings:**
Blue corn tortilla chips
Black olives
Sour Cream
For the guacamole – just mix and serve:
5 avocados, peeled and cubed (remove the pit)
½ cup purple onion, diced
1/6 cup freshly minced cilantro
Salt, pepper to taste
Lime juice to taste (add a bit, taste, etc.)
½ cup diced fresh tomatoes
1 tsp. olive oil mayonnaise (adds creamy texture)
**Directions:**
Prepare your guacamole and place on a platter in a flattened rectangular shape to make the base of your Frankenstein head. With two dollops of sour cream, place the eyes where they should be. With a thinly sliced black olive, place an iris in the middle of each eye. If you want –use a green olive and make the iris and put a tiny circle of a black olive as the pupil in the center.
Cut a few black olives lengthwise into strips and make stitches and put one on the forehead and another by the chin. Add two black olives for the bolts of the neck, and another slice of an end of an olive for the nose. Create a mouth for your monster face with the olive strips. Serve with warmed blue corn
tortilla chips.

## Spooktacular 7 Layer Dip
**Ingredients for ~ 10 servings:**
16 oz. refried beans
1 ¼ ounces of taco seasoning mix (1 packet)
1 cup sour cream (divided)
1 cup salsa of your choice – drained if too runny
1 cup shredded cheddar cheese
2 diced Roma tomatoes (or 1 beefsteak diced tomato)

# Dr. Bonnie

¼ cup green onion
3 ounces of black olives, drained and sliced
1 cup guacamole
Chips for dipping

**Directions:**
Mix the taco seasoning and refried beans, spreading it onto a platter of your choice (11-inch plate preferred). Carefully spread ½ the sour cream onto the bean mixture. Next, add the salsa carefully over the sour cream – don't mix it! Next, guacamole – this may take patience, but add dollops of guacamole over the salsa and very carefully flatten them until they touch. Next is the grated cheese, but place it around the guacamole on the edges, not over it. Top the cheese with olives, diced tomatoes, and sliced green onions. Take the remaining sour cream and place in a sandwich bag, snipping the corner. Squeeze the sour cream in a spider web pattern over the guacamole in the center. Serve with chips.

## Mini Ghost Pizza Bites

**Ingredients for ~10-12 pieces:**
1 can refrigerated pizza dough
Olive oil
Pizza sauce (jar)
Sliced mozzarella cheese
Black olive

**Directions:**
Cut the pizza dough into small circles about the size of your palm. Using a cutting board and a knife, cut your sliced mozzarella into ghost shapes about the size of your pizza dough and set aside. Brush the dough on the bottom side with olive oil and place on nonstick cooking tray. Add the pizza sauce, place the ghostly cheese on top and make a face by cutting the olive into eyes and a mouth. Bake according to the instructions on the pizza dough, keeping an eye on it for when the dough becomes golden brown.

## Rice Jack O'Lanterns

**Ingredients for about 6-8 pieces:**
1.5 cups short grain rice
2 cups of carrot juice
1 cup water
½ teaspoon salt
¼ teaspoon pepper

185

½ cup yellow onion, diced finely
½ cup carrot, diced finely
2 tsp. butter
Bell pepper (green for the stem)
Black olive

**Directions:**

Sauté the onions and carrots in the butter until soft. Boil the rice, carrot juice, sautéed onions, and seasoning until all liquid is absorbed (view the rice package instructions for cooking time). Allow cooling to room temp. To make the Jack O'Lanterns, roll the rice mix into a ball, about the size of a table tennis ball, pressing firmly, so it sticks together. Cut the black olives and use to make the face and with a small rectangle of a bell pepper, make a stem and insert into the top.

## Tiny Bat Cheese Balls

**Ingredients for 14-16 bats:**

16 oz. of cream cheese (softened)
2.5 cups cheddar cheese
Green onion, minced
2 tbsp. port wine
½ cup chopped pecans
¼ cup maple-flavored pancake syrup
Flax seed
Blue corn tortilla chips

**Directions:**

Mix the cheeses, green onion, port wine, syrup until homogenized. Divide into small balls – about the size of a table tennis ball or smaller. Roll each on a pecan – flax seed mixture until covered. Slice green olives with pimentos inside to create the eyes and use blue corn tortilla chips – inserted into the sides – to create the wings of the bat. Serve with extra blue corn tortilla chips &/or crackers.

## Mousy Meatballs

**Ingredients for ~12-16 meatballs:**

1 ½ lb. ground beef or ground turkey
2/3 cup of garlic flavored bread crumbs
1/3 cup minced sweet yellow onion
1 ½ tsp. salt
¼ tsp. ginger
¼ cup half and half
1 egg

# Dr. Bonnie

1 tsp. shortening
2 tsp. cornstarch
½ cup brown sugar, packed
1 can pineapple tidbits (drained) (keep syrup)
1/3 cup balsamic vinegar
1 tsp. soy sauce
1/3 cup diced very finely green and sweet red peppers
Lo Mein noodles for tails

**Directions:**

Mix beef (or turkey), crumbs, onion, egg, salt, ginger and milk. Shape into mouse shaped meatballs (small head, larger body), place the eyes (red pieces of sweet pepper) into the heads and sear the outside of the meatballs in the shortening that is heated to medium in a saucepan. Remove the meatballs and place in a baking dish and cook on 350 for 20 minutes.

Sauce: mix the oil from the skillet with red and green peppers, cornstarch, sugar, pineapple syrup, balsamic vinegar and soy sauce and stir thoroughly.

When it's time, remove the meatballs from the oven and place the meatballs in a crockpot, pouring the sauce over the top and cooking on low until done. Test carefully with a meat thermometer.

Optional for mouse tails: cook a few lo Mein noodles separately per the instructions on the package. Once you remove the mice meatballs from the crockpot, allow cooling before you manipulate them to put in the tails. Using a toothpick, insert a ~ 1-2 inch tail into each mouse, removing the toothpick when the tail is inserted.

## FIRST COURSE

### Fingernail & Brain Salad

**Ingredients for ~4 salads:**
1 pound mixed salad greens
1/2 cup sliced almonds
1/2 red onion, thinly sliced
4 ounces crumbled blue cheese
1 cup raspberry vinaigrette dressing
Salt and pepper to taste.

**Directions:**

Mix the ingredients together and drizzle the dressing on top.

187

### Chamber of Screams Salad

**Ingredients for ~4 salads:**

1 pound mixed salad greens
1/2 cup sliced almonds
1/2 red onion, thinly sliced
4 ounces crumbled blue cheese
1 sliced cucumber. If you are skilled, cut out pumpkin faces in your cucumber slices
1 cup raspberry vinaigrette dressing
Salt and pepper to taste.

**Directions:**

Mix the ingredients together and drizzle the dressing on top.

### Pumpkin Soup

**Ingredients for ~ 10 servings:**

4 cups pumpkin puree
6 cups chicken stock
1 ½ tsp. Salt
1 tsp. Chopped parsley (fresh) (keep sprigs for garnish)
1 cup chopped onion
¼ cup minced shallots
½ tsp. Chopped thyme (fresh)
1 clove of minced garlic
½ cup of heavy whipping cream
Pepper to taste

**Directions:**

Heat stock, salt & pepper, pumpkin, thyme, garlic and shallots. Bring to a boil, reduce heat to low and simmer for 30 minutes uncovered. Puree the soup in small batches (3/4 cup at a time) using a blender or food processor. Return the soup to the pan and bring to a boil again. Reduce heat to low and simmer for another 30 minutes (uncovered). Stir in the whipping cream, stir thoroughly and then pour into soup bowls and garnish with a sprig of fresh parsley.

## ENTREES & SIDE DISHES

### Frankenstein's Face BOO-Ritos

**Ingredients for 10 servings:**

10 spinach tortillas
5 cups Spanish rice (you can make from a box/package)

# Dr. Bonnie

3 cups cubed, cooked chicken
Diced sweet yellow onion
1 tbsp. butter
1 can diced tomatoes
Sour cream
Blue corn tortilla chips
Red pepper
Cubed cheese
Fajita chicken mixed spice
Salt, pepper to taste
Shredded mild cheddar cheese
Black olives
**Directions:**
Prepare your rice according to the package. Heat your spinach tortillas according to the package. Season your chicken with the chicken fajita seasoning, salt, and pepper. Sauté the onion in butter until softened. Drain your diced tomatoes and season. Lay the heated tortilla flat and spoon in rice, chicken, onions, cheddar cheese, and tomatoes. Roll the burrito and place on a platter. Using the remainder of the ingredients, create fun Frankenstein faces on the top side of each boo-rito. Be creative! Serve with sour cream and guacamole on the side.

## Tasty Eyeball Tacos
**Ingredients for 12 servings:**
12 hard taco shells
1 lb. ground meat of your choice (turkey, pork, beef)
Taco seasoning mix (1 package)
½ cup chopped yellow onions
1 large beefsteak tomato, chopped into small cubes
1 bag of pre-washed shredded lettuce
Shredded cheddar cheese 1 – 2 cups
1 can of sliced black olives
1 cup of sour cream in a piping bag
Red food coloring (optional)
**Directions:**
Prepare the shells according to the package. Brown the meat and onions, add the taco seasoning and set aside. When the shells are heated, add the meat, lettuce, tomato, and cheese. Using the piping bag, place two dollops of sour cream on top of the taco contents as the whites of the eyeballs. Place a sliced black olive on top of the sour cream. If you have a great attention to detail, grab some red food

coloring and using a toothpick, make streaks in the sour cream to look like capillaries.

## Stuffed Bloody Bell Peppers

**Ingredients for 6 servings:**
6 bell peppers (red)
1 lb. Of ground beef
1 egg
½ cup of garlic bread crumbs
1 small yellow onion, minced
1 small tomato, diced
2 minced cloves of fresh garlic
½ cup ketchup
3 tablespoons Worcestershire sauce
2 tablespoons of mayonnaise
Salt and pepper to taste
½ teaspoon of basil
½ teaspoon of thyme

**Directions:**
Preheat oven to 350 degrees f (175 degrees c). Grease an 8*8 baking dish. Mix the ingredients in a mixing bowl (set the bell peppers aside). Clean the bell peppers. Slice off the tops and remove the core/seeds. Stuff the insides of the peppers with the mixture and place into the baking sheet. Bake until done, about 1 hour. Drip ketchup along the sides for a 'bloody' effect.

## Bloody Rat Surprise

**Ingredients for ~6-8 servings:**
1 lb. ground beef (or turkey)
½ chopped yellow onion
2 beaten eggs
¾ cup dry garlic-flavored bread crumbs
¼ cup panko crumbs
¾ cup ketchup
1 tsp. of dried mustard
1 tsp. of paprika
½ tsp. salt
¾ tsp. dried thyme
¾ tsp. basil
½ tsp. ground pepper
1 tsp. garlic powder
1 tsp. onion powder

# Dr. Bonnie

1 cup white sugar
1 tbsp. butter
3 10 oz. cans of tomato sauce
1 tbsp. Worcestershire sauce
1 cup cubed cheddar cheese (mild)
1 oz. uncooked spaghetti cut into four pieces each
½ carrot sliced into 1/8 inch sections
1 tablespoon frozen peas

**Directions:**

Preheat oven to 350 degrees f (175 degrees c). In a mixing bowl, combine meat, onion, ketchup egg, bread crumbs, seasoning and use a mashed potato masher to mix thoroughly (use your hands if you can stand it). Take about 1/3 cup of the meat mix and mold it around a cheese cube, shaping it into the shape of a rat's body with a pointy nose and rounded backside. Place your rats into a shallow baking dish and insert a spaghetti tail into each of them on the backsides and you can take another piece, break it into 4 smaller pieces and insert to make whiskers in the snout. Insert deep enough - so they don't slip out after baking.

'Bloody' sauce: mix the tomato sauce, sugar and Worcestershire sauce with a dash of salt and pepper to taste. Pour the sauce over the rats and cover with foil. Bake for ~ 45 minutes in the preheated oven. Uncover and cook for another 20-30 minutes, occasionally glazing the rats with the sauce. Sauté the frozen peas and sliced carrots in a small pan for a few minutes to soften them.

When the rats are finished baking, carefully transfer them to their serving platter (don't mess up your tails!) Gently press two peas for eyes and two carrot slices for the ears into each rat. Spoon some of the bloody sauce around them and serve!

## Vampire Proof Roasted Garlic Chicken

**Ingredients for ~ 6 servings:**

3 tbs. pure olive oil
2 tbs. lime juice
2 tsp. dried thyme
½ tsp. fresh rosemary leaves, minced
½ tsp. fresh sage leaves, minced
½ tsp. fresh black pepper
2 4lb. chickens
8 heads of garlic – thinly sliced
Rosemary sprigs (cleaned)
Salt to taste

**Directions:**

Mix the olive oil, lime juice and herbs in a small bowl. Rinse chickens thoroughly and pat to dry. Rub the olive oil herb mixture on the chickens and place breast side up at least 1 inch away from each other on a roasting pan. Dip the garlic slices in the oil mixture and place all over the chicken.

Roast in a 425-degree oven until done (~ 1.5 hr.). If garlic becomes too brown, remove and set aside in the refrigerator for a while and put back on the last few minutes of cooking. Check with a meat thermometer to determine if the meat is done and juices should run clear and meat should be cooked thoroughly. Put the chickens on a platter and decorate with garlic cloves and rosemary sprigs around the platter. Carve the chickens to serve the guests and add salt/pepper to taste.

## Frankenstein's Stuffed Chicken

**Ingredients for 4 servings:**

2 cups of cooked white rice
1/2 cup chopped mushrooms
1 can cream of mushroom soup
~3/4 stick of butter
1/2 cup chopped green onion
1 teaspoon Worcestershire sauce
Salt and pepper to taste
4 tenderized chicken breast fillets
1 cup garlic flavored bread crumbs

**Directions:**

Mix the white rice, cream of mushroom soup, Worcestershire sauce, sautéed onions and mushrooms, 1/4 stick of butter, salt, pepper, and 1/4 cup of garlic bread crumbs. Tenderize the chicken fillets with a meat tenderizer. At the edge of one end of the chicken fillet, place about 1/2 cup of the rice mixture and roll the chicken fillet around the rice. Place the chicken fillet into a baking pan with the free edge facing down. Microwave the remaining butter for 10 seconds and drizzle over the chicken breast. Lightly sprinkle the garlic flavored bread crumbs over the buttered breast. Cook at 375F until done (~ 40 minutes). Check with a meat thermometer to determine if the meat is done.

# Dr. Bonnie

## Cheesy Enchanted Forest Casserole

**Ingredients for ~8-10 servings:**
2 bags of frozen broccoli
1 tube of Kraft garlic cheese
½ cup jalapeno jack cheese
2 cans of Campbell's cream of mushroom soup
1 can of Campbell's cream of celery soups
½ diced onion
½ stick of butter
Salt and pepper to taste

**Directions:**
Heat the oven to 350F. Thaw out the frozen broccoli and drain the water. Melt the cheeses in a saucepan and add the creamed soups. In a separate pan, sauté the onions in the butter until golden brown. Add the browned onions to the cheese mixture. Pour the cheese mixture over the broccoli in a 9 x 12 baking dish. Sprinkle garlic bread crumbs over the top of the casserole, cover and bake for 1 hour and 15 minutes or until browned and bubbling. Allow cooling on the counter for at least 10 minutes before serving.

# DESSERT & SWEET TREATS

## Brainy Fruit Salad

**Ingredients for 6 servings:**
Blueberry gelatin mix – 1 package (6 oz.)
Small curd cottage cheese (16 oz. carton)
¾ cup frozen blueberries (thawed)
Blue food coloring
Whipped topping

**Directions:**
Prepare the gelatin according to the package instructions and chill until firm. Add 2-3 drops of the blue food coloring to the cottage cheese to turn it a brainy-gray color. Mix the blueberries into this cheese mix. In a clear 6-8 oz. cup, add the gelatin, layer with the cottage cheese/blueberry mix. Add a small layer of whipped topping, another layer of gelatin. Top with the brainy cottage cheese/blueberries.

## Zombie Toes

**Ingredients for 17 servings (per package of cookies):**
1 package of Nutter Butter cookies

Green frosting (white frosting with bright green food coloring)
Black/dark purple gumdrops (or black frosting)
**Directions:**
Cover the Nutter Butter cookies with green frosting and set on parchment paper and allow the frosting to dry out a bit, so it isn't as sticky. Slice the gumdrop and place on one end as a toenail.

## Dead Lady Fingers
**Ingredients for ~15 servings:**
Red food coloring (1 container)
1 2/3 cups all-purpose flour
2 eggs
½ cup butter (softened to room temp)
¼ tsp. vanilla extract
¼ tsp. almond extract
½ cup confectioner's sugar
6 tbsp. granulated sugar
25-30 blanched almonds, sliced into thin fingernail shapes
Red gel frosting (1 tube)
1 pinch of salt
**Directions:**
Turn the oven to 350F to preheat. Line the baking sheets with parchment paper and set aside. Soak the almonds in the food coloring in a small mixing bowl and set aside.
Separate the egg and set aside the white. Mix the yolk, other egg, and vanilla.
In another bowl, mix butter, sugar and salt until thoroughly combined. Then, add the egg mixture and beat until smooth. Add the flour slowly and mix thoroughly. Using plastic wrap, wrap the dough and put into refrigerator until chilled, about 30-45 minutes.
Remove enough of the dough to make a life-sized finger and roll with your hands to shape it. They should be about 3-4 inches long. Pinch the dough to form the two knuckles and using a knife, score the dough (look at your fingers for a reference on where to score the dough.) Be careful not to score the dough to large, as when it cooks, it will enlarge. Arrange your fingers on the baking sheet in rows and lightly brush with egg white. Place the almond slice at the tip of each finger, moving it securely into the dough. Bake until browned, about 12 minutes and cool completely. For an added creep-factor, line the edge of the fingernail with the red gel frosting for a bloody finger effect.

# Dr. Bonnie

*To make witch fingers, add some green food coloring to the dough before chilling/baking.

## Witchy Pumpkin Pie

**Ingredients for 8 servings:**
1 1/2 cups cooked, strained pumpkin (or canned)
2/3 cup sugar
1/4 cup brown sugar
1 1/2 cups evaporated skim milk
3 eggs
3/4 teaspoon cinnamon
1/8 teaspoon ground cloves
1/4 teaspoon ginger
1 teaspoon grated orange peel
1/4 teaspoon nutmeg
1/4 teaspoon salt
1 unbaked pie shell

**Directions:**
Preheat oven to 425 degrees f. Mix pumpkin, sugar(s), orange peel and spices in a large mixing bowl. Add evaporated milk, eggs and mix thoroughly. Pour the pumpkin filling into the pie shell evenly and bake for fifteen minutes. Reduce heat to 350 degrees and bake for 45 minutes more, covering the pie crust with loose aluminum foil if it gets too brown.

## Gross Gelatin Worms

**Ingredients for 8-10 servings:**
1 package raspberry, strawberry &/or grape gelatin mix (6 oz.)
3 envelopes unflavored gelatin (1/4 oz.)
3 cups boiling water
100 flexi-straws
A container the length of the straws (large glass)
¾ cup whipping cream
Green food coloring

**Directions:**
Combine the gelatin in a mixing bowl and add boiling water, stirring until completely dissolved. Chill for about 20 minutes until the mixture is lukewarm. Place the straws in the container. Blend the remaining ingredients and pour the mixture into the straws, ensuring the mix gets to the bottom of each straw.
Chill in the refrigerator for at least 10 hours or until firm – up to a couple of days.

# The Halloween Party Host Handbook

When ready, remove the straws from the container and pull the straws apart. Run hot tap water over the straw for a couple of seconds over each straw and using your little finger or another kitchen tool to push the worms through, remove each worm from the straws and place on waxed paper. Cover and chill until ready to serve. The worms will hold at room temp for about two hours. Serve with a dirt mixture of crushed chocolate cookies and graham crackers on top of chocolate pudding.

## Dirty Q-tips

**Ingredients:**
An empty Q-tip box
Lollipop stick
Marshmallows
Caramel, peanut butter (check for allergies)
**Directions:**
This is super easy but will get tons of laughs and gross-outs. Pierce a marshmallow with the lollipop straw and dip the top end of the marshmallow in caramel for the 'ear wax.' As an alternative, use peanut butter for the ear wax (but note the food allergies of your guests). Then, using the Q-tip box as a display – make your guests queasy with this simple treat.

## Dirt Cups

**Ingredients:**
Chocolate pudding (check servings on your package)
Oreos without the white center
Candy pumpkins
Gummy worms
**Directions:**
In clear cups, add layers of chocolate pudding and crushed up Oreos and top with the candy pumpkins (the pumpkin patch) and insert a gummy worm coming out of the dirt.

## Bloody Band-Aids

**Ingredients:**
Vanilla Sugar Wafers
Strawberry or Raspberry jams
White frosting/icing
**Directions:**

# Dr. Bonnie

On each wafer, create a square in the center of each on the top side for the gauze pad of the Band-Aid and top the icing with a dollop of jam for the blood. Serve on a tray with a box of Band-Aids for a gross yet effective effect.

## Wicked Chocolate Witch Hats
**Ingredients for 20 hats:**
20 Hershey chocolate kisses (unwrapped)
20 fudge-striped cookies (shortbread)
Orange frosting in a piping bag (or purple, green)
**Directions:**
With the chocolate side up and striped side down, affix a chocolate kiss in the center of each cookie using the frosting as the adhesive. The frosting will become the band of the hat and add a festive punch of color.

## Perfect Pumpkin Dip
**Ingredients for 10-12 servings:**
Medium sized pumpkin, cleaned out into a bowl for presenting the dip.
¾ cup cream cheese
¼ cup brown sugar
¾ cup pumpkin (from a can)
2 teaspoons maple syrup
1 tablespoon cinnamon
1 teaspoon pumpkin pie spice
**Directions:**
Mix all ingredients thoroughly and place inside of the pumpkin and serve with apple slices &/or gingerbread cookies.

## Wicked Witch Fingers
**Ingredients for ~15 servings:**
1 cup of salted butter
1 cup of powdered sugar
1 large egg
1 tsp. salt
¾ cup almonds – sliced long-ways, blanched
1 tsp. vanilla extract
2 2/3 cups flour
1/8 tsp. baking powder
1 tube of red icing

**Directions:**
(Makes ~4.5 dozen). Preheat oven to 320F. Mix the butter, egg, sugar, vanilla extract thoroughly. Add the flour, soda, and salt and beat until mixed thoroughly. In a covered bowl, place in the refrigerator for 45 minutes. With chilled dough, form into finger-shaped forms and place on a greased cookie sheet. With a butter knife, make finger markings and then press the almond sliver into the dough as the fingernail. Bake in preheated oven for 15-20 minutes until a golden color. Let cool for 10 minutes. Add the red icing as blood in various places for a fun effect.

## Caramel Apples

**Ingredients for 6 servings:**
1 (14 oz.) package of individually wrapped caramels
6 golden delicious apples
1 tbsp. water
6 wooden Popsicle sticks (sterile)
1 sheet of wax paper

**Directions:**
Wash and dry the apples completely. Remove the stems and push the wooden sticks into the hole where the stem was located until about 1/2 of the stick is in the apple.
Spray the wax paper with non-stick cooking spray. In a medium saucepan, heat up the caramels, stirring until thoroughly melted. Dip the apples in the hot caramel sauce (be careful not to get any on your hands). Coat each apple completely and place on wax paper. Store the apples in the refrigerator.
Alternative – mini caramel apples: using a melon baller, scoop out mini apples from a large apple and insert a lollipop stick. Dip in melted caramel and then dust on some candy sprinkles.

## Candy Apples

**Ingredients for 6 servings:**
2 ¼ cups of sugar
2 ¼ cups of corn syrup
1 cup water
½ tsp. vanilla extract
¼ tsp. pumpkin pie spice
½ tsp. red food coloring

# Dr. Bonnie

6 golden delicious apples (de-waxed by scrubbing with lime juice and baking soda, washed and dipped in boiling water for ~ 10 seconds)
1 sheet of wax paper
**Directions:**
Wash and dry the apples completely. Remove the stems and push the wooden sticks into the hole where the stem was located until about 1/2 of the stick is in the apple.
Spray the wax paper with non-stick cooking spray. In a medium saucepan, heat up the sugar, corn syrup, food coloring, water and heat up to 300 F (check with a candy thermometer). Remove the mix from the heat source and using thermal gloves for protection, dip the apples in the hot mixture (be careful). Coat each apple completely and place on wax paper. Store the apples in the refrigerator. Set coated apples on a greased wax paper and allow reaching room temperature before eating.

## Poison (not really) Apples

**Ingredients for 6 servings:**
Collect some small branches/twigs (washed and one end sharped to a point)
6 apples (de-waxed by scrubbing with lime juice and baking soda, washed and dipped in boiling water for ~ 10 seconds)
2 ¼ cups of sugar
2 ¼ cups of corn syrup
1 cup water
Black food coloring
Blue food coloring
**Directions:**
Wash and dry the apples completely. Remove the stems and push the branches into the hole where the stem was located until about 1/2 of the stick is in the apple.
Spray the wax paper with non-stick cooking spray. Make a black batch and a blue batch to mix it up a bit. In a medium saucepan, heat up the sugar, corn syrup, food coloring, water and heat up to 300F (check with a candy thermometer). Remove the mix from the heat source and using thermal gloves for protection, dip the apples in the hot mixture (be careful). Coat each apple completely and place on wax paper. Store the apples in the refrigerator. Set coated apples on a greased wax paper and allow reaching room temperature before eating.

## Mummified Candy Apples

**Ingredients for 8 servings:**
8 small apples (de-waxed by scrubbing with lime juice and baking soda, washed and dipped in boiling water for ~ 10 seconds)
8 Popsicle sticks
2.5 cups white candy melts (14 oz.)
Black tube icing/frosting

**Directions:** wash and dry the apples completely. Remove the stems and push the wooden sticks into the hole where the stem was located until about 1/2 of the stick is in the apple.

Spray the wax paper with non-stick cooking spray. In a microwave, melt the candy melts and stir until smooth. Dip each apple in the white candy, ensuring that the apple is coated (reheat the candy melt in between apples and stir). Draw two black eyes on each candy apple with the black frosting. If you have a white frosting, add a white first and then tip with a black dot. When the apples are coated and placed on the wax paper, take the remaining white candy melt and drizzle on the apples to where it appears as gauze.

## Breakable Bone Treats

**Ingredients for 8-10 servings:**
4 large egg whites
1/3 tsp. cream of tartar
1/8 tsp. salt
2/3 sugar
½ tsp. vanilla

**Directions:**
Preheat the oven to 210F and line a cookie sheet with parchment. Beat the egg whites, tartar, and salt at medium speed until light and very fluffy. Gradually add the sugar while beating on medium speed and then add the vanilla. Using a piping tip, add the fluffy mix into a piping bag and create tiny finger-sized bone-shaped snacks on the cookie sheet. Bake 1 hour until done. Dry in the oven (after turning the oven off) for another hour and fifteen minutes. Makes ~ 5 -5.5 dozen. Store in an airtight container.

## Graveyard Dirt Cups

**Ingredients:**
2 cups of milk
1 package of instant chocolate pudding (check serving size)
4 cups of whipped topping

16 oz. Oreo cookies
12 gummy worms
**Directions:**
Follow the instructions on the package of instant pudding. Crush Oreos and add ½ to the pudding mix with the whipped topping and stir thoroughly. Using 8 oz. cups, add a small layer of crushed Oreos to the bottom of the cup, layer with the chocolate pudding mix and then top with crushed Oreos. Add the gummy worm to the top.

## Halloween Carrot Cake
**Ingredients for over 25 servings:**
6 cups of grated carrots
2 teaspoons of vanilla extract
1 cup of brown sugar
1 cup of raisins
4 large eggs
1 1/2 cups of white sugar
1 cup smart balance vegetable oil
1 cup of crushed pineapple (drained)
3 cups of all-purpose flour
1 1/2 teaspoons of baking soda
1 teaspoon of salt
3 ½ teaspoons of ground cinnamon
1 cup of evenly chopped walnuts
**Directions:**
Preheat oven to 350 degrees f (175 degrees c). In a mixing bowl, mix the grated carrots and brown sugar. Set aside for 1 hour. Prepare two 10 inch cake pans for baking (grease/flour). Stir the raisins into the carrot and brown sugar mixture. In a large bowl, beat eggs until they are light and fluffy. Fold in the white sugar, vegetable oil and vanilla extract. Mix for a minute before adding the crushed pineapple. Mix the dry ingredients: flour, baking soda, salt, and cinnamon before stirring into the mixture. Finally, add the chopped walnuts and the carrot mixture. Pour the batter evenly into the baking pans.
Bake for 45 to 50 minutes in the preheated oven. Test the cake for doneness before removing. Cool the pans for 25 min before removing from pan. When the layers have cooled, frost the cake with a cream cheese frosting.

# The Halloween Party Host Handbook

## Candy Corn Ice Cream Treats
**Ingredients for 8 servings:**
1-quart vanilla ice cream (any brand)
Orange and yellow food coloring
Clear plastic or glass cups
Whipped cream
Sprinkles
**Directions:**
Take the ice cream out of the freezer and allow softening for 20-30 minutes. Spoon about 1/3 of the ice cream in a medium bowl, adding orange food coloring to color a bright orange (or as desired). In another bowl, repeat the process with the yellow food coloring. Stir the remaining ice cream until it is smooth and creamy. Spoon the yellow ice cream into the bottom of the glass, flattening and avoiding bubbles. You may wish to wipe the glass from any residue on the sides. Then, add the orange and top with the white. Add whipped cream and sprinkles (if you wish) on top. Serve with a spoon.

## Scary Lemon Eyeballs
**Ingredients for ~8 servings:**
3 oz. (small box) lemon-flavored gelatin
1 cup hot water
½ cup mini marshmallows
1 cup pineapple juice
8 oz. Cream cheese
**Directions:**
Dissolve gelatin in the hot water in a double boiler. Add marshmallows and stir thoroughly until melted. Once melted, remove from heat and add the juice and cheese and mix thoroughly. Cover and place into the refrigerator for 5 minutes. Spray with non-stick cooking spray - either a candy mold (truffles) or round ice cube tray or any other rounded mold and pour the mixture into each mold and place in the refrigerator. *as an alternative, chill in a large mixing bowl and use a melon baller to make eyeball shapes once it thickens. To make the eyeball décor, use food coloring and a paintbrush. Draw the iris (colored portion), pupil (black circle in the center), and wicked capillaries as you wish. Be creative! Makes about 8 dozen eyeballs.

## Chocolate'y Tarantulas
**Ingredients for 25-32 tarantulas (depending upon size):**
2 cups of semisweet chocolate chips (baking chips)

# Dr. Bonnie

Sprinkles of any kind for eyes
**Directions:**
Melt the chips in the top of a double boiler. Let the chocolate mix stand over the water until cooled for about 10 minutes – 15 minutes as you do not want the chocolate too liquid. Place wax paper on a cookie sheet. Pour chocolate mix into a piping bag with a ¼ inch piping tip. Squeeze chocolate onto wax paper in the shape of spiders. Allow cooling further and then peel off of the wax paper and store in an airtight container in the refrigerator. Can add sprinkles as the eyes, but add before cooling.

## Halloween Rock Candy
**Ingredients for a variable amount of servings depending upon size:**
2 cups of granulated sugar
Orange food coloring (1-2 drops)
1 cup water
Heavy string (sterile)
**Directions:**
In a medium saucepan, heat up the water and add sugar until you see that no more sugar can dissolve in the water (you'll see sugar on the bottom of the pan). Remove the pot from the stove, add the drops of food coloring and stir. Pour the liquid into a clean glass jar and tie one piece of the heavy string around a pencil and dip into the water mixture. Crystals will start to form and within 6 hours, you'll see them coming up the string! Every 24 hours, remove the jar, heat it up and then re-set this apparatus as you did before and more and more crystals will grow!

## Batty Sugar Cookies
**Ingredients for 48 servings:**
1 cup softened butter
1 tsp. baking soda
½ tsp. baking powder
1 ½ cups granulated sugar
1 large egg
½ tsp. salt
1 tsp. vanilla
2 ¾ cups of flour
Black squeeze frosting (or another color for other shapes)
**Directions:**
Preheat the oven at 375f. Mix the ingredients together in a mixing bowl and chill in the refrigerator for at least 1 hour. Roll out the dough until

¼ inch thick and by either using a cookie cutter or with a butter knife, cut out bat shapes (pumpkins, witch fingers, etc.) And place on a greased cookie sheet. Cook for 10 minutes or until a light golden brown. Frost with the black frosting (or orange if you prefer to make pumpkins).

## Coffin Cake

**Ingredients for 25+ servings:**

12 tablespoons (1 ½ sticks) unsalted butter, softened
1 ½ cups sugar
2 cups all-purpose flour
2 teaspoons baking powder
1/4 teaspoon salt
6 large egg whites (3/4 cup)
3/4 cup milk
2 teaspoons vanilla extract
Chocolate frosting. Black squeeze frosting for the lining and orange squeeze frosting for any messages (e.g. Welcome to the Witch's Coven, Happy Birthday ___, Happy Halloween, etc.).

**Directions:**

Set rack at the middle level in the oven and preheat to 350 degrees. Butter the bottom of two 9-inch round or one 13 by 9 by 2-inch pan and line with flour. In a large bowl, beat butter and sugar for about 5 minutes, until light and fluffy. Stir together flour, baking powder, and salt. Set aside. Combine egg whites, milk, and vanilla extract. Add 1/3 of the flour mixture to the butter mixture then add half the milk mixture. Continue to alternate beginning and ending with flour mixture. Scrape the bowl and beater often.

Pour the batter into prepared rectangular pan(s) and smooth top with a metal spatula. Bake cake(s) about 25 to 30 minutes, or until a toothpick inserted in the center emerges clean.

Cool in pan on a rack for 5 minutes, then turn out onto a rack, remove paper and let cool completely. Put into the freezer for about 20-30 minutes, remove and then cut the rectangle in the shape of a coffin. Cover the cake with the chocolate frosting; line the coffin with the black squeeze frosting and then write a festive *Happy Halloween* (or other) message on the top of the cake.

## Candy Corn Pudding Parfaits

**Ingredients for 6 servings:**

10 Hershey's Kisses brand candy corn flavored candies
1 package (6-serving size) vanilla flavored cook and serve pudding

# Dr. Bonnie

3 cups milk
1/2 cup whipped cream topping
Additional candy corn candies (or Hershey's brand candy corn-flavored candies) for garnish on top

**Directions:**
Stir together pudding mix and milk in medium saucepan. Cook per the directions on the box and then divide the cooked pudding into 3 groups: ½ cup and 1 cup is separately refrigerated. The remainder is left in the pan. After the refrigerated pudding has cooled, evenly divide the 1 cup of pudding among 4 to 6 clear parfait glasses. Put these back into the refrigerator and cover loosely with plastic wrap.
To the remaining pudding in the pan, add the 10 candy corn flavored candies and stir until melted. The pudding should turn a nice orange color. Once it is uniform, remove from the heat and allow cooling. Once cooled, layer the parfait by adding a layer of the orange pudding. Stir the 1/2 cup of refrigerated pudding with whipped topping. Evenly layer onto the orange layer in serving dishes. Cover; refrigerate until ready to serve. Garnish with additional whipped topping and candy piece, if desired. 4 to 6 servings.

# COCKTAILS

## The Spectral

**Ingredients for 3 cocktails:**
4 oz. hypnotiq® liqueur
2 oz. Malibu® coconut rum
4 oz. pineapple juice

**Directions:**
Combine all ingredients over ice in a cocktail shaker and shake well and strain into a martini or cocktail glass and serve.

## The Coffin Nail

**Ingredients for 1 cocktail:**
1/2 shot Godiva liquor
1/2 shot bailey's Irish cream liquor
Fill the coffee mug with 1/2 coffee and 1/2 milk to taste
Top with whipped cream

**Directions:**
Mix the liquors together in a shaker and strain into a coffee mug. Fill the mug with coffee and milk to taste and top with whipped cream.

# The Halloween Party Host Handbook

## The Ghostbuster Slime Attack
**Ingredients for 3-4 cocktails:**
¼ cup light corn syrup
Green food coloring
1 oz. vodka
1 oz. peach schnapps
1 oz. sour apple schnapps
1 oz. coconut rum
1 oz. sweet and sour mix
10 oz. lemon/lime soda
**Directions:**
Frost your glasses and when ready to serve, make your slime by adding green food coloring to the corn syrup – drop by drop until you get the right color. Dip the rim of the frosted glass into the slime and turn right side up, allowing the slime to ooze on the side of the glass. Mix the liquors together in a shaker to chill them and then add soda and stir. Fill the glass with your delicious fruity mix and serve.

## Get That Ghoul A Breath Mint!
**Ingredients for 1 cocktail:**
1.5 oz. Bacardi Silver
Club soda
Lime juice
12 mint leaves
1.5 oz. sugar syrup (sugar dissolved in water)
Ice
**Directions:**
Add Bacardi silver over ice in a highball glass and nearly fill the glass with club soda
Add 1 oz. Lime juice and drop in a wedge of lime and 12 mint leaves (fresh)
Add 1.5 oz. of sugar syrup (which is dissolved sugar water) and mix before serving.

## Bloody Syringes
**Ingredients for 4-5 cocktails:**
4 oz. vodka (any brand)
2 oz. licor43
3 oz. raspberry syrup
½ cup fresh raspberries

# Dr. Bonnie

2 oz. orange juice
I med sized orange
Plastic syringes (available at any party supply store)
6 oz. club soda

**Directions:**
To make the raspberry syrup (or purchase it premade) puree the raspberries and press through a fine-mesh strainer, discarding the thick solids. Take the raspberry liquid and heat in a saucepan on medium heat, adding ¼ cup of sugar. Stir until mixed thoroughly and heat until it darkens to a nice burgundy blood color. Fill each syringe with this delicious mix and set aside.

In a shaker with ice, add the alcohols and shake for about 30 seconds. Then, add the OJ and club soda and stir (don't shake the club soda or you'll lose your bubbles). Pour into glasses with ice and insert your 'bloody' syringe into each glass. Garnish with an orange wedge.

## Black Magic Screwdriver

**Ingredients for 1 cocktail:**
½ cup orange juice
1.5 oz. black vodka
½ oz. triple sec
Orange for garnish
Ice

**Directions:**
Using an iced cocktail shaker, add the orange juice and triple sec, shake until chilled, straining into a glass. Pour the black vodka over the back of a spoon – very slowly – so it sets on top of the orange juice/triple sec. If you pour it straight, it will mix. You don't want that – you want the black vodka to sit in a layer on top.

Dip the orange wedge into the black vodka – very carefully – and use as a garnish.

## Bloody Mary

**Ingredients for 1 cocktail:**
1.5 oz. vodka (any brand)
.5 oz. lime juice
3 oz. Tomato juice or v8 juice
1 dash of salt
1 dash of Tabasco sauce
1 dash of Worcestershire sauce

**Directions:**
Mix in a highball glass and garnish with chilled celery and a lime wedge on the rim.

## The Walking Dead
**Ingredients for 1 cocktail:**
.5 oz. crème de almond
1 oz. Bacardi Silver
.5 oz. triple sec
1.5 oz. orange juice
1.5 oz. sour mix
Cherries for garnish
**Directions:**
Shake everything in a shaker with ice and strain into a Collins glass with ice. Garnish with cherries.

## The Vampire Shot
**Ingredients for 1 cocktail:**
1.5 oz. black vodka
½ oz. cranberry juice
Red sugar
**Directions:**
In an iced cocktail shaker, add the vodka, chill and set aside. In another iced shaker, add the cranberry, shake until chilled and pour into a shot glass. Then, using the back of a spoon to ensure you get the black vodka on top, gently pour the black vodka on the top layer of a red sugar rimmed shot glass.

## Halloween Martini
**Ingredients for 5-6 cocktails:**
2 oz. dark rum
½ oz. dry vermouth
2 black olives
Orange sugar
**Directions:**
Add the rum and vermouth into an iced shaker and chill the mix. Rim the martini glass with orange sugar and pierce a couple of olives with a stir stick. The sugar is the sweet treat, and the olive does the trick.

# Dr. Bonnie

## Hogsteins Butterbeer
**Ingredients for 5-6 cocktails:**
1 cup butterscotch schnapps liqueur – put into a freezer to chill
before serving
8 cups cream soda (~ 1 l bottle) - chilled
**Directions:**
Mix the ingredients together and stir well. Makes about 5-6 servings.

## Ghostly Delight
**Ingredients for 5-6 cocktails:**
2 oz. vodka (Titos or other)
1 oz. vanilla simple syrup
1 oz. heavy cream
2 oz. club soda
Marshmallow and black frosting are optional
**Directions:**
Mix the ingredients together in an iced shaker (minus the club soda)
and shake until chilled. Add the club soda and stir well. Pour into a
martini glass (frosted is best). Skewer a marshmallow on a stir stick for
an optional garnish. If you have some black frosting – dab on a quick
ghost face on your marshmallow.

## Monster-ritas
**Ingredients for 4-5 cocktails:**
¼ cup light corn syrup
Green food coloring
½ cup fresh lime juice
¾ cup Patron (or other) tequila
3 oz. triple sec
4 maraschino cherries with 4 tsp. of syrup
**Directions:**
Mix the green food coloring with the light corn syrup until it's a bright
green (add drop-by-drop and stir until you have a good monster'y
color.
Freeze the glasses you will use to frost the glass. When you are ready
to serve, dip the rim into the green syrup and abruptly turn right-side
up, allowing the green monster juice to drip down the sides. The frozen
glass will put a halt to it in just the right places.
For the 'rita' combine the ingredients (minus the cherry syrup/cherries)
in a shaker filled with ice. Take your monstrous glass and add a
teaspoon of cherry juice to the bottom of each glass, pour in the

margarita mix ¾ high in the glass. Pierce a cherry on a stir stick for an added touch.

## Vampire Tonic

**Ingredients for 1 cocktail:**
1 oz. vodka
1/2 oz. triple sec
1/2 oz. lime juice
1/2 oz. cranberry juice

**Directions:**
Shake vodka, triple sec, lime, and cranberry juice vigorously in a shaker with ice. Strain into a martini glass, garnish with a lime wedge on the rim and serve.

## Graveyard Mud

**Ingredients for 1 cocktail:**
1/2 shot Godiva liquor
1/2 shot bailey's Irish cream liquor

**Directions:**
Mix the liquors together in a shaker and strain into a coffee mug. Fill the mug with coffee and milk to taste and top with whipped cream.

## Bloody Brain Shot

**Ingredients for 1 cocktail:**
1 oz. strawberry vodka (chilled)
1/8 oz. lime juice
¾ oz. Bailey's Irish Cream
Splash of grenadine

**Directions:**
Add vodka and lime juice to an iced shaker and shake until fully chilled. Add the mix to a shot glass (straining it to avoid adding ice). Submerge a straw end into the Bailey's and suck up some of the liqueur and transfer it to your chilled shot. Slowly, allow the Bailey's to add to the vodka/lime mix and it should curdle and form 'brain-like' floaties. Repeat this process until you've got a nice brain at the top of your drink. Take a splash of grenadine and make some creepy blood on your brain. Time to gross out your guests!

## Bleeding Sun

**Ingredients for 1 cocktail:**
1.5 oz. Bacardi

# Dr. Bonnie

.5 oz. Cointreau
2 oz. pineapple juice
1 tbsp. strawberry puree
## Directions:
Mix the ingredients in an iced shaker and pour over ice into glass. Dip a stir stick into your puree and allow dripping into the glass to create blood drips.

## The Pumpkin Wizard Smasher
### Ingredients for 1 cocktail:
2 oz. Vanilla vodka
½ oz. Pumpkin liqueur (if you can find it…substitute with pumpkin spice syrup or pumpkin puree)
½ oz. Sylk cream liqueur
1 tsp. Whipped cream
Pumpkin pie spice shaker
Cinnamon sticks for garnish
### Directions:
Pour the liquors into a shaker filled with ice and shake well. Strain into a cocktail glass (chilled) and top with whipped cream. Shake the pumpkin pie spice on the whipped cream and garnish with cinnamon stick.

## Blood Orange Martini
### Ingredients for 8 cocktails:
1 cup Tito's vodka (or another vodka)
1 cup chilled blood orange or pomegranate juice
1 cup chilled apple juice
½ cup of orange liqueur
*red food coloring to boost the color and make it spooky
### Directions:
Mix thoroughly with an ice shaker and pour into martini glasses.

## Spooky Messages
Spooky messages: for any of the cocktails and beverages served, if you are using glass – add a few drops of dishwashing detergent to a small glass of water. Dip your finger into the soapy mix and write a spooky message on the outside of the glass and put the glass into the freezer for at least 20 minutes. Remove the glass and the spooky letters will be revealed. Your guests will certainly love looking for their hidden messages throughout the night!

## Tap a Pumpkin

Google *tap a pumpkin*. There are pumpkin tap kits you can purchase from a few retailers. Clean out your pumpkin's seeds and pulp and then insert the faucet in the lower third portion. Make your favorite beverage – hopefully, it's pumpkin flavored. Fill up your pumpkin with the beverage you created. Your guests will love serving themselves.

# VIII. Halloween Safety Guidelines

## COSTUMES:

Safe, fire-retardant materials only. Since trick-or-treaters or party goers are likely to walk next to candles, votive or illuminated bags – it is best to wear safe materials. Check for costumes that have 'flame resistant' in the advertisement &/or on the tag.

In the event of freezing weather, wear loose fitting costumes and thermal underclothing to retain heat since you are likely to be outside. Costumes should not be too long as that can be a dangerous tripping hazard not only to the wearer but everyone surrounding. If you are walking at night (child to adult), you should place reflective tape along the costume lengthways so cars can see you. The same goes for your flashlight and bag (in the event of trick-or-treating). Face: Masks, masks, masks. Masks are a Halloween staple and a large part of the tradition. However, they can reduce a child's (or even an adults) visibility tremendously! When you can, switch to face makeup. Unless you are in a Halloween costume contest, you don't need a mask!

Masks can be constricting – make sure you (or the child) are getting enough oxygen. You don't want to asphyxiate slowly (or your child). When you purchase Halloween makeup – check for packages that contain statements such as 'laboratory tested,' 'non-toxic,' 'meets federal standards for cosmetics,' 'made with US approved color additives.' Always read the manufacturer's instructions for application and be extremely careful next to the eyes and mouth. Make a small test spot to determine if the wearer is sensitive to the product. Always remove makeup before bedtime to prevent skin/eye irritation.

Refrain from wearing decorative contact lenses. It's not worth the risk. Contacts should only be prescribed by a licensed ophthalmologist.

Swords, knives, and other accessories should be rounded, soft and flexible. Some cheaper versions can be used as weapons with sharp plastic points, etc.

## AS A MOTORIST:

Children are quick, excited and forgetful of pedestrian laws on Halloween. They will dart across the street and from behind parked cars. As you drive down a neighborhood street, assume that children are about jump in front of your car – keep on your toes and drive very, very slow – especially in densely populated residential areas. Enter and exit alleyways with extreme caution. Assume that not all parents have read this safety section and realize that most Halloween costumes are black - so children might blend in with the night after dark. Keep alert as you watch for kids! Don't drive too close to the sidewalks or curbs as crowded walkways might cause a child to tumble into the street.

## PARENTAL CHECK-LIST:

- No child under fourteen-years-old should trick-or-treat without an adult or responsible, older teen. Even at fourteen, some kids may still need parental guidance.

- Map out the route for trick-or-treating. If parents are not going to be with the kids (i.e. for fourteen-year-olds and older), make sure you know every person who is going with the group and write down their (home/cell) phone numbers.

- Talk to kids about the rules of Halloween – do not go up to a home /apartment without the lights on.

- Discuss and agree upon a return time if you will not be chaperoning them.

- It wouldn't hurt to make sure at least one of the kids has a phone on them – nowadays, most kids possess mobile phones and don't leave home without them. Ask that they set their ringtones on max volume – preferably with vibrations.

- Discuss the rules of trespassing and how they are to stay on the sidewalk and respect others' property during the trick-or-treating runs.

- Instruct the kids not to eat any candy until they return to the home and allow you to inspect it. No snacking from the goody bag while trick-or-treating! When your trick-or-treater returns home, view each piece of candy and look for sharp objects, tiny pinholes, discoloring, torn wrappers, and anything else that may be suspicious. If the candy doesn't look right for any reason – toss it!

# Dr. Bonnie

Throw away all home-made treats – only allow factory-made candy to make it to the final pile.

- If your child has a food allergy, check every label – common sense, but just a reminder.

- Enforce that the kids never accept a ride from a stranger.

- Review the proper pedestrian/traffic rules with the group and make sure they understand that cars might not see them, so they need to be extra careful crossing the street! They should walk on the sidewalk as far away from the street as possible.

- Write on a piece of tape - your child's name, address and phone and tape this securely to the inside of your child's costume. Tell the child that this information is there and if the child gets lost, s/he is to go to a house with a light on and tell them to call the number. Do this with younger kids – especially if you are responsible for a big group - even if you are with the child, as in the dark among many kids, the worst can happen, and your child can get lost.

- Explain to kids they are never to enter a home – even if asked to by an adult. They are only there for a treat – and they can get this treat from a well-lit porch.

- Explain to kids they are to walk, not run, from house to house. They are to stay on the sidewalks and never cross on the lawns – not only for safety, but it is rude to trample someone's property especially when they just treated you to some free candy!

- Make sure that each child has a flashlight.

- Instruct the kids to never walk near a luminary or lit pumpkin/candles. Even if they have flame-resistant costumes, you don't want to take a chance.

**Expecting trick-or-treaters? Here are some tips:**

- Provide healthier treats for trick-or-treaters such as low-calorie treats (e.g. Halloween pretzel bags, fruit snacks).

215

# The Halloween Party Host Handbook

- Offer child-safe Halloween toys as fun alternatives such as novelty items, glow sticks, balloons.

- Only serve factory-made treats. It's extra nice to go the extra mile and bake some treats, but you're liable if a child gets sick from eating your food. Maybe they have a hidden allergy, etc., and you are providing food without a nutrition facts label. It's best to protect the children's interests – and yours as well.

- Be sure sidewalks and stairs are well-lit and free of obstacles that could cause someone to fall.

- Keep candles and candle-lit pumpkins and luminaries away from doorsteps, walkways, stoops, and curtains. Place them on sturdy surfaces and keep them out of the reach of pets and small children. Never leave a fire in any form unattended.

## HOSTING A PARTY? HERE'S A CHECKLIST

*The following is not a substitute for legal advice/guidance. These are simply tips and talking points. Always check with your local authorities to get the details of all local laws regarding party hosting before committing to hosting a party.*

**General parties:**
- Only serve pasteurized beverages. Unpasteurized beverages (i.e. ciders, juices) can have harmful bacteria such as *Salmonella.*

- Do not serve raw cookie dough – for the same reason above.

- Keep all perishable items that you will serve on ice/in the refrigerator until time to serve and do not allow them to stay out for more than 2 hours (or 1 hour if the temp is ~ 85F or above, which is unlikely on Halloween, nevertheless). Perishable items would include but is not limited to finger sandwiches, cheese/cheese ball/cream cheese platters, fruit salads, tossed salads, cold pasta dishes, meats/poultry/seafood, cream pies/cakes &/or anything containing whipped cream.

# Dr. Bonnie

- Switch out your flame candles for LED – it's not worth the risk of a guest burning themselves &/or catching your home on fire.

- Don't post things publicly about your party online or you may receive unwanted guests.

- Make the start and finish times very clear on your invite.

- Clearly state the food/alcohol expectations on your invite – is it BYOB, alcohol-free, potluck, or everything is host provided.

- Give your neighbors a heads-up so they don't complain about you for noise/traffic at your home. Some areas have 'noise permits' – so check with your local government/police to see if there's such a thing to apply for in advance of your party.

- Ensure your valuables are locked away. It's just best to never have a dispute if something turns up missing.

- Ensure your first aid kit is well-stocked and accessible.

- Check your liability insurance and be aware of your coverage in the case of personal injury to a third party or damage to your property.

- Ensure there is proper lighting in all areas for guests – no darkened hallways on the way to a restroom, etc.

- If some of your guests will smoke, designate a smoking area with proper ashtrays, etc.

- As the host, you can be found liable if a guest at your party causes property damage or harms another person. Be a responsible host and set appropriate standards for behavior.

- Make certain out-of-bound areas are properly secured.

- Have a safe and secure place where guests can store their valuables (i.e. handbags, coats).

# The Halloween Party Host Handbook

- Other areas that may be potential hazards: swimming pools, ponds, gas heaters, barbecue pits, fire pits, etc. Pay attention to the guests' accessibility to these items.

- Out of control parties can become a criminal offense for the host unless you have taken reasonable steps to prevent the party from becoming out of control. You could face a significant fine or prison sentence if you are negligent and people/property are harmed. If the host is a child/minor and the parent gives permission for the child to host a party, and the party gets out of control, the parent could become guilty of the offense. Check your local laws before hosting a party. It's best to call 9-1-1 immediately if your party gets out of control. It's negligent not to call, so do the right thing.

- Coordinate parking so your guests do not get towed. Make sure you have ample 'legal' spaces for them and if not, encourage carpooling &/or Uber.

- Have one main entrance to your event to monitor guests.

- It's always best to limit your guest list to people you know.

**Parties with alcohol:**
*The following is not a substitute for legal advice/guidance. These are only tips and talking points.*
*Alcohol laws vary from state to state. There is such a thing as 'social host liability.' Anybody who provides alcohol is responsible if the drinker is harmed by the alcohol &/or has an accident and injures or kills themselves, or someone else. By serving your guests alcohol, please realize that you, as the host, have a responsibility to ensure your guests' safety. If your guests are drinking, be sure they are of legal age and take their keys away at the door. Make sure all guests have a safe ride home with a sober driver. Also, ensure they do not drink a dangerous/harmful amount of alcohol during your party – you have a duty to prevent over-indulgence – so hire a licensed bartender and serve from one location to ensure nobody is over-served. Watch out for any guests who might consume too much and realize the dangers of alcohol poisoning and other alcohol-related conditions and diseases. If a guest has consumed alcohol and isn't acting right – do not hesitate to get this guest medical assistance. Check the alcohol liability laws in your state before serving alcohol at your party. Designated drivers should not consume even one drink during your event. This also goes for the host and the bartender.*

# Dr. Bonnie

- If a guest becomes too intoxicated (see above), call 9-1-1 and keep the guest's airway free and stay with them until the ambulance arrives. You may be liable for this person's overindulgence if you have been negligent and haven't put the proper steps in play – however, please realize it is **far worse of an outcome** for you and this guest if you do not get this person help.

- It's a smart trick to limit full-strength drinks – serve lower strength selections and plenty of non-alcoholic options.

- Schedule plenty of activities, such as party games that do not involve alcohol consumption. Never host a party that centers on drinking alcohol for the entertainment – you're asking for trouble.

- Only serve alcohol from one location. This way, you can track consumption.

- If you are the party host, it is your obligation to refrain from using any drugs/alcohol. You're the one in charge. Stay sober.

- Make sure food and water are available to the guests at all time. If you are serving alcohol, snacks high in fat and carbs such as cheese, dips, crackers, seafood, can delay the absorption of alcohol. Avoid salty foods, as these encourage more drinking.

- Your bartender must also remain sober. You should hire a professional bartender that is licensed. They are trained to recognize signs of intoxication. The bartender makes the call of when someone has been over-served and cuts them off. You need this person to do their job. Hiring a licensed bartender is cheaper than having to hire a criminal attorney &/or paying fees, etc.

- Refrain from serving alcohol at least an hour before your party is over. Switch to coffee or milkshakes and serve food. Do not allow any designated drivers to have drinks – not even one. You also want your guests that have been drinking to sober up before they go in public. They can get into trouble for public intoxication, and you may be liable. Do not allow them to take a 'roadie' – that's the worst thing to do at the end of the night.

219

# The Halloween Party Host Handbook

- Do not have servers walking around topping off glasses – you can't track consumption this way, and it encourages over-indulgence.

- It is against the law to serve minors. Don't do it. You could face criminal charges in court and a significant fine or prison time if something bad happens as a result of your actions.

- A smart option is to include a checkbox on your RSVP that includes the guests confirming they have a safe ride home if they intend to have a couple of drinks.

- Never push alcohol consumption. Adult drinking games may happen, but do not pressure anybody to drink alcohol – have alternatives such as drinking a 'mocktail' or eating a cookie instead, etc.

- Realize only time will sober a guest. Coffee or other caffeinated beverages will not serve to sober your guests. Be prepared to arrange for drivers (i.e. Uber, Lyft, taxi, limousine, etc.) or offer a couch.

- Check your liability insurance and be aware of your coverage for liquor liability in the case of any issue involving alcohol. Homeowner policies will not cover illegal alcohol consumption such as serving to minors.

- Consider hosting your party at a public venue instead of your home to minimize your risks.

- Employers hosting a party that serves alcohol should check their comprehensive general liability policy to determine their third-party liquor liability coverage. Charging employees for beverages doesn't negate your liability.

- If you are a frequent party host, it may be worth it to look into a 1 million dollar umbrella policy offered by standard homeowners or renters policies. This coverage can run you as little as ~$125 per year and is well worth it for the peace of mind.

# FOR MORE INFORMATION ON PARTY HOSTING:

The Official Party Host Handbook is available for purchase on most book retailer online sites. This is an essential guide for party hosting. From birthdays to baby showers there are unique party themes for all ages, party food recipes, party etiquette, over 100 party games, and more! There's also a master party planning checklist for any event.

Head over to http://partyhost411.com/ for upcoming events to celebrate, party tips, party themes, etiquette advice, and more.

For specific party hosting tips with an emphasis on murder mystery parties, check out the MyMysteryParty.com blog: http://mymysteryparty.com/murder-mystery-blog/

Follow Dr. Bonnie on social media:
 @bonblossman  @bonblossman  @bonblossman

Made in the USA
Coppell, TX
04 October 2022

84062677R00132